Lecture Notes in Computer Science 13559

More information about this series at https://link.springer.com/bookseries/558

Ghada Zamzmi · Sameer Antani · Ulas Bagci ·
Marius George Linguraru ·
Sivaramakrishnan Rajaraman · Zhiyun Xue (Eds.)

Medical Image Learning with Limited and Noisy Data

First International Workshop, MILLanD 2022
Held in Conjunction with MICCAI 2022
Singapore, September 22, 2022
Proceedings

Editors
Ghada Zamzmi ⓘ
National Institutes of Health
Bethesda, MD, USA

Sameer Antani ⓘ
National Institutes of Health
Bethesda, MD, USA

Ulas Bagci ⓘ
Northwestern University
Chicago, IL, USA

Marius George Linguraru ⓘ
Children's National Hospital
Washington, WA, USA

Sivaramakrishnan Rajaraman ⓘ
National Institutes of Health
Bethesda, MD, USA

Zhiyun Xue ⓘ
National Institutes of Health
Bethesda, MD, USA

ISSN 0302-9743   ISSN 1611-3349 (electronic)
Lecture Notes in Computer Science
ISBN 978-3-031-16759-1   ISBN 978-3-031-16760-7 (eBook)
https://doi.org/10.1007/978-3-031-16760-7

This Springer imprint is published by the registered company Springer Nature Switzerland AG
The registered company address is: Gewerbestrasse 11, 6330 Cham, Switzerland

Preface

Deep learning (DL)-based computer-aided diagnostic systems have been widely and successfully studied for analyzing various image modalities such as chest X-rays, computed tomography, ultrasound, and optical imaging including microscopic imagery. Such analyses help in identifying, localizing, and classifying disease patterns as well as staging the extent of the disease and recommending therapies. Although DL approaches have a huge potential to advance medical imaging technologies and potentially improve quality and access to healthcare, their performance relies heavily on the quality, variety, and size of training data sets as well as appropriate high-quality annotations. In the medical domain, obtaining such data sets is challenging due to several privacy constraints and tedious annotation processes. Further, real-world medical data tends to be noisy and incomplete leading to unreliable and potentially biased algorithm performance. To mitigate or overcome training challenges in imperfect or data-limited scenarios, several training techniques have been proposed. Despite the successful application of these techniques in a wide range of medical image applications, there is still a lack of theoretical and practical understanding of their learning characteristics and decision-making behavior when applied to medical images.

This volume presents novel approaches for handling noisy and limited medical image data sets. This collection is derived from articles presented in the workshop titled "Medical Image Learning with Noisy and Limited Data (MILLanD)" that was held in conjunction with the 25th International Conference on Medical Image Computing and Computer Assisted Intervention (MICCAI 2022). The workshop brought together machine learning scientists, biomedical engineers, and medical doctors to discuss the challenges and limitations of current deep learning methods applied to limited and noisy medical data and present new methods for training models using such imperfect data. The workshop received 54 full-paper submissions in various topics including efficient data annotation and augmentation strategies, new approaches for learning with noisy/corrupted data or uncertain labels, weakly-supervised learning, semi-supervised learning, self-supervised learning, and transfer learning strategies. Each submission was reviewed by 2–3 reviewers and further assessed by the workshop's chairs. The workshop's reviewing process was double-blind, i.e., both the reviewer and author identities were concealed throughout the review process. This process resulted in the selection of 22 high-quality papers that are included in this volume.

August 2022

Ghada Zamzmi
Sameer Antani
Ulas Bagci
Marius George Linguraru
Sivaramakrishnan Rajaraman
Zhiyun Xue

Organization

General Chair

Ghada Zamzmi   National Institutes of Health, USA

Program Committee Chairs

Sameer Antani   National Institutes of Health, USA
Ulas Bagci   Northwestern University, USA
Marius George Linguraru   Children's National Hospital, USA
Sivaramakrishnan Rajaraman   National Institutes of Health, USA
Zhiyun Xue   National Institutes of Health, USA
Ghada Zamzmi   National Institutes of Health, USA

Program Committee

Sema Candemir   Eskişehir Technical University, Turkey
Somenath Chakraborty   University of Southern Mississippi, USA
Amr Elsawy   National Institutes of Health, USA
Prasanth Ganesan   Stanford Medicine, USA
Loveleen Gaur   Amity University, India
Peng Guo   National Institutes of Health, USA
Mustafa Hajij   University of San Francisco, USA
Alba García Seco Herrera   University of Essex, UK
Alexandros Karargyris   Institute of Image-Guided Surgery, IHU
                                        Strasbourg, France
Ismini Lourentzou   Virginia Tech, USA
Rahul Paul   Harvard Medical School, USA
Anabik Pal   SRM University, Andhra Pradesh, India
Harshit Parmar   Texas Tech University, USA
Sirajus Salekin   University of South Florida, USA
Ahmed Sayed   Milwaukee School of Engineering, USA
Mennatullah Siam   York University, Canada
Sudhir Sornapudi   Corteva Agriscience, USA
Lokendra Thakur   MIT and Harvard Broad Institute, USA
Lihui Wang   Guizhou University, China
Feng Yang   National Institutes of Health, USA
Mu Zhou   Stanford University, USA

Additional Reviewers

Kexin Ding
M. Murugappan
Venkatachalam Thiruppathi
Zichen Wang
Miaomiao Zhang
Qilong Zhangli

Contents

Active and Continual Learning

Transfer Representation Learning

Imbalanced Data and Out-of-Distribution Generalization

Approaches for Noisy, Missing, and Low Quality Data

Efficient and Robust Annotation Strategies

Heatmap Regression for Lesion Detection Using Pointwise Annotations

Chelsea Myers-Colet[1]([✉]), Julien Schroeter[1], Douglas L. Arnold[2], and Tal Arbel[1]

[1] Centre for Intelligent Machines, McGill University, Montreal, Canada
{cmyers,julien,arbel}@cim.mcgill.ca
[2] Montreal Neurological Institute, McGill University, Montreal, Canada
douglas.arnold@mcgill.ca

Abstract. In many clinical contexts, detecting all lesions is imperative for evaluating disease activity. Standard approaches pose lesion detection as a segmentation problem despite the time-consuming nature of acquiring segmentation labels. In this paper, we present a lesion detection method which relies only on point labels. Our model, which is trained via heatmap regression, can detect a variable number of lesions in a probabilistic manner. In fact, our proposed post-processing method offers a reliable way of directly estimating the lesion existence uncertainty. Experimental results on Gad lesion detection show our point-based method performs competitively compared to training on expensive segmentation labels. Finally, our detection model provides a suitable pre-training for segmentation. When fine-tuning on only 17 segmentation samples, we achieve comparable performance to training with the full dataset.

Keywords: Lesion detection · Lesion segmentation · Heatmap regression · Uncertainty · Multiple sclerosis

1 Introduction

For many diseases, detecting the presence and location of all lesions is vital for estimating disease burden and treatment efficacy. In stroke patients, for example, the location of a cerebral hemorrhage was shown to be an important factor in assessing the risk of aspiration [1] thus, failing to locate even a single one could drastically impact the assessment. Similarly, in patients with Multiple Sclerosis (MS), detecting and tracking all gadolinium-enhancing lesions (Gad lesions), whether large or small, is especially relevant for determining treatment response in clinical trials [2]. Detecting all Gad lesions is imperative as just one new lesion indicates new disease activity.

To achieve this goal, standard practice in deep learning consists of training a lesion segmentation model with a post-processing detection step [3,4]. However, segmentation labels are expensive and time consuming to acquire. To this end, we

© The Author(s), under exclusive license to Springer Nature Switzerland AG 2022
G. Zamzmi et al. (Eds.): MILLanD 2022, LNCS 13559, pp. 3–12, 2022.
https://doi.org/10.1007/978-3-031-16760-7_1

develop a lesion detection model trained on pointwise labels thereby reducing the manual annotation burden. Unlike previous point annotation-based methods [5–7], ours combines the ability to detect a variable number of lesions with the benefit of leveraging a probabilistic approach. Indeed, our refinement method is not only independent of a specific binarization threshold, it offers a unique way of estimating the lesion existence probability. Our contributions are threefold:

(1) We demonstrate the merit of training on point annotations via heatmap regression over segmentation labels on the task of Gad lesion detection. With weaker labels, our models still achieve better detection performance.
(2) Our proposed refinement method allows for a reliable estimation of lesion existence uncertainty thus providing valuable feedback for clinical review.
(3) When the end goal is segmentation, our detection models provide a suitable pre-training for fine-tuning on a limited set of segmentation labels. When having access to only 17 segmentation samples, we can achieve comparable performance to a model trained on the entire segmentation dataset.

2   Related Work

Point annotations are often extremely sparse which leads to instability during training of deep neural networks. Therefore, most state-of-the-art methods rely on the application of a smoothing operation to point labels. A Gaussian filter is commonly applied to create a heatmap as was done in [5,6] for suture detection. Others have found success applying distance map transformations. For instance, Han et al. [8] and van Wijnen et al. [9] used Euclidean and Geodesic distance maps to perform lesion detection. We demonstrate the benefits of training with Gaussian heatmaps over distance maps as they offer a more precise and interpretable probabilistic prediction yielding superior detection performance.

Irrespective of the choice of smoothing used for training, detection methods will often differ in their post-processing refinement step, i.e. in extracting lesion coordinates from a predicted heatmap. The simplest approach consists in finding the location with the maximum mass [5,10,11] or computing the centre of mass [6]. Although these approaches easily allow for the detection of multiple lesions, they require careful tuning of the binarization threshold and are susceptible to missing both isolated and overlapping peaks. More sophisticated methods exist which aim to fit a Gaussian distribution to the predicted heatmap thus retaining its probabilistic interpretation, e.g. [12,13]. Specifically, to perform cephalogram landmark detection Thaler et al. [7] align a Gaussian distribution via Least Squares curve fitting. Since the approach taken in [7] is limited to a set number of landmarks, we extend it to detect a variable number of lesions. Our method thus offers the flexibility of simpler approaches, without any dependence on a binarization threshold, while providing a probabilistic interpretation.

3   Method

In this work, we propose a strategy to detect the presence and location of multiple lesions from brain MRIs of patients with a neurodegenerative disease. Our model

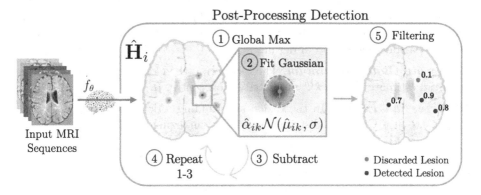

Fig. 1. Overview of detection method given a predicted heatmap $\hat{\mathbf{H}}_i$: lesion candidates are found by (1) locating the global maximum, (2) fitting a Gaussian distribution to an extracted region and (3) subtracting the influence of this lesion from the heatmap. (4) Repeat steps 1–3 before (5) filtering out unlikely lesions.

is trained via heatmap regression (Sect. 3.1) while lesion detection is performed in a post-processing step (Sect. 3.2). Finally, we present a transfer learning scheme to perform segmentation on a limited dataset (Sect. 3.3).

3.1 Training via Heatmap Regression

The proposed heatmap regression training scheme requires a domain expert to label only a single point identifying each lesion, e.g. by marking the approximate centre of the lesion. To stabilize training, we apply a Gaussian filter with smoothing parameter σ to the point annotations thus creating a multi-instance heatmap [5–7,14–16]. Since all lesions are represented by a single point and smoothed using the same value of σ, equal importance is attributed to lesions of all sizes. We train a model f_θ to map a sequence of input MRIs to a predicted heatmap $\hat{\mathbf{H}}_i$.

3.2 Detection During Inference

Given a continuous heatmap $\hat{\mathbf{H}}_i$, we now aim to detect individual lesions. Specifically, for patient i, we wish to represent the kth detected lesion by a single point, $\hat{\mu}_{ik}$, which can be extracted from the heatmap. We assume the predicted heatmap $\hat{\mathbf{H}}_i$ will model a sum of Gaussian distributions (each describing a single lesion) to mimic the target heatmap:[1]

$$\hat{\mathbf{H}}_i = \sum_K \hat{\mathbf{H}}_{ik} = \sum_K \mathcal{N}(\hat{\mu}_{ik}, \sigma) \tag{1}$$

---

[1] Valid as long as f_θ sufficiently minimizes the loss and thus models the target.

Our method essentially aims to find the individual Gaussian distributions comprising the sum in Eq. 1 in an iterative manner as shown in Fig. 1. We now describe each depicted step in detail.

(1) Locate Global Maximum. The location of the global maximum serves as an initial estimate for the kth predicted lesion centre, $\hat{\boldsymbol{\mu}}_{ik}$.

(2) Gaussian Fitting. In the region surrounding a detected lesion with centre $\hat{\boldsymbol{\mu}}_{ik}$, we fit a Gaussian distribution with normalizing constant $\hat{\alpha}_{ik}$:

$$\hat{\mathbf{H}}_{ik} = \hat{\alpha}_{ik} \mathcal{N}(\hat{\boldsymbol{\mu}}_{ik}, \sigma) \qquad (2)$$

Provided there is minimal overlap between neighbouring lesions, we can use a Least Squares curve fitting algorithm to estimate $\hat{\alpha}_{ik}$ and $\hat{\boldsymbol{\mu}}_{ik}$.[2] The normalizing constant, $\hat{\alpha}_{ik}$, represents the prior probability of producing a peak in this region (from Bayes' Theorem), i.e. it is the belief that a lesion exists in the given region. We thus refer to $\hat{\alpha}_{ik}$ as the lesion existence probability (similar to [17]). As an initial estimate for $\hat{\alpha}_{ik}$, we sum within the extracted region, i.e. the hypothesis space, as shown in Fig. 1 (2).

(3) Subtract. Now that potential lesion k has been identified and fitted with a continuous Gaussian function, we remove its contribution to the sum in Eq. 1. This allows our method to more easily detect the individual contributions of neighbouring lesions with overlapping Gaussian distributions.

$$\hat{\mathbf{H}}'_i = \hat{\mathbf{H}}_i - \hat{\alpha}_{ik} \mathcal{N}(\hat{\boldsymbol{\mu}}_{ik}, \sigma) \qquad (3)$$

(4) Repeat. Since we have subtracted the contribution of lesion k from the aggregated heatmap, the global maximum now corresponds to a different candidate lesion. Steps 1 to 3 are repeated until a maximum number of lesions have been found or when the lesion existence probability drops below a threshold, e.g. 0.01.

(5) Filtering. Lesions with a low probability of existence are discarded (threshold optimized on the validation set). By overestimating the lesion count and subsequently discarding regions unlikely to contain a lesion, we can better account for noisy peaks in the heatmap. We evaluate the calibration of these probabilities and demonstrate the validity of this filtering step (Sect. 4.2).

3.3   Segmentation Transfer Learning

In addition to detection, estimating a lesion segmentation can be beneficial for assessing lesion load. We therefore design a transfer learning scheme which first relies on building a strong lesion detector using point annotations before fine-tuning on a small segmentation dataset. Specifically, we (1) train a detection model on point annotations until convergence; (2) build a small segmentation training set; (3) fine-tune the detection model on segmentation samples only. Training in this manner minimizes the amount of detailed segmentation labels that must be generated.

---

[2] Valid for Gad lesions given a sufficiently small smoothing parameter σ.

4   Experiments and Results

The proposed heatmap regression model is compared against three benchmarks in terms of detection performance. We train models on (1) segmentation labels, (2) Euclidean distance maps and (3) Geodesic distance maps [8,9]. Similar to our method, lesions are detected from the output prediction in a post-processing step. Here, we instead binarize the output at threshold τ (optimized on the validation set), cluster connected components to form detected lesions and use the centre of mass (segmentation) or the maximum (detection) to represent the lesion (referred to as CC). As an additional benchmark, we apply this method to heatmap outputs from our proposed regression models. This is in line with detection methods used by [18,19] for segmentation outputs and [5,6] for heatmap predictions.

4.1   Experimental Setup

Dataset. We evaluate our method on Gad lesion detection as they are a relevant indicator of disease activity in MS patients [20]. However, their subtlety and extreme size variation makes them difficult to identify. Experiments are performed using a large, multi-centre, multi-scanner proprietary dataset consisting of 1067 patients involved in a clinical trial to treat Relapsing-Remitting MS. Multi-modal MRIs, including post-contrast T1-weighted MRI, are available for each patient and are provided as inputs to our system. For fairness, we create train (60%), validation (20%) and test (20%) sets by first splitting at the patient level. We have access to manually derived Gad lesion segmentation masks. Each sample is first independently rated by two experts who then meet to produce a consensus. Point labels were generated directly from segmentation masks by calculating the centre of mass of each lesion and transformed into either heatmaps, using a Gaussian kernel with smoothing parameter σ, or distance maps (baseline methods), using decay parameter p. Hyperparameters were selected based on validation performance.

Model. We train a modified 5-layer U-Net [21] with dropout and instance normalization using a Mean-Squared Error loss for heatmap regression and a weighted cross-entropy loss for segmentation. See code for details[3].

Evaluation. We apply the Hungarian algorithm [22] to match predicted lesions to ground truth lesions using Euclidean distance as a cost metric. Assignments with large distances are considered both a false positive and a false negative.

---

[3] https://github.com/ChelseaM-C/MICCAI2022-Heatmap-Lesion-Detection.

Table 1. Lesion detection results as a mean over 3 runs. Reported is the detection F1-score, precision, recall and small lesion recall for models trained with segmentation, Gaussian heatmap or distance map (Geodesic, Euclidean) [8,9] labels using connected components (CC) or Gaussian fitting (GAUSSIAN).

Label type	Detection method	F1-score	Precision	Recall	Small lesion recall
Segmentation	CC	85.4 ± 0.02	85.3 ± 1.10	85.5 ± 1.15	67.7 ± 3.58
Euclidean map	CC	80.6 ± 1.01	**92.6 ± 1.28**	71.4 ± 2.14	51.0 ± 3.28
Geodesic map	CC	73.7 ± 4.89	81.0 ± 7.97	67.8 ± 2.98	47.8 ± 2.81
Gaussian heatmap	CC	83.9 ± 0.27	80.9 ± 4.43	87.3 ± 2.64	**75.0 ± 5.75**
	GAUSSIAN	**86.3 ± 0.24**	87.0 ± 1.89	**85.7 ± 1.44**	70.4 ± 4.47

4.2   Lesion Detection Results

Despite only having access to point annotations, the proposed Gaussian heatmap approach performs competitively with the segmentation baseline (see Table 1). In fact, our proposed iterative detection method (GAUSSIAN) even slightly outperforms the segmentation model on all detection metrics. By contrast, both distance map approaches show notably worse performance with especially low recall scores indicating a high number of missed lesions. The proposed model additionally outperforms competing methods for the task of small lesion detection (3 to 10 voxels in size) underlining the merit of training directly for detection. Segmentation models will typically place more importance on larger lesions since they have a higher contribution to the loss, a bias not imposed by our detection model. Our model additionally does not sacrifice precision for high recall on small lesions; we perform on par with segmentation.

Lesion Existence Probability Evaluation. We evaluate the quality of our fitted lesion existence probabilities on the basis of calibration and derived uncertainty to justify both the curve fitting and filtering steps.

(1) Calibration. We compare the calibration [23] of the lesion existence probabilities before and after Least Squares curve fitting. Recall the initial estimate for α_{ik} is found by summing locally within the extracted region. Our proposed existence probabilities are well calibrated (Fig. 2a), with little deviation from the ideal case thus justifying our proposed filtering step. As well, the fitted probabilities are significantly better calibrated than the initial estimates demonstrating the benefit of curve fitting.

(2) Uncertainty. While it is important to produce accurate predictions, quantifying their uncertainty is of equal importance in the medical domain. We can compute the entropy of our lesion existence probabilities without sampling and show it is well correlated with detection accuracy. As we consider only the least uncertain instances, we observe a monotonic increasing trend, even achieving an accuracy of 100% (Fig. 2b). Similar results are achieved with the more standard MC Dropout approach [24] applied to segmentation outputs (calculated at a lesion level as in [18]).

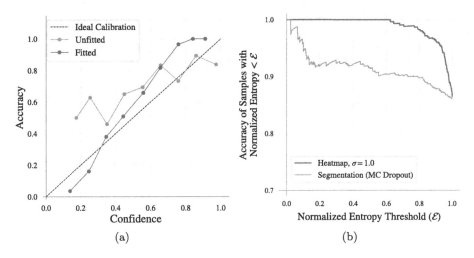

Fig. 2. Lesion existence probability evaluation. (a) Calibration of unfitted (pink) vs. fitted (green) probabilities. (b) Detection accuracy of least uncertain samples according to our model (green) vs. MC Dropout applied to segmentation (pink). (Color figure online)

Our derived lesion existence probabilities are not only well-calibrated, they produce meaningful uncertainty estimates. With only a single forward pass, our uncertainty estimates perform on par with standard sampling-based approaches.

4.3   Lesion Segmentation via Transfer Learning

To demonstrate the adaptability of our method, we fine-tune the trained heatmap regression models with a small segmentation dataset as described in Sect. 3.3. Specifically, we use segmentation labels for a randomly chosen 1% of our total training set for fine-tuning. To account for bias in the selected subset, we repeat this process 3 times and average the results. For comparison, we train from scratch with this limited set as well as on the full segmentation training set. We additionally include results on random subsets of 5% and 10% in the appendix along with the associated standard deviation of each experiment.

Remarkably, our pre-trained models show only a 3% drop in segmentation F1-score performance with a mere 1% of the segmentation labels compared to the model trained on the full segmentation dataset (see Table 2). By contrast, the model trained from scratch with the same 1% of segmentation labels shows a 10% drop in segmentation F1-score. This emphasizes the importance of detecting lesions since models trained from scratch in the low data regime show considerably lower detection F1-score. It is clear the models do not require very much data in order to properly segment lesions as demonstrated by competitive performance of our pre-trained models. However, as indicated by poor detection performance of the pure segmentation models in the low data regime, it is clear these models need help localizing lesions before they can be segmented. We can

Table 2. Segmentation transfer learning results averaged over 3 random subsets. We present segmentation F1-score (Seg F1.) and detection (Det.) metrics on the fine-tuned segmentation models: F1-score, precision, recall. Pre-trained models are distinguished by their smoothing hyperparameter σ.

Quantity seg. labels	Pre-trained model	Seg. F1	Det. F1	Det. precision	Det. recall
100%	None	70.5 ± 0.31	85.4 ± 0.02	85.3 ± 1.10	85.5 ± 1.15
1%	None	60.7 ± 2.48	69.7 ± 5.92	79.0 ± 6.47	62.7 ± 7.69
	$\sigma = 1.0$	67.2 ± 0.71	**85.4 ± 0.62**	83.9 ± 1.74	**87.0 ± 2.40**
	$\sigma = 1.25$	**67.6 ± 1.31**	84.5 ± 0.38	**86.0 ± 0.67**	83.1 ± 1.32
	$\sigma = 1.5$	67.2 ± 1.51	85.0 ± 0.50	83.6 ± 1.01	86.6 ± 1.10
	Euclidean	66.3 ± 0.18	84.7 ± 1.45	83.3 ± 3.24	86.1 ± 1.67
	Geodesic	59.9 ± 1.44	77.9 ± 4.36	85.6 ± 7.33	71.7 ± 3.49

see a similar trend with the models pre-trained on distance maps. The Euclidean distance maps offered higher detection scores than the Geodesic ones (Table 1) and therefore serve as a better pre-training for segmentation, although still lower than our models.

5 Discussion and Conclusion

In this work, we have demonstrated how training a heatmap regression model to detect lesions can achieve the same, and at times better, detection performance compared to a segmentation model. By requiring clinicians to indicate a single point within each lesion, our approach significantly reduces the annotation burden imposed by deep learning segmentation methods. Our proposed method of iteratively fitting Gaussian distributions to a predicted heatmap produces well-calibrated existence probabilities which capture the underlying uncertainty.

Perhaps most significantly, our transfer learning experiments have revealed an important aspect about segmentation models. Our results demonstrate that segmentation models must learn first and foremost to find lesions. Indeed, our models, which are already adept at lesion detection, can easily learn to delineate borders with only a few segmentation samples. By contrast, the models provided with the same limited set of segmentation labels trained from scratch fail primarily to detect lesions thus lowering their segmentation scores. It therefore presents an unnecessary burden on clinicians to require them to manually segment large datasets in order to build an accurate deep learning segmentation model.

Although we have demonstrated many benefits, Gaussian heatmap matching has its limitations. The smoothing hyperparameter requires careful tuning to both maintain stable training and to avoid a significant overlap in peaks (especially for densely packed lesions). As well, the method still requires an expert annotator to mark approximate lesion centres however, this is much less time-consuming than fully outlining each lesion. We recognize this could introduce high variability in the labels regarding where the point is placed within each lesion. Though the current model was trained on precise centres of mass, the proposed method does not necessarily impose any such constraints, in theory. Future work is needed to evaluate the robustness of the model to high variability in the label space.

In summary, our proposed training scheme and iterative Gaussian fitting post-processing step constitute an accurate and label-efficient method of performing lesion detection and segmentation.

Acknowledgements. This work was supported by awards from the International Progressive MS Alliance (PA-1412-02420), the Canada Institute for Advanced Research (CIFAR) Artificial Intelligence Chairs program (Arbel), the Canadian Natural Science and Engineering Research Council (CGSM-NSERC-2021-Myers-Colet) and the Fonds de recherche du Québec (303237). The authors would also like to thank Justin Szeto, Kirill Vasilevski, Brennan Nichyporuk and Eric Zimmermann as well as the companies who provided the clinical trial data: Biogen, BioMS, MedDay, Novartis, Roche/Genentech, and Teva. Supplementary computational resources were provided by Calcul Québec, WestGrid, and Compute Canada.

References

1. Daniels, S.K., Foundas, A.L.: Lesion localization in acute stroke. J. Neuroimaging **9**(2), 91–98 (1999)
2. Rudick, R.A., Lee, J.-C., Simon, J., Ransohoff, R.M., Fisher, E.: Defining interferon β response status in multiple sclerosis patients. Ann. Neurol. Official J. Am. Neurol. Assoc. Child Neurol. Soc. **56**(4), 548–555 (2004)
3. Lundervold, A.S., Lundervold, A.: An overview of deep learning in medical imaging focusing on MRI. Zeitschrift für Medizinische Physik **29**(2), 102–127 (2019)
4. Doyle, A., Elliott, C., Karimaghaloo, Z., Subbanna, N., Arnold, D.L., Arbel, T.: Lesion detection, segmentation and prediction in multiple sclerosis clinical trials. In: Crimi, A., Bakas, S., Kuijf, H., Menze, B., Reyes, M. (eds.) BrainLes 2017. LNCS, vol. 10670, pp. 15–28. Springer, Cham (2018). https://doi.org/10.1007/978-3-319-75238-9_2
5. Sharan, L., et al.: Point detection through multi-instance deep heatmap regression for sutures in endoscopy. Int. J. Comput. Assist. Radiol. Surg. **16**(12), 2107–2117 (2021). https://doi.org/10.1007/s11548-021-02523-w
6. Stern, A., et al.: Heatmap-based 2d landmark detection with a varying number of landmarks. arXiv preprint arXiv:2101.02737 (2021)
7. Thaler, F., Payer, C., Urschler, M., Stern, D.: Modeling annotation uncertainty with gaussian heatmaps in landmark localization. arXiv preprint arXiv:2109.09533 (2021)
8. Han, X., Zhai, Y., Yu, Z., Peng, T., Zhang, X.-Y.: Detecting extremely small lesions in mouse brain MRI with point annotations via multi-task learning. In: Lian, C., Cao, X., Rekik, I., Xu, X., Yan, P. (eds.) MLMI 2021. LNCS, vol. 12966, pp. 498–506. Springer, Cham (2021). https://doi.org/10.1007/978-3-030-87589-3_51
9. van Wijnen, K.M.H., et al.: Automated lesion detection by regressing intensity-based distance with a neural network. In: Shen, D., et al. (eds.) MICCAI 2019. LNCS, vol. 11767, pp. 234–242. Springer, Cham (2019). https://doi.org/10.1007/978-3-030-32251-9_26
10. Donné, S., De Vylder, J., Goossens, B., Philips, W.: Mate: machine learning for adaptive calibration template detection. Sensors **16**(11), 1858 (2016)

11. Chen, B., Xiong, C., Zhang, Q.: CCDN: checkerboard corner detection network for robust camera calibration. In: Chen, Z., Mendes, A., Yan, Y., Chen, S. (eds.) ICIRA 2018. LNCS (LNAI), vol. 10985, pp. 324–334. Springer, Cham (2018). https://doi.org/10.1007/978-3-319-97589-4_27

12. Zhang, F., Zhu, X., Dai, H., Ye, M., Zhu, C.: Distribution-aware coordinate representation for human pose estimation. In: Proceedings of the IEEE/CVF Conference on Computer Vision and Pattern Recognition, pp. 7093–7102 (2020)

13. Graving, J.M., et al.: Deepposekit, a software toolkit for fast and robust animal pose estimation using deep learning. Elife 8, e47994 (2019)

14. Wang, X., Bo, L., Fuxin, L.: Adaptive wing loss for robust face alignment via heatmap regression. In: Proceedings of the IEEE/CVF International Conference on Computer Vision, pp. 6971–6981 (2019)

15. Pfister, T., Charles, J., Zisserman, A.: Flowing convnets for human pose estimation in videos. In: Proceedings of the IEEE International Conference on Computer Vision, pp. 1913–1921 (2015)

16. Hervella, Á.S., Rouco, J., Novo, J., Penedo, M.G., Ortega, M.: Deep multi-instance heatmap regression for the detection of retinal vessel crossings and bifurcations in eye fundus images. Comput. Methods Programs Biomed. 186, 105201 (2020)

17. Schroeter, J., Myers-Colet, C., Arnold, D., Arbel, T.: Segmentation-consistent probabilistic lesion counting. Med. Imaging Deep Learn. (2022)

18. Nair, T., Precup, D., Arnold, D.L., Arbel, T.: Exploring uncertainty measures in deep networks for multiple sclerosis lesion detection and segmentation. Med. Image Anal. 59, 101557 (2020)

19. De Moor, T., Rodriguez-Ruiz, A., Mérida, A.G., Mann, R., Teuwen, J.: Automated lesion detection and segmentation in digital mammography using a u-net deep learning network. In: 14th International Workshop on Breast Imaging (IWBI 2018), vol. 10718, p. 1071805. International Society for Optics and Photonics (2018)

20. McFarland, H.F., et al.: Using gadolinium-enhanced magnetic resonance imaging lesions to monitor disease activity in multiple sclerosis. Ann. Neurol. 32(6), 758–766 (1992)

21. Ronneberger, O., Fischer, P., Brox, T.: U-Net: convolutional networks for biomedical image segmentation. In: Navab, N., Hornegger, J., Wells, W.M., Frangi, A.F. (eds.) MICCAI 2015. LNCS, vol. 9351, pp. 234–241. Springer, Cham (2015). https://doi.org/10.1007/978-3-319-24574-4_28

22. Kuhn, H.W.: The Hungarian method for the assignment problem. Naval Res. Logist. Q. 2(1–2), 83–97 (1955)

23. Guo, C., Pleiss, G., Sun, Y., Weinberger, K.Q.: On calibration of modern neural networks. In: International Conference on Machine Learning, pp. 1321–1330. PMLR (2017)

24. Gal, Y., Ghahramani, Z.: Dropout as a Bayesian approximation: Representing model uncertainty in deep learning. In: International Conference on Machine Learning, pp. 1050–1059. PMLR (2016)

Partial Annotations for the Segmentation of Large Structures with Low Annotation Cost

Bella Specktor Fadida[1]([⊠]), Daphna Link Sourani[2], Liat Ben Sira[3,4], Elka Miller[5], Dafna Ben Bashat[2,3], and Leo Joskowicz[1]

[1] School of Computer Science and Engineering, The Hebrew University of Jerusalem, Jerusalem, Israel
{bella.specktor,josko}@cs.huji.ac.il
[2] Sagol Brain Institute, Tel Aviv Sourasky Medical Center, Tel Aviv-Yafo, Israel
[3] Sackler Faculty of Medicine and Sagol School of Neuroscience, Tel Aviv University, Tel Aviv-Yafo, Israel
[4] Division of Pediatric Radiology, Tel Aviv Sourasky Medical Center, Tel Aviv-Yafo, Israel
[5] Medical Imaging, Children's Hospital of Eastern Ontario, University of Ottawa, Ottawa, Canada

Abstract. Deep learning methods have been shown to be effective for the automatic segmentation of structures and pathologies in medical imaging. However, they require large annotated datasets, whose manual segmentation is a tedious and time-consuming task, especially for large structures. We present a new method of partial annotations of MR images that uses a small set of consecutive annotated slices from each scan with an annotation effort that is equal to that of only few annotated cases. The training with partial annotations is performed by using only annotated blocks, incorporating information about slices outside the structure of interest and modifying a batch loss function to consider only the annotated slices. To facilitate training in a low data regime, we use a two-step optimization process. We tested the method with the popular soft Dice loss for the fetal body segmentation task in two MRI sequences, TRUFI and FIESTA, and compared full annotation regime to partial annotations with a similar annotation effort. For TRUFI data, the use of partial annotations yielded slightly better performance on average compared to full annotations with an increase in Dice score from 0.936 to 0.942, and a substantial decrease in Standard Deviations (STD) of Dice score by 22% and Average Symmetric Surface Distance (ASSD) by 15%. For the FIESTA sequence, partial annotations also yielded a decrease in STD of the Dice score and ASSD metrics by 27.5% and 33% respectively for in-distribution data, and a substantial improvement also in average performance on out-of-distribution data, increasing Dice score from 0.84 to 0.9 and decreasing ASSD from 7.46 to 4.01 mm. The two-step optimization process was helpful for partial annotations for both in-distribution and out-of-distribution data. The partial annotations method with the two-step optimizer is therefore recommended to improve segmentation performance under low data regime.

Keywords: Deep learning segmentation · Partial annotations · Fetal MRI

G. Zamzmi et al. (Eds.): MILLanD 2022, LNCS 13559, pp. 13–22, 2022.
https://doi.org/10.1007/978-3-031-16760-7_2

1 Introduction

Fetal MRI has the potential to complement US imaging and improve fetal development assessment by providing more accurate volumetric information about the fetal structures [1, 2]. However, volumetric measurements require manual delineation, also called segmentation, of the fetal structures, which is time consuming, annotator-dependent and error-prone.

In this paper, we focus on the task of fetal body segmentation in MRI scans. Several automatic segmentation methods were proposed for this task. In an early work, Zhang et al. [3] proposed a graph-based segmentation method. More recently, automatic segmentation methods for fetal MRI are based on deep neural networks. Dudovitch et al. [4] describes a fetal body segmentation network that reached high performance with only nine annotated examples. However, the method was tested only on data with similar resolutions and similar gestational ages for the FIESTA sequence. Lo et al. [5] proposed a 2D deep learning framework with cross attention squeeze and excitation network with 60 training scans for fetal body segmentation in SSFP sequences.

While effective, robust deep learning methods usually require a large, high-quality dataset of expert-validated annotations, which is very difficult and expensive to obtain. The annotation process is especially time consuming for structures with large volumes, as they require the delineation of many slices. Therefore, in many cases, the annotation process is performed iteratively, when first initial segmentation is obtained with few annotated datasets, and subsequently manual segmentations are obtained by correcting network results. However, the initial segmentation network trained on few datasets is usually not robust and might fail for cases that are very different from the training set.

To address the high cost associated with annotating structures with large volumes, one approach is to use sparse annotations, where only a fraction of the slices or pixels are annotated [6]. Çiçek et al. [7] describes a 3D network to generate a dense volumetric segmentation from sparse annotations, in which uniformly sampled slices were selected for manual annotation. Goetz et al. [8] selectively annotated unambiguous regions and employed domain adaptation techniques to correct the differences between the training and test data distributions caused by sampling selection errors. Bai et al. [9] proposed a method that starts by propagating the label map of a specific time frame to the entire longitudinal series based on the motion estimation, and then combines FCN with a Recurrent Neural Network (RNN) for longitudinal segmentation. Lejeune et al. [10] introduced a semi-supervised framework for video and volume segmentation that iteratively refined the pixel-wise segmentation within an object of interest. However, these methods impose restrictions on the way the partial annotations are sampled and selected that may be inconvenient for the annotator and still require significant effort.

Wang et al. [11] proposed using incomplete annotations in a user-friendly manner of either a set of consecutive slices or a set of typical separate slices. They used a combined cross-entropy loss with boundary loss and performed labels completion based on the network output uncertainty that was incorporated in the loss function. They showed that their method with 30% of annotated slices was close to the performance using full annotations. However, the authors did not compare segmentation results using full versus partial annotations with the same annotation effort. Also, a question remains if user-friendly partial annotations can be leveraged in the context of the Dice loss as well, a widely used loss function that is robust to class imbalance [12].

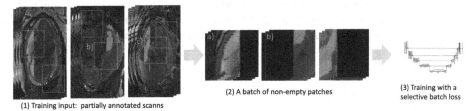

(2) A batch of non-empty patches

(3) Training with a selective batch loss

(1) Training input: partially annotated scanns

Fig. 1. Training flow with partial annotations. 1) Non-empty blocks are picked from the partially annotated scans (sagittal view, example of relevant blocks is shown in yellow). 2) A batch of non-empty blocks is used as input along with information about non-empty slices. The black areas of the blocks correspond to unselected voxels (voxels that are not used by the loss function). 3) The network is trained with a selective loss that uses only the pixels in annotated slices. (Color figure online)

Training with limited data usually makes the training optimization more difficult. Therefore, to facilitate optimization, we seek a scheme that will help in avoiding convergence to a poor local minimum. Smith [13] proposed the usage of a cyclic learning rate to remove the need for finding the best values and schedule for the global learning rates. Loshchilov et al. [14] showed the effectiveness of using warm learning rate restarts to deal with ill-conditioned functions. They used a simple learning rate restart scheme after a predefined number of epochs.

In this paper, we explore the effectiveness of using partial annotations under low data regime with the Soft Dice loss function. We also explore the usefulness of a warm restarts optimization scheme in combination with fine-tuning to deal with the optimization difficulties under low data regime.

2   Method

Our segmentation method with small annotation cost consists of two main steps: 1) manual partial delineations, where the user partially annotates scans with the guidance of the algorithm; 2) training with partial annotations, where a 3D segmentation network is trained with blocks of the partially annotated data using a selective loss function.

The manual partial delineations step is performed as follows. First, the uppermost and lowermost slices of the organ are manually selected by the annotator, which is a quick and easy task. Then, the algorithm randomly chooses a slice within the structure of interest. Finally, the slices to annotate around this slice are selected. The number of slices is determined by the chosen annotation percentage. The annotation percentage is taken from the slices that include the structure of interest, i.e., non-empty segmentation slices. The slices to annotate are chosen consecutively to reduce annotation time, as often the annotations depend on the 3D structure of the organ seen by scrolling and viewing nearby slices during the annotation.

The training with partial annotations is performed as follows. Only the non-empty blocks of the partially annotated data are used for training, as some of the blocks may not include annotations at all. To enrich the annotated data, we also use the border slices information in the loss function and treat the slices outside the structure of interest as annotated slices. We add as input to the network a binary mask specifying the locations of the annotated slices during training. The network is trained with a selective loss function that takes into account only the annotated slices. Also, we use a relatively large batch size of 8 to include enough information during each optimization iteration. Figure 1 shows the training flow.

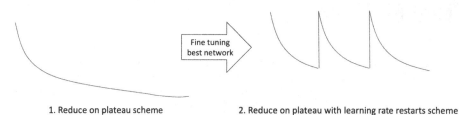

1. Reduce on plateau scheme   2. Reduce on plateau with learning rate restarts scheme

Fig. 2. Illustration of the two-step optimization process with the proposed learning rate regimes (graphs of learning rate as a function of epoch number).

2.1 Selective Dice Loss

To train a network with partially annotated data, we modify the loss function to use only the annotated slices information. We illustrate the use of a selective loss for the commonly used Soft Dice loss. A batch loss is used, meaning that the calculation is performed on the 4-dimentional batch directly instead of averaging the losses of single data blocks.

Let the number of image patches be I and let the image patch consist of C pixels. The number of voxels in a minibatch is therefore given by $I \times C = N$. Let t_i be a voxel at location i in the minibatch for the ground truth delineation $t_i \in T$ and r_i be a voxel at the location i in the minibatch for the network result $r_i \in R$.

The Batch Dice loss [15] is defined as:

$$Batch\ Dice\ Loss\ (L_{CD}) = -\frac{2\sum_N t_i r_i}{\sum_N t_i + \sum_N r_i} \qquad (1)$$

Since we have partial annotations, we will use only the annotated slices locations in the loss calculation. Let $T' \subset T$ and $R' \subset R$ be the ground truth in the annotated slices and the network result in the annotated slices, with minibatch voxels $t_i' \in T'$ and $r_i' \in R'$ respectively. The number of voxels that we consider in the minibatch is now $N' < N$, corresponding only to the annotated slices. The batch dice loss for partial annotations is defined as:

$$Selective\ Batch\ Dice\ Loss\ (L_{CD}) = -\frac{2\sum_{N'} t_i' r_i'}{\sum_{N'} t_i' + \sum_{N'} r_i'} \qquad (2)$$

2.2 Optimization

To facilitate the optimization process under small data regime, we perform the training in two steps. First, a network is trained with reduction of learning rate on plateau. Then, we use the weights of the network with best results on the validation set to continue training. Similarly to the first phase, the training in the second phase is performed with reduction in plateau, but this time with learning rate restarts every predefined number of epochs (Fig. 2).

3 Experimental Results

To evaluate our method, we retrospectively collected fetal MRI scans with the FIESTA and TRUFI sequences and conducted two studies.

Datasets and Annotations: We collected fetal body MRI scans of patients acquired with the true fast imaging with steady-state free precession (TRUFI) and the fast imaging employing steady-state acquisition (FIESTA) sequences from the Sourasky Medical Center (Tel Aviv, Israel) with gestational ages (GA) 28–39 weeks and fetal body MRI scans acquired with the FIESTA sequence from Children's Hospital of Eastern Ontario (CHEO), Canada with GA between 19–37 weeks. Table 1 shows detailed description of the data.

Table 1. Datasets description.

MRI sequence	ID/ OOD	Clinical site	Scanners	Resolution (mm^3)	Pixels/ slice	# Slices	GA	#
TRUFI	ID	Sourasky Medical Center	Siemens Skyra 3T, Prisma 3T, Aera 1.5T	0.6 − 1.34 × 0.6 − 1.34 × 2 − 4.8	320 − 512 × 320 − 512	50–120	28–39	101
FIESTA	ID	Sourasky Medical Center	GE MR450 1.5T	1.48 − 1.87 × 1.48 − 1.8 × 2 − 5	256 × 256	50–100	28–39	104
	OOD	Children's Hospital	Mostly GE Signa HDxt 1.5T; Signa 1.5T, SIEMENS Skyra 3T	0.55 − 1.4 × 0.55 − 1.4 × 3.1 − 7.5	256 × 256512 × 512	19–55	19–37, mostly 19–24	33

Ground truth segmentations were created as follows. First, 36 FIESTA cases were annotated from scratch. Then, 68 ID and 33 OOD cases were manually corrected from network results. For the TRUFI data all cases were created by correcting network results:

first, a FIESTA network was used to perform initial segmentation and afterwards a TRUFI network was trained for improved initial segmentation. Both the annotations and the corrections were performed by a clinical trainee. All segmentations were validated by a clinical expert.

Studies: We conducted two studies that compare partial annotations to full annotations with the same number of slices. Study 1 evaluates the partial annotations method for the TRUFI body dataset and performs ablation for the two-step optimization process and the usage of slices outside of the fetal body structure. Study 2 evaluates the partial annotations method for the FIESTA body dataset for both ID and OOD data.

For both studies, we compared training with 6 fully annotated cases to 30 partially annotated cases with annotation of 20% of the slices. The selection of cases and the location for partial annotations was random for all experiments. Because of the high variability in segmentation quality for the low-data regime, we performed all the experiments with four different randomizations and averaged between them. The segmentation quality is evaluated with the Dice, Hausdorff and 2D ASSD (slice Average Symmetric Surface Difference) metrics.

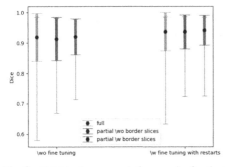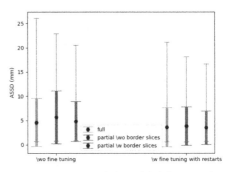

Fig. 3. Fetal body segmentation results for the FIESTA sequence. Training with full annotations (full) is compared to training with partial annotations with (\w) and without (\wo) border slices. The colored bars show the STD of the metric and the grey bars show the range of the metric (minimum and maximum).

A network architecture similar to Dudovitch et al. [4] was utilized with a patch size of $128 \times 128 \times 48$ to capture a large field of view. A large batch size of 8 was used in all experiments to allow for significant updates in each iteration for the partial annotations regime. Since the TRUFI sequence had a higher resolution compared to FIESTA, the scans were downscaled by $\times 0.5$ in the in-plane axes to have a large field of view [16]. The segmentation results were refined by standard post-processing techniques of holes filling and extraction of the main connected component.

Both partially annotated and fully annotated networks were trained in a two-step process. First, the network was trained with a decreasing learning rate, with an initial learning rate of 0.0005. The network that yielded the best validation result was selected, and this network was then fine-tunned on the same data. For fine-tuning, we again used a decreasing learning rate scheme with an initial learning rate of 0.0005, but this time we performed learning rate restarts every 60 epochs.

Study 1: partial annotations for TRUFI sequence and ablation
The method was evaluated on 30/13/58 training/validation/test split for partially annotated cases with 20% of annotated slices and 6/13/58 for fully annotated cases. The 6
fully annotated training cases were randomly chosen out of the 30 partially annotated
training cases. Ablation experiments were performed to evaluate the effectiveness of the
two-step optimization scheme and the usage of slices outside the body structure.

Six scenarios were tested: 1) full annotations without fine tuning; 2) partial annotations without fine tuning and without borders information; 3) partial annotations without
fine-tuning and with borders information; 4) full annotations with fine tuning; 5) partial
annotations with fine tuning but without borders information; 6) partial annotations with
fine tuning and borders information.

Figure 3 shows the fetal body segmentation results with the Dice score and ASSD
evaluation metrics. Fine tuning with restarts was helpful for both full and partial annotations regimes, increasing the full annotations segmentation Dice score from 0.919 to
0.937 and partial annotations with borders segmentation Dice score from 0.92 to 0.942.
Incorporating border information with the selective Dice loss function improved partial
annotation setting, increasing the Dice score from 0.936 to 0.942 and decreasing the
Dice Standard Deviation (STD) from 0.056 to 0.049. Finally, partial annotations with
borders information had slightly better average results to the full annotations regime
with a Dice score of 0.937 and 0.942 and ASSD of 3.61 and 3.52 for the full and partial
annotations respectively, with a substantially smaller STD: a Dice score STD of 0.063
compared to 0.049 and ASSD STD of 4.04 compared to 3.45 for the full annotations
and partial annotations regimes respectively.

Table 2. Segmentation results comparison between partial and full annotations for FIESTA body
sequence on ID and OOD data. Best results are shown in bold. Unusual behavior for fine-tuning
(two step optimization) is indicated with italics.

Data distribution	Network training	Dice	Hausdorff (mm)	2D ASSD (mm)
In-Distribution (ID)	Full	0.959 ± 0.044	34.51 ± 37.26	2.15 ± 2.33
	Full fine-tuned	0.964 ± 0.040	32.98 ± 36.86	1.88 ± 2.07
	Partial	0.959 ± 0.034	34.15 ± 35.96	2.21 ± 1.67
	Partial fine-tuned	$0.965 \pm \mathbf{0.029}$	31.89 ± 35.82	$1.90 \pm \mathbf{1.39}$
Out-of-Distribution (OOD)	Full	0.836 ± 0.178	39.34 ± 29.26	7.46 ± 10.61
	Full fine-tuned	*0.826 ± 0.214*	*39.61 ± 32.66*	*8.86 ± 16.54*
	Partial	0.875 ± 0.091	36.19 ± 21.44	5.47 ± 3.92
	Partial fine-tuned	$\mathbf{0.899 \pm 0.067}$	$\mathbf{30.37 \pm 18.86}$	$\mathbf{4.00 \pm 2.26}$

Study 2: partial annotations for FIESTA sequence for ID and OOD data
For partial annotations regime, the network was trained on 30 cases and for the full
annotations regime the network was trained on 6 cases randomly chosen out of the

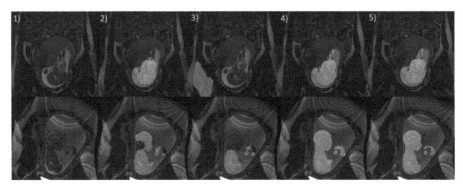

Fig. 4. Illustrative fetal body segmentation results for the FIESTA OOD data. Left to right (columns): 1) original slice; 2) Full annotations without fine-tuning; 3) Full annotations with fine-tuning; 4) Partial annotations with fine-tuning; 5) ground truth.

30 partially annotated training cases. For both methods, we used the same 6 cases for validation, 68 test cases for ID data and 33 test cases for OOD data.

The OOD data was collected from a different clinical site than the training set and included mostly smaller fetuses (28 out of 33 fetuses had GA between 19–24 weeks compared to GA between 28–39 in the training set). For both partial and full annotations regimes we used Test Time Augmentations (TTA) [17] for the OOD setting to reduce over-segmentation. Because of large resolution differences, we rescaled OOD data to the resolution of $1.56 \times 1.56 \times 3.0\,mm^3$, similar to the resolution of the training set.

In total, eight scenarios were tested, four for ID data and four for OOD data. For both ID and OOD data the following was tested: 1) full annotations without fine tuning. 2) full annotations with fine tuning. 3) partial annotations without fine-tuning. 4) partial annotations with fine-tuning.

Table 2 shows the results. For the ID data, partial annotations results were similar to full annotations with the same annotation effort, but again the STD was much smaller: Dice STD of 0.04 compared to 0.029 and ASSD STD of 2.07 compared to 1.39 for full and partial annotations respectively. For both full and partial annotations regimes the fine tuning slightly improved the segmentation results.

For the OOD data, the differences between segmentation results using full and partial annotations were much larger, with better results for partial annotations regime. Using partial annotations, results improved from a Dice score of 0.836 to 0.899 and from ASSD of 7.46 mm to 4 mm. Unlike in the ID setting, fine-tuning with restarts hurt performance on OOD data in the full annotations regime, potentially indicating an overfitting phenomenon. This was not the case for partial annotations, where again fine tuning with learning rate restarts further improved segmentation results as in the ID setting.

Figure 4 shows illustrative body segmentation results for the OOD data. Partial annotations showed better performance on these cases compared to full annotations, indicating higher robustness. Also, fine tuning full annotations resulted in decreased performance with a complete failure to the detect the case in the top row, which may indicate an overfitting to the training set.

4 Conclusion

We have presented a new method for using partial annotations for large structures. The method consists of algorithm-guided annotation step and a network training step with selective data blocks and a selective loss function. The method demonstrated significantly better robustness under low data regime compared to full annotations.

We also presented a simple two-step optimization scheme for low data regime that combines fine-tuning with learning rate restarts. Experimental results show the effectiveness of the optimization scheme for partial annotations method on both ID and OOD data. For full annotations, the two-step optimization was useful only for ID data but hurt performance on OOD data, indicating potential overfitting.

The selected partial annotations are user-friendly and require only two additional clicks in the beginning and end of the structure of interest, which is negligible compared to the effort required for segmentation delineations. Thus, they can be easily used to construct a dataset with a low annotation cost for initial segmentation network.

Acknowledgements. This research was supported in part by Kamin Grant 72061 from the Israel Innovation Authority.

References

1. Reddy, U.M., Filly, R.A., Copel, J.A.: Prenatal imaging: ultrasonography and magnetic resonance imaging. Obstet. Gynecol. **112**(1), 145–150 (2008)
2. Rutherford, M., et al.: MR imaging methods for assessing fetal brain development. Dev. Neurobiol. **68**(6), 700–711 (2008)
3. Zhang, T., Matthew, J., Lohezic, M., Davidson, A., Rutherford, M., Rueckert, D et al.: Graph-based whole body segmentation in fetal MR images. In: Proceedings of the Medical Image Computing and Computer-Assisted Intervention Workshop on Perinatal, Preterm and Paediatric Image Analysis (2016)
4. Dudovitch, G., Link-Sourani, D., Ben Sira, L., Miller, E., Ben Bashat, D., Joskowicz, L.: Deep learning automatic fetal structures segmentation in MRI scans with few annotated datasets. In: Martel, A.L., et al. (eds.) MICCAI 2020. LNCS, vol. 12266, pp. 365–374. Springer, Cham (2020). https://doi.org/10.1007/978-3-030-59725-2_35
5. Lo, J., et al.: Cross attention squeeze excitation network (CASE-Net) for whole body fetal MRI segmentation. Sensors **21**(13), 4490 (2021)
6. Tajbakhsh, N., Jeyaseelan, L., Li, Q., Chiang, J.N., Wu, Z., Ding, X.: Embracing imperfect datasets: a review of deep learning solutions for medical image segmentation. Med. Image Anal. **63**(1), 101693 (2020)
7. Çiçek, O., Abdulkadir, A., Lienkamp, S.S., Brox, T., Ronneberger, O.: 3D U-net: learning dense volumetric segmentation from sparse annotation. In: Ourselin, S., Joskowicz, L., Sabuncu, M., Unal, G., Wells, W. (eds.) Proceedings of the international Conference Medical Image Computing and Computer-Assisted Intervention – MICCAI 2016. MICCAI 2016, LNIP, vol 9901, pp. 424–432. Springer, Cham. https://doi.org/10.1007/978-3-319-46723-8_49
8. Goetz, M., et al.: DALSA: domain adaptation for supervised learning from sparsely annotated MR images. IEEE Trans. Med. Imag. **35**(1), 184–196 (2016)

9. Bai, W., et al..: Recurrent neural networks for aortic image sequence segmentation with sparse annotations. In: Frangi, A.F., Schnabel, J.A., Davatzikos, C., Alberola-López, C., Fichtinger, G. (eds.) MICCAI 2018. LNCS, vol. 11073, pp. 586–594. Springer, Cham (2018). https://doi.org/10.1007/978-3-030-00937-3_67

10. Lejeune, L., Grossrieder, J., Sznitman, R.: Iterative multi-path tracking for video and volume segmentation with sparse point supervision. Med. Image Anal. **50**, 65–81 (2018)

11. Wang, S., et al.: CT male pelvic organ segmentation via hybrid loss network with incomplete annotation. IEEE Trans. Med. Imaging **39**(6), 2151–2162 (2020)

12. Sudre, C.H., Li, W., Vercauteren, T., Ourselin, S., Jorge Cardoso, M.: Generalised dice overlap as a deep learning loss function for highly unbalanced segmentations. In: Cardoso, M.J., et al. (eds.) DLMIA/ML-CDS -2017. LNCS, vol. 10553, pp. 240–248. Springer, Cham (2017). https://doi.org/10.1007/978-3-319-67558-9_28

13. Smith, L.N.: Cyclical learning rates for training neural networks. In: 2017 IEEE Winter Conference on Applications of Computer Vision (WACV) 24 Mar 2017, pp. 464–472. IEEE

14. Loshchilov, I., Hutter, F.: SGDR: Stochastic gradient descent with warm restarts. arXiv preprint arXiv:1608.03983 (2016)

15. Kodym, O., Španěl, M., Herout, A.: Segmentation of head and neck organs at risk using CNN with batch dice loss. In: Brox, T., Bruhn, A., Fritz, M. (eds.) GCPR 2018. LNCS, vol. 11269, pp. 105–114. Springer, Cham (2019). https://doi.org/10.1007/978-3-030-12939-2_8

16. Isensee, F., Jaeger, P.F., Kohl, S.A., Petersen, J., Maier-Hein, K.H.: nnU-Net: a self-configuring method for deep learning-based biomedical image segmentation. Nat. Meth. **18**(2), 203–211 (2021)

17. Wang, G., Li, W., Aertsen, M., Deprest, J., Ourselin, S., Vercauteren, T.: Aleatoric uncertainty estimation with test-time augmentation for medical image segmentation with convolutional neural networks. Neurocomputing **338**, 34–45 (2019)

Abstraction in Pixel-wise Noisy Annotations Can Guide Attention to Improve Prostate Cancer Grade Assessment

Hyeongsub Kim, Seo Taek Kong, Hongseok Lee, Kyungdoc Kim, and Kyu-Hwan Jung[✉]

VUNO Inc., Seoul, Korea
khwan.jung@vuno.co
https://www.vuno.co/

Abstract. Assessing prostate cancer grade from whole slide images (WSIs) is a challenging task. While both slide-wise and pixel-wise annotations are available, the latter suffers from noise. Multiple instance learning (MIL) is a widely used method to train deep neural networks using WSI annotations. In this work, we propose a method to enhance MIL performance by deriving weak supervisory signals from pixel-wise annotations to effectively reduce noise while maintaining fine-grained information. This auxiliary signal can be derived in various levels of hierarchy, all of which have been investigated. Comparisons with strong MIL baselines on the PANDA dataset demonstrate the effectiveness of each component to complement MIL performance. For 2,097 test WSIs, accuracy (Acc), the quadratic weighted kappa score (QWK), and Spearman coefficient were increased by 0.71%, 5.77%, and 6.06%, respectively, while the mean absolute error (MAE) was decreased by 14.83%. We believe that the method has great potential for appropriate usage of noisy pixel-wise annotations.

Keywords: Multiple instance learning · Weak supervision · Noisy labels · Prostate cancer grade assessment · Whole slide image

1 Introduction

Prostate cancer is one of the most common cancers in the world [8,10]. Important prognostic information is inferred from Gleason patterns and grades which are categorized into international society of urological pathology (ISUP) grade groups [5] based on their severity. Assessing prostate cancer grades in whole slide images (WSIs) with giga-scale resolutions is time-consuming and pixel-wise annotations have significant noisiness [1].

Deep neural networks when used to assist diagnosis of cancer must indicate regions where Gleason patterns present for further confirmation. However, pixel-wise Gleason pattern annotations are known to be excessively noisy and its

© The Author(s), under exclusive license to Springer Nature Switzerland AG 2022
G. Zamzmi et al. (Eds.): MILLanD 2022, LNCS 13559, pp. 23–31, 2022.
https://doi.org/10.1007/978-3-031-16760-7_3

noise levels outweigh its potential benefits. Optimizing patch-wise metrics was insufficient to translate to slide-wise performance, and consequently learning algorithms typically have used pixel-wise annotations have been used only for feature extraction, while the final classifiers have been trained on the less noisy slide-wise annotations [9]. Multiple instance learning (MIL) is a widely used paradigm when classifying histopathological WSIs because slide-wise annotations can be obtained through medical information systems while pixel-wise annotations are not readily available [4]. Attention-based MIL emphasizes regions to locate sparsely-positioned lesions in core needle biopsy tissues but never directly accesses pixel-wise information.

Several attempts to utilize both WSI and pixel-wise annotations are outlined in [2,9]. Instead of relying on noisy Gleason patterns, the studies use annotations indicating presence of tumor and separate localization from classification. Specifically, Strom and Kartasalo et al. applied boosting on ensembles of detection and grading networks and evaluated their patch-wise performances [9]. Bulten et al. mimicked a clinical setting where a feature extraction network learns to identify tumor positions [2]. Features were then extracted to train a classification model predicting ISUP grade groups. Without training on segmentation masks, [4] ranks of the top-K relevant patches and MIL were utilized. Relevant patches were subjected to recurrent neural network to diagnose malignant or benign tumors.

This work seeks to complement MIL by eliciting useful information from statistical approach in pixel-wise noisy annotations. Our experiments demonstrate that without carefully filtering pixel-wise noise, a combination with MIL amplifies errors in already mis-classified cases, e.g. ISUP grade 3 classified as 2 by a MIL model is classified as 1 by their combination. To allay such issues, we propose to construct weak-supervisory signals from noisy pixel-wise annotations. Annotation abstraction derived from Gleason patterns was shown to enhance spatial attention by reducing pixel-wise noise. Experiments demonstrated how coarse auxiliary signals effectively enhance an attention module's accuracy and improve ISUP grading of prostate WSIs.

2   Materials and Method

2.1   Data

The Prostate cANcer graDe Assessment (PANDA) dataset containing 10,516 WSIs was used for this study [3]. Data were split into 8,419 and 2,097 WSIs of digitized hematoxylin and eosin (H&E)-stained biopsies for training and test. Slide-wise annotations are provided in the form of Gleason scores and corresponding severity grade ranging 0 to 5 according to the international society of urological pathology (ISUP) standard [5], and endpoints indicating no tumor or malignancy. Mask values in pixel-wise annotation depend on the data provider [3]. Masks acquired from different institutions come with different semantics and are converted to another mask indicating tumor presence. In this work, we excluded slide-wise Gleason scores to focus on the effect of annotation abstraction. The distribution of dataset is detailed in Table 1.

Table 1. Dataset description separated by ISUP grade groups.

Grading group	Train	Val	Test	Total
No tumor	1,726	575	572	2,873
ISUP group 1	1,572	524	520	2,616
ISUP group 2	805	269	267	1,341
ISUP group 3	735	244	247	1,226
ISUP group 4	750	249	246	1,245
ISUP group 5	727	243	245	1,215
Total	6,315	2,104	2,097	10,516

2.2 Architecture

The end-to-end network architecture commonly used throughout this work is described. An ImageNet-pretrained ResNeXt-50 extracted 2,048 channel pre-global average pooling features from a batch of $b_g = 16$ WSI inputs. Each WSI was split into $b_s = 32$ patches, with resolution of $H = W = 224$. A learnable global convolution filter followed by sigmoid activation was used to compute attention A and multiplied with the input feature. Post-attention features were fed to the classification layers to predict the ISUP grading group. The classification layer consists of max-pooling, average pooling layer, and fully connected layer(FC layer) as in Fig. 1(a).

2.3 Multiple Instance Learning for Cancer Grade Assessment

Let $\mathcal{Y} = \{0, \dots, 5\}$ be the set of possible ordinal annotations describing ISUP grades. A classifier is trained to predict slide-wise ordinal annotations $y \in \mathcal{Y}$. Its softmax prediction is denoted by $\hat{p}$. Because classes share ordinal relations, the mean variance loss [7] is added to the standard cross entropy loss:

$$L_{mv} = H\left(y, \hat{p}\right) + \mathbb{E}_{\hat{y} \sim \hat{p}}\left[(\hat{y} - y)^2\right] + \left(\mathbb{E}_{\hat{y} \sim \hat{p}}\left[\hat{y}\right] - y\right)^2. \tag{1}$$

2.4 Noisy Labels and Weak Supervision

Raw pixel-wise annotations are extremely noisy [3], therefore have often been discarded [1]. Models trained using only MIL often weighed each patch equally because only ISUP grade groups were learnt. Appropriately processed fine-grained annotations can potentially inform the model to utilize local morphological features whose importance should be weighed differently.

The consensus of fine-grained pixel-wise annotations was rarely achievable, so that, the annotations method itself could be major component the noise of pixel-wise annotations. However, their abstraction at the increased coarseness

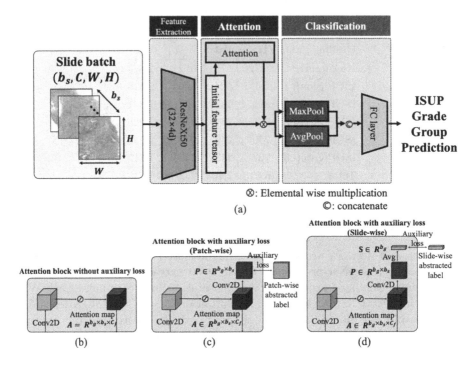

Fig. 1. (a) An overview of the proposed method. Attention mechanism for multiple instance learning and additional network layers when using (b) no auxiliary loss, (c) patch-wise auxiliary loss, and (d) slide-wise auxiliary loss. b_g: Global batch size, b_s: slide batch size, C: Input channel size, W: Input width, H: Input height, C_f: Initial feature channel

releases pixel-wise noise in WSI annotations. Let γ_p, γ_s be ratio of tumor to total tissue area in each patch and slide:

$$\gamma_\ell = \frac{1}{|\Omega_\ell|} \sum_{\omega \in \Omega_\ell} \mathbf{1}\{M_\omega = 1\}, \; \ell \in \{p, s\} \tag{2}$$

where $\Omega_\ell = \{1, \ldots, H_\ell\} \times \{1, \ldots, W_\ell\}$ is the resolution set of a patch or slide, i.e. its pixel indices, and M_ω is the tumor indicator mask. The masks (Fig. 2(a)) are obtained from WSI using Akensert method [1], resolution being 1.0 micron per pixel (mpp). To ensure representation capacity for well-separability, we added a learnable block followed by sigmoid for each coarseness level p, s, shown in Fig. 1(b–d). The auxiliary losses (L_ℓ) are then computed as the binary cross entropy H_2 between predictions and the above ratio:

$$L_\ell = H_2(\gamma_\ell, \hat{p}_\ell). \tag{3}$$

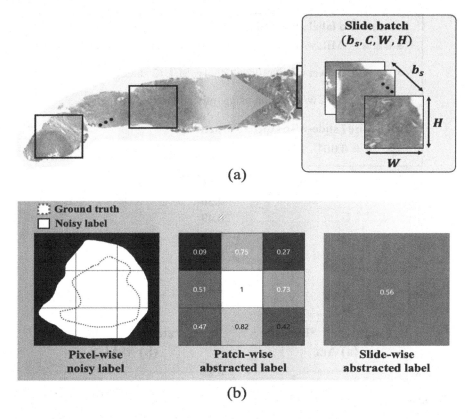

Fig. 2. (a) Slide batch generation; b_s: slide batch size, C: channel size, W: Patch width, H: Patch height, (b) Abstraction in noisy annotation method based on the noisy pixel-wise annotation.

Combining all the losses considered, the total loss is then a convex combination between MIL and the auxiliary loss computed at varying levels of abstraction $\ell \in \{p, s\}$. Here, w is the for the auxiliary loss as follows:

$$L = wL_\ell + (1 - w)L_{mv}. \tag{4}$$

3   Experiments

3.1   Implementation and Evaluation

We compared the performance of three baselines without the auxiliary loss and conducted an ablation study assessing the effectiveness of each auxiliary loss according to abstraction type and its weight (w). All models shared the same ResNeXt-50 (32 × 4d) encoder. The first baseline is MIL model without both attention and auxiliary loss. This MIL baseline model already achieved high performance by positioning in the top-10 rank in the challenge. [1]. The second

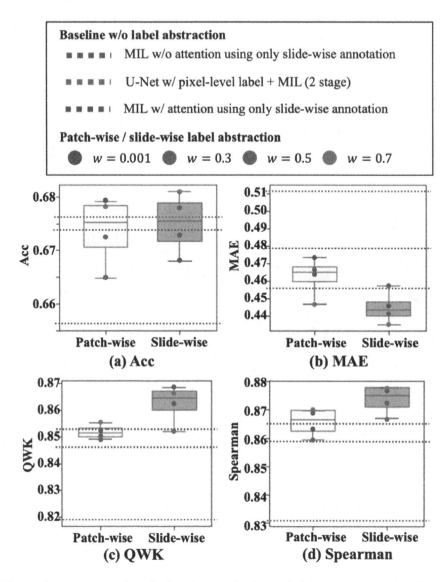

Fig. 3. A comparison of methods using patch-wise and slide-wise annotation abstractions evaluated with respect to the following criteria: (a) Accuracy (Acc), (b) Mean absolute error (MAE), (c) Quadratic weighted kappa (QWK), and (d) Spearman correlation. (Color figure online)

baseline model consisted of two stages. In the first stage, a U-Net model with ResNeXt-50 backbone networks was trained on pixel-wise annotations for feature extraction. In second stage, MIL with the freezed ResNeXt-50 in the end of first stage in Fig. 1(a) was trained on only slide-wise annotation based on the first stage's output as typical methods [2,9]. The third baseline adds only attention module without abstraction on top of the second baseline.

Ablation study proceeds with increasing levels of abstraction (patch/slide) with various coefficients (w). A coefficient of 0.7 on the auxiliary loss was found to work best via grid search which weighs the abstraction loss during the training of the model. AdamW optimizer [6] with 16 slides in each mini-batch was used with cosine annealing, and the initial learning rate was set to 1e−4. Performance for ISUP grade group prediction were evaluated with respect to accuracy, mean absolute error (MAE), quadratic weighted kappa (QWK), and spearman rank correlations.

3.2   Results

As shown in Fig. 3(a), the accuracy of the model trained on pixel-wise noisy annotations was improved with the use of slide-wise annotations. This margin is similar to the gain achieved by adding attention to the MIL baseline (green dotted line in Fig. 3). However, inspecting other criteria (b–d) which penalizes incorrect predictions far from true annotations demonstrates how pixel-wise labels are detrimental in amplifying incorrect predictions. Acc, QWK, and Spearman coefficient were increased by 0.71%, 5.77%, and 6.06%, and MAE was decreased by 14.83% when adding slide-wise label abstraction to the MIL baseline. For such cases, models trained using either patch or slide-wise abstraction predicted ISUP grades closer to true annotations'. The higher levels of abstraction, the more noise filtered naturally, thereby the slide-wise annotations with high noise have achieved benefit. These results support that the use of auxiliary loss using abstracted annotations is more helpful in improving model performance.

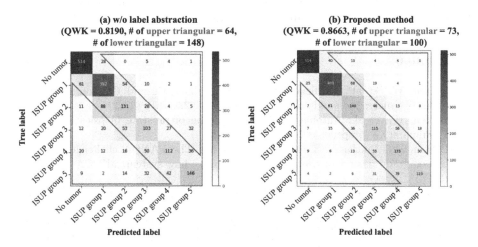

Fig. 4. Confusion matrices comparing (a) Pixel-wise annotation based baseline model without the abstraction with (b) Proposed method trained on abstracted annotations.

We also visualized the distribution of predictions and true ISUP grade groups in Fig. 4. The QWK increased from 0.8190 to 0.8663 when using slide-wise abstractions. Under and over-estimated predictions with margin ≥ 2 are highlighted in blue and red triangles, respectively. The implications of under and over-estimates differ: over-estimations (blue) lead to unnecessary costs of care. Under-estimating the severity of cancer (red) is critical because a patient would not receive proper treatment. The cumulative number of upper triangular cases slightly increased by 9 cases (from 64 to 73), but the number of lower triangular cases decreased by 30% from 148 cases to 100 cases. This implies that the potential risk of a patient can be mitigated with the use of our method.

In this study, we tested the effective use of pixel-wise noisy labels in slide-wise inference. It showed a performance improvement in terms of QWK compared to slide-wise classification after attention based on the results of the segmentation model. Compared with the PANDA challenge, the source of the dataset we used, we note that there may be a slight performance difference because the train set and test set used are different from the challenge.

4   Conclusion

We proposed a method to guide a MIL attention network by performing abstraction to filter annotation noise. Our method demonstrated superior performance in comparison with strong baselines. In particular, the performance was improved for samples that were difficult to predict due to noisy annotations, thereby reducing the severity of misdiagnosis. We believe that this study has potential not only for pathology, but also for large-scale environments when fine-grained annotations are contaminated with substantial noise levels.

References

1. Bulten, W., et al.: Artificial intelligence for diagnosis and Gleason grading of prostate cancer: the panda challenge. Nat. Med. **24**, 1–10 (2022)
2. Bulten, W., et al.: Automated Gleason grading of prostate biopsies using deep learning. arXiv preprint arXiv:1907.07980 (2019)
3. Bulten, W., Pinckaers, S., Eklund, K., et al.: The PANDA challenge: prostate cancer grade assessment using the Gleason grading system. MICCAI challenge (2020)
4. Campanella, G., et al.: Clinical-grade computational pathology using weakly supervised deep learning on whole slide images. Nat. Med. **25**(8), 1301–1309 (2019)
5. Egevad, L., Delahunt, B., Srigley, J.R., Samaratunga, H.: International society of urological pathology (ISUP) grading of prostate cancer-an ISUP consensus on contemporary grading (2016)
6. Loshchilov, I., Hutter, F.: Decoupled weight decay regularization. arXiv preprint arXiv:1711.05101 (2017)
7. Pan, H., Han, H., Shan, S., Chen, X.: Mean-variance loss for deep age estimation from a face. In: Proceedings of the IEEE Conference on Computer Vision and Pattern Recognition, pp. 5285–5294 (2018)

8. Society, A.C.: About prostate cancer. https://www.cancer.org/cancer/prostate-cancer/about/key-statistics.html
9. Ström, P., et al.: Pathologist-level grading of prostate biopsies with artificial intelligence. arXiv preprint arXiv:1907.01368 (2019)
10. UK, P.C.: What is the prostate? https://prostatecanceruk.org/prostate-information/about-prostate-cancer

Meta Pixel Loss Correction for Medical Image Segmentation with Noisy Labels

Zhuotong Cai[✉], Jingmin Xin, Peiwen Shi, Sanping Zhou, Jiayi Wu, and Nanning Zheng

Xi'an Jiaotong University, Xi'an, China
cai99624@stu.xjtu.edu.cn

Abstract. Supervised training with deep learning has exhibited impressive performance in numerous medical image domains. However, previous successes rely on the availability of well-labeled data. In practice, it is a great challenge to obtain a large high-quality labeled dataset, especially for the medical image segmentation task, which generally needs pixel-wise labels, and the inaccurate label (noisy label) may significantly degrade the segmentation performance. In this paper, we propose a novel Meta Pixel Loss Correction (MPLC) based on a simple meta guided network for the medical segmentation that is robust to noisy labels. The core idea is to estimate a pixel transition confidence map by meta guided network to take full advantage of noisy labels for pixel-wise loss correction. To achieve this, we introduce a small size of meta dataset with the meta-learning method to train the whole model and help the meta guided network automatically learn the pixel transition confidence map in an alternative training manner. Experiments have been conducted on three medical image datasets, and the results demonstrate that our method is able to achieve superior segmentation with noisy labels compared to the existing state-of-the-art approaches.

Keywords: Label noise · Loss correction · Meta learning

1 Introduction

With the recent emergence of large-scale datasets supervised by high-quality annotations, deep neural networks (DNNs) have exhibited impressive performance in numerous domains, particularly in medical applications. It has proved itself to be a worthy computer assistant in solving many medical problems, including disease early diagnosis, disease progression prediction, patient classification, and many other crucial medical image processing tasks like image registration and segmentation [7]. However, the former success is mostly contributed to the availability of well-labeled data. In practice, it is a great challenge to obtain large high-quality datasets with accurate labels in medical imaging. Because such labeling is

Supplementary Information The online version contains supplementary material available at https://doi.org/10.1007/978-3-031-16760-7_4.

G. Zamzmi et al. (Eds.): MILLanD 2022, LNCS 13559, pp. 32–41, 2022.
https://doi.org/10.1007/978-3-031-16760-7_4

not only time-expensive but also expertise-intensive. In most cases, the labeled datasets more or less have potential noisy labels, especially for the segmentation task, which generally needs pixel-wise annotation. Therefore, a segmentation model that is robust to such noisy training data is highly required.

To overcome this problem, a few recent approaches had been proposed. Mirikharaji et al. [11] proposed a semi-supervised method to optimize the weights on the images in the noisy dataset by reducing the loss on a small clean dataset for skin lesion segmentation. Inspired by [13], Zhu et al. [20] detected incorrect labels in the segmentation of heart, clavicles, and lung in chest radiographs through decreasing the weight of samples with incorrect labels. Wang et al. [18] combined the meta learning with the re-weighting method to adapt for corrupted pixels and re-weight the relative influenced loss for lung and liver segmentation.

All these methods are built on the basis of exclusion or simply re-weighting the suspected noisy samples to reduce their negative influence for training. However, simple exclusion or re-weighting can not make full use of noisy labels and ignores the reason leading to these noise labels, which makes them still have room for further performance improvement. This motivates us to explore the feasibility of taking full advantage of noisy labels by estimating the pixel transition confidence map, so as to do further pixel loss correction to make the model noise-robust and improve the segmentation performance with corrupted pixels.

In this paper, we propose a novel meta pixel loss correction(MPLC) to address the problem of medical image segmentation with noisy labels. Specifically, we design a meta guided network by feeding the segmentation network prediction as input to generate the pixel transition confidence map. The obtained pixel transition confidence map can represent the possibility of transitioning from the latent clean label to the observed noisy label, which can lead to improved robustness to noisy labels in the segmentation network through further pixel loss correction processing. The contributions of this paper can be summarized as follows: 1) We propose a novel meta pixel loss correction method to generate a noise-robust segmentation model to make full use of the training data. 2) With the introduction of noise-free meta-data, the whole model can be trained in an alternative manner to automatically estimate a pixel transition confidence map, so as to further do pixel loss correction. 3) We conduct experiments on a combination of three medical datasets, including LIDC-IDRI, LiTS and BraTS19 for segmentation tasks with noisy labels. The results show that our method achieves state-of-art performance in medical image segmentation with noisy labels.

2   Methodology

We propose a novel meta pixel loss correction method (MPLC) to correct loss function and generate a noise-robust segmentation network with noisy labels. The detailed architecture of our proposed framework and workflow are shown in Fig. 1. And it consists of two components: (1) a segmentation network based on U-Net (2) a meta guided network for generating the pixel transition confidence map to do further pixel loss correction. The components are trained in an end-to-end manner and are described as follows.

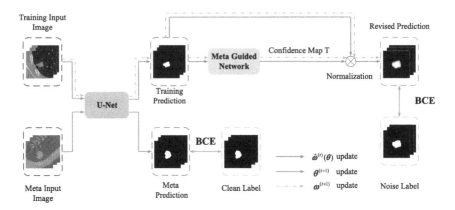

Fig. 1. Overview of our workflow in one loop.

2.1   Meta Pixel Loss Correction

Given a set of training noisy label samples $S = \left\{(X^i, \tilde{Y}^i), 1 \leq i \leq N\right\}$, where X^i is training input images, $\tilde{Y}^i \in \{0,1\}^{h \times w \times c}$ represent the observed noisy labels, denote training images with noisy segmentation annotations. We use U-Net [14] as the backbone DNN for segmentation and it generates a prediction P^i from the function $P^i = f(X^i, \omega)$, where f denotes the U-Net and ω denotes the parameters of U-Net. For a conventional segmentation task, cross entropy is used as the loss function $Loss = l(P^i, \tilde{Y}^i)$ to learn the parameters ω.

However, there may exist many noisy labels in the training dataset which contributes to the poor performance of the trained U-Net. Because the influences of these errors in the loss function can lead the gradient into the probably wrong direction and cause overfitting issues [16]. Instead of simply excluding the corrupted unreliable pixel [11,18], we aim to take advantage of these noisy labels.

T Construction. Assuming that there is a pixel transition confidence map T, which can bridge clean label and noisy label, specifying the probability of clean label flipping to noisy label. T will be applied to the segmentation prediction through the transition function and finally we get the revised prediction, which resembles the relative noisy mask. Thus, the noisy labels are used properly and the original cross entropy loss between the revised prediction and the noisy mask can work as usual, which approximately equals to training on clean labels.

In this paper, we design a learning framework with prediction P^i which could adaptively generate pixel transition confidence map T for every training step

$$T^i = g(P^i, \theta), \tag{1}$$

where θ indicates the parameters of that framework. Specifically, for T in every pixel, we have

$$T^i_{xy} = p(\tilde{Y}^i_{xy} = m | Y^i_{xy} = n), \forall m, n \in \{0, 1\}, \tag{2}$$

where T_{xy}^i represents the confidence of transitioning from the latent clean label Y_{xy}^i to the observed noisy label $\tilde{Y}_{xy}^i$ at pixel (x,y). Corrupted pixels have low pixel confidence but high transition probability. Due to binary segmentation, we assume the size of the pixel transition matrix is $N \times C \times H \times W$, where $C = 2$ represents the foreground and background in our paper. Each value in the transition matrix from different C represents the confidence that the pixel in foreground and background keep not flipping to other.

We can use T_{xy}^i to do pixel loss correction and the loss function of the whole model can be written as:

$$Loss = -\frac{1}{Nhw} \sum_{i=1}^{N} \sum_{x=1}^{h} \sum_{y=1}^{w} l(\mathcal{H}_{trans}(T_{xy}^i, f(X_{xy}^i, \omega)), \tilde{Y}_{xy}^i), \tag{3}$$

$$\mathcal{H}_{trans}(T_{xy}^i, f(X_{xy}^i, \omega)) = P_{xy}^i * T_{xy}^i(C = 1) + (1 - P_{xy}^i) * (1 - T_{xy}^i(C = 0)) \tag{4}$$

where l is BCE loss function, $\mathcal{H}_{trans}$ is the transition function between foreground and background. In our method, the transition function Eq. 4 represents the foreground of prediction keeps no change and the background of prediction flips into the foreground.

Optimization. Given a fixed θ, the optimized solution to ω can be found through minimizing the following objective function:

$$\omega^*(\theta) = \arg\min_{\omega} \frac{1}{Nhw} \sum_{i=1}^{N} \sum_{x=1}^{h} \sum_{y=1}^{w} l(\mathcal{H}_{trans}(T_{xy}^i, f(X_{xy}^i, \omega)), \tilde{Y}_{xy}^i). \tag{5}$$

We then introduce how to learn the parameters θ through our meta guided network. Motivated by the success of meta-parameter optimization, our method takes advantage of a small trusted dataset to correct the probably wrong direction of the gradient and guide the generation of pixel loss correction map. Specifically, we leverage an additional meta data set $\mathcal{S} = \{(\mathcal{X}^j, \mathcal{Y}^j), 1 \leq j \leq M\}$ which has clean annotations. M is the number of meta-samples and $M \ll N$. Given a meta input $\mathcal{X}^j$ and optimized parameters $\omega^*(\theta)$, through segmentation network, we can obtain the prediction map as $\mathcal{P}^j = f(\mathcal{X}^j, \omega^*(\theta))$, the meta loss for the meta dataset can be written as:

$$Loss_{meta} = -\frac{1}{Mhw} \sum_{j=1}^{M} \sum_{x=1}^{h} \sum_{y=1}^{w} l(f(\mathcal{X}_{xy}^i, \omega^*(\theta)), \mathcal{Y}_{xy}^i), \tag{6}$$

Combined with Eq.(5) and Eq.(6), it is formulated into a bi-level minimization problem and the optimized solution to θ^* can be acquired through minimizing the following objective function:

$$\theta^* = \arg\min_{\theta} \frac{1}{Mhw} \sum_{j=1}^{M} \sum_{x=1}^{h} \sum_{y=1}^{w} l(f(\mathcal{X}_{xy}^i, \omega^*(\theta)), \mathcal{Y}_{xy}^i). \tag{7}$$

After achieving θ^*, we can then get the pixel transition confidence map, which estimates the transition confidence from correct labels to be corrupted ones to help train a noise-robust segmentation model.

Input	GroundTruth	Prediction	Revised Prediction	Noise Mask

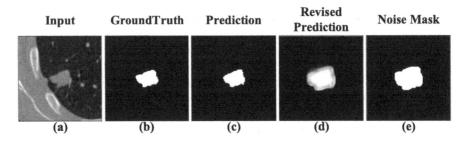

| (a) | (b) | (c) | (d) | (e) |

Fig. 2. Illustration of working processing about meta guided network. (Dilation operator is used to generate noise)

Meta Guided Network. For the meta guided network g in the Eq. (1), we explore the different architectures, which need to satisfy the auto-encoder structure of U-Net and be also easy trained for the small meta dataset by meta-learning. In this paper, SENet [5] has been used as the backbone, which is a simple and easy trained structure and generates the same size result as U-Net for transition. By feeding the prediction P^i, this meta guide network can adaptively recalibrate latent transition confidence by explicitly modeling interdependencies between channels, especially in favor of finding the transition confidence from correct labels to the corrupted ones.

From Fig. 2, we can see that how our meta guided network work to build a noise-robust model. By feeding the prediction (c) to the meta guided network, the relative pixel transition confidence map can be obtained. Corrupted pixels have low pixel confidence but high transition probability. After the transition function with the confidence map, the prediction is turned into the revised prediction (d), which is very similar to the noisy mask (e). Finally, cross entropy can be used between revised prediction and observed noisy mask to train the segmentation model. This enables our method to train a noise-robust segmentation network with noisy labels.

2.2   Optimization Algorithm

The algorithm includes mainly following steps. Given the training input $(X^i, \tilde{Y}^i)$, we can then deduce the formulate of one-step w updating with respect to θ as

$$\hat{\omega}(\theta) = \omega^{(t)} - \alpha \frac{1}{Nhw} \sum_{i=1}^{N} \sum_{x=1}^{h} \sum_{y=1}^{w} \nabla_w l(\mathcal{H}_{trans}(T_{xy}^{i(t)}, f(X_{xy}^i, \omega)), \tilde{Y}_{xy}^i), \quad (8)$$

where α is the learning rate and $T_{xy}^{i(t)}$ is computed by feeding the pixel-level prediction into meta guided network with parameters $\theta^{(t)}$.

Then, with current mini-batch meta data samples$(\mathcal{X}^j, \mathcal{Y}^j)$, we can perform one-step updating for solving

$$\theta^{(t+1)} = \theta^{(t)} - \beta \frac{1}{Mhw} \sum_{j=1}^{M} \sum_{x=1}^{h} \sum_{y=1}^{w} \nabla_\theta l(f(\mathcal{X}_{xy}^i, \hat{\omega}(\theta)), \mathcal{Y}_{xy}^i), \quad (9)$$

Algorithm 1: The proposed learning Algorithm

Input: Training data S, meta data $\mathcal{S}$, batch size n m, the number of iterations I

1 Initialize segmentation network parameter ω and meta guided network parameter θ;

2 **for** $t = 1$ **to** I **do**

3      $X, Y \leftarrow$ Sample minibatch (S, n);

4      $\mathcal{X}^m, \mathcal{Y}^m \leftarrow$ Sample minibatch $(\mathcal{S}, m)$;

5   Update $\theta^{(t+1)}$ by Eq.(9);

6   Update $\omega^{(t+1)}$ by Eq.(10);

7   Update T by the current segmentation network with parameter $\omega^{(t+1)}$;

8 **end**

Output: Segmentation network parameter ω^{I+1}

---

where β is learning rate and we use autograd to calculate Jacobian. After we achieve $\theta^{(t+1)}$, we can update w, that is

$$\omega^{(t+1)} = \omega^{(t)} - \alpha \frac{1}{Nhw} \sum_{i=1}^{N} \sum_{x=1}^{h} \sum_{y=1}^{w} \nabla_w l(\mathcal{H}_{trans}(T_{xy}^{i(t+1)}, f(X_{xy}^i, \omega), \tilde{Y}_{xy}^i), \quad (10)$$

The predict $T_{xy}^{i(t+1)}$ is updated with the parameters of $\omega^{(t+1)}$ of the segmentation network. The entire algorithm is then summarized in Algorithm 1.

3 Experiment Results

3.1 Dataset

We evaluate our method on three medical segmentation datasets: LIDC-IDRI [1], LiTS [4] and BraTS2019 [10], which were selected for lesion segmentation. We follow the same preprocessing and experiment settings with [18] on the LIDC-IDRI and LiTS datasets with 64×64 cropped lesion patches. **LIDC-IDRI** is a lung CT dataset consisting of 1018 lung CT scans. 3591 patches are adopted, which are split into a training set of 1906 images, a testing set of 1385 images and the last 300 images for the meta set. **LiTS** contains 130 abdomen CT liver scans with tumors and liver segmentation challenge. 2214 samples are sampled from this dataset. 1471, 300 and 443 images are used for training, meta weight learning, and testing respectively. **BraTS19** is a brain tumor challenge dataset. It consists of 385 labeled 3D MRI scans and each MRI scan has four modalities (T1, T1 contrast-enhanced, T2 and FLAIR). 3863 ET lesion patches are adopted and training dataset, meta dataset and testing dataset contain 1963 samples, 300 samples and 1600 samples respectively. Specifically, because our input is cropped lesion patch, the challenge results can not be cited in our experiments.

Table 1. Results of segmentation models on LIDC-IDRI. ($r = 0.4$)

Noise	Dilation			ElasticDeform		
Model name	mIOU	Dice	Hausdorff	mIOU	Dice	Hausdorff
U-Net [14]	62.53	75.56	1.9910	65.01	76.17	1.9169
Prob U-Net [9]	66.42	78.39	1.8817	68.43	79.50	1.8757
Phi-Seg [3]	67.01	79.06	1.8658	68.55	81.76	1.8429
UA-MT [19]	68.18	80.98	1.8574	68.84	82.47	1.8523
Curriculum [8]	67.78	79.54	1.8977	68.18	81.30	1.8691
Few-Shot GAN [12]	67.74	78.11	1.9137	67.93	77.83	1.9223
Quality Control [2]	65.00	76.50	1.9501	68.07	77.68	1.9370
U2 Net [6]	65.92	76.01	1.9666	67.20	77.05	1.9541
MWNet [15]	71.56	81.17	1.7762	71.89	81.04	1.7680
MCPM [18]	74.69	84.64	1.7198	75.79	84.99	1.7053
Our MPLC	**77.24**	**87.16**	**1.6387**	**77.52**	**87.44**	**1.6157**

3.2   Experiment Setting

Noise Setting: Extensive experiments have been conducted under different types of noise. We artificially corrupted the target lesion mask with two types of label degradation: dilation morphology operator and ElasticDeform. 1) Dilation morphology operator: the foreground region is expanded by several pixels (randomly drawn from [0, 6]). 2) ElasticDeform [17]: label noise is generated by complicated operations such as rotation, translation, deformation and morphology dilation on groundtruth labels. Specifically, we set a probability r as the noisy label ratio to represent the proportion of noisy corrupted labels in all data.

Implementation Detail: We train our model with SGD at initial learning rate $1e{-}4$ and a momentum 0.9, a weight decay $1e{-}3$ with mini-batch size 60. Set $\alpha = 1e{-}4, \beta = 1e{-}3$ in all the experiments. The learning rate decay 0.1 in 30th epoch and 60th epoch for a total of 120 epoch. mIOU, Dice and Hausdorff were used to evaluate our method.

3.3   Experimental Results

Comparisons with State-of-the-Art Methods. In this section, we set r to 40% for all experiments, which means 40% training labels are noisy labels with corrupted pixels. There are 9 existing segmentation methods for the similarity task on the LIDC-IDRI dataset, including: Prob U-Net [9], Phi-Seg [3], UA-MT [19], Curriculum [8], Few-Shot GAN [12], Quality Control [2], U2 Net [6], MWNet [15] and MCPM [18]. Visualization results are shown in Fig. 3.

Table 1 shows the results of all competing methods on the LIDC-IDRI dataset with the aforementioned experiment setting. It can be observed that our method gets the best performance. Specifically, compared with MCPM and MWNet, which use the re-weighting method, our algorithm has the competitive Dice result (87.16) and it outperforms the second best method(MCPM) by 2.52%.

An extra **t-test comparison** experiment has been done between our method and the second best method(MCPM), and the result shows that P-value < 0.01, which represents there is a statistical difference between our method and MCPM.

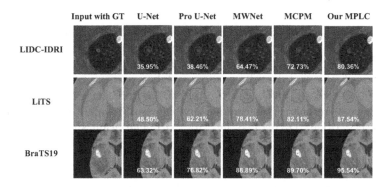

Fig. 3. Visualization of segmentation results under $r = 0.8$ in this section. Green and red contours indicate the ground-truths and segmentation results, respectively. The Dice value is shown at the bottom line, and our method produces much better results than other methods on every dataset. (Color figure online)

Robustness to Various R-S. We explore the robustness of our MPLC under the various percent of noise label ratio r {0.2, 0.4, 0.6, 0.8}. It has been evaluated on LIDC-IDRI, LiTS and BraTS19 datasets under the dilation operation. Table 2 shows the results compared with baseline approaches. It shows that our method consistently outperforms other methods across all the noise ratios on all datasets, showing the effectiveness of our meta pixel loss correction strategy.

Table 2. Results (mIOU) of segmentation methods using various r-s.(Noise=Dilation)

Dataset	LIDC-IDRI				LiTS				BraTS19			
r	0.8	0.6	0.4	0.2	0.8	0.6	0.4	0.2	0.8	0.6	0.4	0.2
U-Net [14]	42.64	51.23	62.53	69.88	37.18	43.55	46.41	51.20	32.51	50.02	56.27	63.65
Prob U-Net	52.13	60.81	66.42	71.03	40.16	45.90	49.22	53.97	55.04	56.25	58.08	62.64
MWNet [15]	61.28	67.33	71.56	72.07	43.14	44.97	51.96	58.65	60.63	66.06	67.99	69.50
MCPM [18]	67.60	68.97	74.69	74.87	45.09	48.76	55.17	62.04	61.74	67.39	67.93	69.52
Our MPLC	**73.04**	**76.07**	**77.24**	**78.16**	**62.25**	**64.53**	**65.56**	**66.44**	**63.67**	**67.79**	**69.09**	**71.79**

3.4   Limitation

Because our approach is based on the instance-independent assumption that $P(\tilde{y}|y) = P(\tilde{y}|x, y)$. It is more suitable to model single noise distribution but fails in real-world stochastic noise like the complicated noise setting with multi noises(erosion, dilation, deformity, false negatives, false positives). When it is extended to instance-dependent, we should model the relationship among clean label, noisy label and instance for $P(\tilde{y}|x, y)$ in future work.

4   Conclusion

We present a novel Meta Pixel Loss Correction method to alleviate the negative effect of noisy labels in medical image segmentation. Given a small number of high-quality labeled images, the deduced learning regime makes our meta guided network able to take full use of noisy labels and estimate the pixel transition confidence map, which can be used to do further pixel loss correction and train a noise-robust segmentation. We extensively evaluated our method on three datasets, LIDC-IDRI, LiTS and BraTS19. The result shows that the proposed method can outperform state-of-the-art in medical image segmentation with noisy labels.

Acknowledgment. This work was supported by by the National Natural Science Foundation of China under Grant 61790562 and Grant 61773312.

References

1. Armato, S.G., et al.: The lung image database consortium (LIDC) and image database resource initiative (IDRI): a completed reference database of lung nodules on CT scans. Acad. Radiol. **14**(12), 1455–1463 (2007)
2. Audelan, B., Delingette, H.: Unsupervised quality control of image segmentation based on Bayesian learning. In: Shen, D., et al. (eds.) MICCAI 2019. LNCS, vol. 11765, pp. 21–29. Springer, Cham (2019). https://doi.org/10.1007/978-3-030-32245-8_3
3. Baumgartner, F., et al.: PHiSeg: capturing uncertainty in medical image segmentation. In: Shen, D., et al. (eds.) MICCAI 2019. LNCS, vol. 11765, pp. 119–127. Springer, Cham (2019). https://doi.org/10.1007/978-3-030-32245-8_14
4. Han, X.: Automatic liver lesion segmentation using a deep convolutional neural network method (2017)
5. Hu, J., Shen, L., Albanie, S., Sun, G., Wu, E.: Squeeze-and-excitation networks. IEEE Trans. Pattern Anal. Mach. Intell. **42**(8), 2011–2023 (2020). https://doi.org/10.1109/TPAMI.2019.2913372
6. Huang, C., Han, H., Yao, Q., Zhu, S., Zhou, S.K.: 3D U^2-net: a 3D universal u-net for multi-domain medical image segmentation. In: Shen, D., et al. (eds.) MICCAI 2019. LNCS, vol. 11765, pp. 291–299. Springer, Cham (2019). https://doi.org/10.1007/978-3-030-32245-8_33
7. Karimi, D., Dou, H., Warfield, S.K., Gholipour, A.: Deep learning with noisy labels: Exploring techniques and remedies in medical image analysis. Med. Image Anal. **65**, 101759 (2020)
8. Kervadec, H., Dolz, J., Granger, É., Ben Ayed, I.: Curriculum semi-supervised segmentation. In: Shen, D., et al. (eds.) MICCAI 2019. LNCS, vol. 11765, pp. 568–576. Springer, Cham (2019). https://doi.org/10.1007/978-3-030-32245-8_63

9. Kohl, S.A., et al.: A probabilistic u-net for segmentation of ambiguous images. arXiv preprint arXiv:1806.05034 (2018)

10. Menze, B.H., Jakab, A., Bauer, S., et al.: The multimodal brain tumor image segmentation benchmark (brats). IEEE Trans. Med. Imaging **34**(10), 1993–2024 (2015). https://doi.org/10.1109/TMI.2014.2377694

11. Mirikharaji, Z., Yan, Y., Hamarneh, G.: Learning to segment skin lesions from noisy annotations. In: Wang, Q., et al. (eds.) DART/MIL3ID -2019. LNCS, vol. 11795, pp. 207–215. Springer, Cham (2019). https://doi.org/10.1007/978-3-030-33391-1_24

12. Mondal, A.K., Dolz, J., Desrosiers, C.: Few-shot 3d multi-modal medical image segmentation using generative adversarial learning. arXiv preprint arXiv:1810.12241 (2018)

13. Ren, M., Zeng, W., Yang, B., Urtasun, R.: Learning to reweight examples for robust deep learning. In: International Conference on Machine Learning, pp. 4334–4343. PMLR (2018)

14. Ronneberger, O., Fischer, P., Brox, T.: U-net: convolutional networks for biomedical image segmentation. In: Navab, N., Hornegger, J., Wells, W.M., Frangi, A.F. (eds.) MICCAI 2015. LNCS, vol. 9351, pp. 234–241. Springer, Cham (2015). https://doi.org/10.1007/978-3-319-24574-4_28

15. Shu, J., et al.: Meta-weight-net: learning an explicit mapping for sample weighting. arXiv preprint arXiv:1902.07379 (2019)

16. Song, H., Kim, M., Park, D., Shin, Y., Lee, J.G.: Learning from noisy labels with deep neural networks: a survey. IEEE Transactions on Neural Networks and Learning Systems (2022)

17. van Tulder, G.: Package elsticdeform. http://github.com/gvtulder/elasticdeform/. Accessed 4 Dec 2018

18. Wang, J., Zhou, S., Fang, C., Wang, L., Wang, J.: Meta corrupted pixels mining for medical image segmentation. In: Martel, A.L., et al. (eds.) MICCAI 2020. LNCS, vol. 12261, pp. 335–345. Springer, Cham (2020). https://doi.org/10.1007/978-3-030-59710-8_33

19. Yu, L., Wang, S., Li, X., Fu, C.-W., Heng, P.-A.: Uncertainty-aware self-ensembling model for semi-supervised 3D left atrium segmentation. In: Shen, D., et al. (eds.) MICCAI 2019. LNCS, vol. 11765, pp. 605–613. Springer, Cham (2019). https://doi.org/10.1007/978-3-030-32245-8_67

20. Zhu, H., Shi, J., Wu, J.: Pick-and-learn: automatic quality evaluation for noisy-labeled image segmentation. In: Shen, D., et al. (eds.) MICCAI 2019. LNCS, vol. 11769, pp. 576–584. Springer, Cham (2019). https://doi.org/10.1007/978-3-030-32226-7_64

Re-thinking and Re-labeling LIDC-IDRI for Robust Pulmonary Cancer Prediction

Hanxiao Zhang[1], Xiao Gu[2], Minghui Zhang[1], Weihao Yu[1], Liang Chen[3], Zhexin Wang[3(✉)], Feng Yao[3], Yun Gu[1,4(✉)], and Guang-Zhong Yang[1(✉)]

[1] Institute of Medical Robotics, Shanghai Jiao Tong University, Shanghai, China
{geron762,gzyang}@sjtu.edu.cn
[2] Imperial College London, London, UK
[3] Department of Thoracic Surgery, Shanghai Chest Hospital,
Shanghai Jiao Tong University, Shanghai, China
wangzhexin001@hotmail.com
[4] Shanghai Center for Brain Science and Brain-Inspired Technology,
Shanghai, China

Abstract. The LIDC-IDRI database is the most popular benchmark for lung cancer prediction. However, with subjective assessment from radiologists, nodules in LIDC may have entirely different malignancy annotations from the pathological ground truth, introducing label assignment errors and subsequent supervision bias during training. The LIDC database thus requires more objective labels for learning-based cancer prediction. Based on an extra small dataset containing 180 nodules diagnosed by pathological examination, we propose to re-label LIDC data to mitigate the effect of original annotation bias verified on this robust benchmark. We demonstrate in this paper that providing new labels by similar nodule retrieval based on metric learning would be an effective re-labeling strategy. Training on these re-labeled LIDC nodules leads to improved model performance, which is enhanced when new labels of uncertain nodules are added. We further infer that re-labeling LIDC is current an expedient way for robust lung cancer prediction while building a large pathological-proven nodule database provides the long-term solution.

Keywords: Pulmonary nodule · Cancer prediction · Metric learning · Re-labeling

1 Introduction

The LIDC-IDRI (Lung Image Database Consortium and Image Database Resource Initiative) [1] is a leading source of public datasets. Since the introduction of LIDC, it is used extensively for lung nodule detection and cancer prediction using learning-based methods [4,6,11,12,15–17,21,23].

G. Zamzmi et al. (Eds.): MILLanD 2022, LNCS 13559, pp. 42–51, 2022.
https://doi.org/10.1007/978-3-031-16760-7_5

When searching papers in PubMed[1] with the following filter: *("deep learning" OR convolutional) AND (CT OR "computed tomography") AND (lung OR pulmonary) AND (nodule OR cancer OR "nodule malignancy") AND (prediction OR classification)*, among 53 papers assessed for eligibility of nodule malignancy classification, 40 papers used LIDC database, 5 papers used NSLT (National Lung Screening Trial) database[2] [10,18,19] (no exact nodule location provided), and 8 papers used other individual datasets. LIDC is therefore the most popular benchmark in cancer prediction research.

A careful examination of the LIDC database, however, reveals several potential issues for cancer prediction. During the annotation of LIDC, characteristics of nodules were assessed by multiple radiologists, where the rating of malignancy scores (1 to 5) was based on the assumption of a **60-year-old male smoker**. Due to the lack of clinical information, these malignancy scores were subjective. Although a subset of LIDC cases possesses patient-based pathological diagnosis [13], its nodule-level binary labels can not be confirmed.

Since it is hard to recapture the pathological ground truth for each LIDC nodule, we apply the extra SCH-LND dataset [24] with pathological-proven labels, which is used not only for establishing a truthful and fair evaluation benchmark but also for transferring pathological knowledge for different clinical indications.

In this paper, we first assess the nodule prediction performances of LIDC driven model in six scenarios and their fine-tuning effects using SCH-LND with detailed experiments. Having identified the problems of the undecided binary label assignment scheme on the original LIDC database and unstable transfer learning outcomes, we seek to re-label LIDC nodule classes by interacting with the SCH-LND. The first re-labeling strategy adopts the state-of-the-art nodule classifier as an end-to-end annotator, but it has no contribution to LIDC re-labeling. The second strategy uses metric learning to learn similarity and discrimination between the nodule pairs, which is then used to elect new LIDC labels based on the similarity ranking in a pairwise manner between the under-labeled LIDC nodule and each nodule of SCH-LND. Experiments show that the models trained with re-labeled LIDC data created by metric learning model not only resolve the bias problem of the original data but also transcend the performance of our model, especially when the new labels of the uncertain subset are added. Further statistical results demonstrate that the re-labeled LIDC data suffers class imbalance problem, which indicates us to build a larger nodule database with pathological-proven labels.

2   Materials

LIDC-IDRI Database: According to the practice in [14], we excluded CT scans with slice thickness larger than 3 mm and sampled nodules identified by at least three radiologists. We only involve solid nodules in SCH-LND and LIDC databases because giving accurate labels for solid nodules is of great challenge.

---

[1] https://pubmed.ncbi.nlm.nih.gov/.

[2] https://cdas.cancer.gov/datasets/nlst/.

Extra Dataset: The extra dataset called SCH-LND [24] consists of 180 solid nodules (90 benign/90 malignant) with exact spatial coordinates and radii. Each sample is very rare because all the nodules are confirmed and diagnosed by immediate pathological examination via biopsy with ethical approval.

To regulate variant CT formats, CT slice thickness is resampled to 1mm/pixel if it is larger than 1 mm/pixel, while the X and Y axes are fixed to 512×512 pixels. Each pixel value is unified to the HU (Hounsfield Unit) value before nodule volume cropping.

3   Study Design

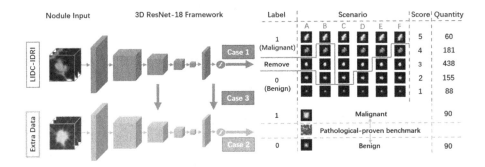

Fig. 1. Illustration of the study design for nodule cancer prediction. **Case 1:** training from scratch over the LIDC database after assigning nodule labels according to the average malignancy scores in 6 scenarios. **Case 2:** training over extra data based on accurate pathological-proven labels by 5-fold cross-validation. **Case 3:** testing or fine-tuning LIDC models of Case 1 using extra data.

The preliminary study follows the instructions of Fig. 1 where two types of cases (Case 1 and Case 2) conduct training and testing in each single data domain and one type of case (Case 3) involves domain interaction (cross-domain testing and transfer learning) between LIDC and SCH-LND. In Case 1 and Case 3, we identify 6 different scenarios by removing uncertain average scores (Scenarios A and B) or setting division threshold (Scenarios C, D, E, and F) to assign binary labels for LIDC data training. Training details are described in Sect. 5.1.

To evaluate the model performance comprehensively, we additionally introduce Specificity (also called Recall$_b$, when treating benign as positive sample) and Precision$_b$ (Precision in benign class) [20], besides regular evaluation metrics including Sensitivity (Recall), Precision, Accuracy, and F1 score.

Based on the visual assessment of radiologists, human-defined nodule features can be easily extracted and classified by a commonly used model (3D ResNet-18 [5]), whose performance can emulate the experts' one (Fig. 2, Case 1). Many studies still put investigational efforts for better results across the LIDC board, overlooking inaccurate radiologists' estimations and bad model capability in the real world. However, once the same model is revalidated under

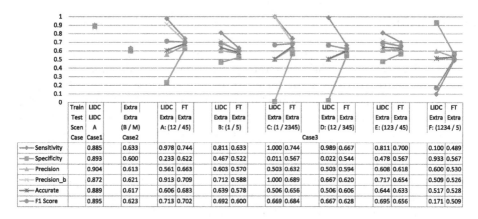

	Train	LIDC		Extra		LIDC	FT	LIDC	FT	LIDC	FT	LIDC	FT	LIDC	FT	LIDC	FT
	Test	LIDC		Extra		Extra	Extra	Extra	Extra	Extra	Extra	Extra	Extra	Extra	Extra	Extra	Extra
	Scen	A		(B / M)		A: (12 / 45)		B: (1 / 5)		C: (1 / 2345)		D: (12 / 345)		E: (123 / 45)		F: (1234 / 5)	
	Case	Case1		Case2		Case3											
Sensitivity		0.885		0.633		0.978	0.744	0.811	0.633	1.000	0.744	0.989	0.667	0.811	0.700	0.100	0.489
Specificity		0.893		0.600		0.233	0.622	0.467	0.522	0.011	0.567	0.022	0.544	0.478	0.567	0.933	0.567
Precision		0.904		0.613		0.561	0.663	0.603	0.570	0.503	0.632	0.503	0.594	0.608	0.618	0.600	0.530
Precision_b		0.872		0.621		0.913	0.709	0.712	0.588	1.000	0.689	0.667	0.620	0.717	0.654	0.509	0.526
Accurate		0.889		0.617		0.606	0.683	0.639	0.578	0.506	0.656	0.506	0.606	0.644	0.633	0.517	0.528
F1 Score		0.895		0.623		0.713	0.702	0.692	0.600	0.669	0.684	0.667	0.628	0.695	0.656	0.171	0.509

Fig. 2. Performance comparisons between different Cases or Scenarios (Scen) in Fig. 1. For instance, 'A:(12/45)' represents 'Scenario A' that treats LIDC scores 1 & 2 as benign labels and scores 4 & 5 as malignant labels. FT denotes fine-tuning using extra data by 5-fold cross-validation based on the pre-trained model in each scenario.

the pathological-proven benchmark (Fig. 2, Case 3, Scenario A), its drawback is objectively revealed that LIDC model decisions take up too many false-positive predictions. These two experimental outcomes raise a suspicion that whether the visual assessment of radiologists might have a bias toward malignant class.

To resolve this suspicion, we compare the performances of 6 scenarios in Case 3. Evidence reveals that, under the testing data from SCH-LND, the number of false-positive predictions has a declining trend when the division threshold moves from the benign side to the malignant side, but the bias problem is still serious when reaching Scenario E, much less of Scenario A and B. Besides, as training on the SCH-LND dataset from scratch can hardly obtain a high capacity model (Fig. 2, Case 2), we use transfer learning in Case 3 to get the model fine-tuned on the basis of weights of different pre-trained LIDC models.

Observing the inter-comparison within each scenario in Case 3, transfer learning can push scattered metric values close. However, compared with Case 2, the fine-tuning technique would bring both positive and negative transfer, depending upon the property of the pre-trained model.

Thus, either for training from scratch or transfer learning process, the radiologists' assessment of LIDC nodule malignancy can be hard to properly use. In addition to its inevitable assessment errors, there is a thorny problem to assign LIDC labels (how to set division threshold) and removing uncertain subset (waste of data). We thus expect to re-label the LIDC malignancy classes with the interaction of SCH-LND, to correct the assessment bias as well as utilize the uncertain nodules (average score = 3). Two independent approaches are described in the following section.

4   Methods

We put forward two re-labeling strategies to obtain new ground truth labels on the LIDC database. The first strategy generates the malignancy label from a machine annotator: the state-of-the-art nodule classifier that has been pre-trained on LIDC data and fine-tuned on SCH-LND to predict nodule class. The second strategy ranks the top nodules' labels using a machine comparator: a metric-based Network that measures the correlation between nodule pairs.

Considering that the knowledge from radiologists' assessments could be a useful resource, in each strategy, two modes of LIDC re-labeling are proposed. **For Mode 1 (Substitute):** LIDC completely accepts the re-label outcomes from other label machines. **For Mode 2 (Consensus):** The final LIDC re-label results would be decided by the consensus of label machine outcomes and its original label (Scenario A). In other words, this mode will leave behind the nodules with the same label and discard controversial ones, which may cause data reduction. We evaluate the LIDC re-labeling effect by using SCH-LND to test the model which is trained with re-labeled data from scratch.

4.1   Label Induction Using Machine Annotator

The optimized model with fine-tuning technique can correct the learning bias initiated by LIDC data. Some fine-tuned models even surpass the LIDC model performance in large scales of evaluation metrics. We wonder whether the current best performance model can help classify and annotate new LIDC labels. Experiments will be conducted using two annotation models from Case 2 and Case 3 (Scenario A) in Sect. 3.

4.2   Similar Nodule Retrieval Using Metric Learning

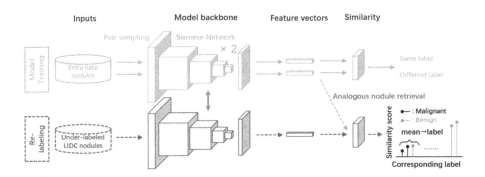

Fig. 3. The second strategy of LIDC re-labeling that using a metric learning model to search for the most similar nodules and give new labels.

Metric learning [2,7] provides a few-shot learning approach that aims to learn useful representations through distance comparisons. We use Siamese Network

[3,9] in this study which consists of two networks whose parameters are tied to each other. Parameter tying guarantees that two similar nodules will be mapped by their respective networks to adjacent locations in feature space.

For training a Siamese Network in Fig. 3, we pass the inputs in the set of pairs. Each pair is randomly chosen from SCH-LND and given the label whether two nodules of this pair are in the same class. Then these two nodule volumes are passed through the 3D ResNet-18 to generate a fixed-length feature vector individually. A reasonable hypothesis is given that: if the two nodules belong to the same class, their feature vectors should have a small distance metric; otherwise, their feature vectors will have a large distance metric. In order to distinguish between the same and different pairs of nodules when training, we apply contrastive loss over the Euclidean distance metric (similarity score) induced by the malignancy representation.

During re-labeling, we first pair each nodule from SCH-LND used in training up with an under-labeled LIDC nodule and sort each under-labeled nodule partner by their similarity scores. Then the new LIDC label is awarded by averaging the labels of the top 20% partner nodules in the ranking list of similarity scores.

5   Experiments and Results

5.1   Implementation

We apply 3D ResNet-18 [5] in this paper with adaptive average pooling (output size of $1 \times 1 \times 1$) following the final convolution layer. For the general cancer prediction model, we use a fully connected layer and a Sigmoid function to output the prediction score (binary cross-entropy loss). While for Siamese Network, we use a fully connected layer to generate the feature vector (8 neurons). Due to various nodule sizes, the batch size is set to 1, and group normalization [22] is adopted after each convolution layer.

All the experiments are implemented in PyTorch with a single NVIDIA GeForce GTX 1080 Ti GPU and learned using the Adam optimizer [8] with the learning rate of 1e–3 (100 epochs) and that of 1e–4 for fine-tuning in transfer learning (50 epochs). The validation set occupies 20% of the training set in each experiment. All the experiments and results involving or having involved the training of SCH-LND are strictly conducted by 5-fold cross-validation.

5.2   Quantitative Evaluation

To evaluate the first strategy using machine annotator, we first use Case 2 model to re-label LIDC nodules (a form of 5-fold cross-validation) other than the uncertain subset (original average score = 3). The re-labeled nodules are then fed into the 3D ResNet-18 model, which will be trained from scratch and tested on the corresponding subset of SCH-LND for evaluation. The result (4th row) shows

Table 1. Performances of different re-labeling methods based on each mode of re-labeling strategies. Under-labeled LIDC data are chosen by their original average score.

Row	Baselines	Method	Training	Testing	Sensitivity	Specificity	Precision	Precision$_b$	Accuracy	F1
1		Case 3-A	LIDC	Extra	0.9778	0.2333	0.5605	0.9130	0.6056	0.7126
2		Case 2	Extra	Extra	0.6333	0.6000	0.6129	0.6207	0.6167	0.6230
3		Siamese	Extra	Extra	0.6667	0.6000	0.6250	0.6429	0.6333	0.6452
LIDC re-labeling										
	Strategy	Mode	Method	Under-label	Sensitivity	Specificity	Precision	Precision$_b$	Accuracy	F1
4	Annotator	Substitute	Case 2	1;2;4;5	0.5778	0.5667	0.5714	0.5730	0.5722	0.5746
5			Case 3-A		0.4630	0.6667	0.5814	0.5538	0.5648	0.5155
6		Consensus	Case 2		0.8778	0.3667	0.5809	0.7500	0.6222	0.6991
7			Case 3-A		0.8556	0.3778	0.5789	0.7234	0.6167	0.6906
8	Comparator	Substitute	Siamese	1;2;4;5	0.6111	0.6556	0.6395	0.6277	0.6333	0.6250
9				1;2;3;4;5	0.6778	**0.6667**	**0.6703**	0.6742	**0.6722**	**0.6740**
10		Consensus		1;2;4;5	0.8000	0.3778	0.5625	0.6538	0.5889	0.6606
11				1;2;3;4;5	0.7333	0.5889	0.6408	0.6883	0.6611	0.6839

that although this action greatly fixes label bias to a balanced state, this group of new labels can hardly build a model tested well on SCH-LND. Contrary to common sense, the state-of-the-art nodule classifier makes re-label performance worse (5th row), which is much lower than that of learning from scratch using SCH-LND (2nd row), indicating that the best model optimized with fine-tuning technique is not suitable for LIDC re-labeling. The initial two experiments adopting Mode 2 (Consensus) achieved better comprehensive outcomes than Mode 1 (Substitute) but with low Specificity (Table 1).

Metric learning takes a different re-label strategy that retrieves similar nodules according to the distance metric. Metric learning on a small dataset can obtain a better performance (3rd row) compared with general learning from scratch (2nd row). The re-label outcomes (8th and 9th row) also show great comprehensive improvement over baselines by Mode 1, where the re-labeling of uncertain nodules (average score = 3) is an important contributing factor.

Overall, there is a trade-off between Mode 1 and Mode 2. But Mode 2 seems to remain the LIDC bias property because testing results often have low Specificity and introduce data reduction. Re-labeling by consensus (Mode 2) may integrate the defects of both original labels and models, especially for malignant labels, while re-labeling uncertain nodules can help mitigate the defect of Mode 2.

We finally re-labeled the LIDC database with the Siamese Network trained using all of SCH-LND. As shown in Fig. 4, our re-labeled results are in broad agreement with the low malignancy score ones. In score 3 (uncertain data), the majority of the nodules are re-labeled to benign class, which explains the better performance when the nodules of score 3 are assigned to benign label in Scenario E (Fig. 2, Case 3). The new labels correct more than half of the original nodule labels with score 4 which could be the main reason leading to the data bias.

5.3   Discussion

Re-labeling through metric learning is distinct from the general supervised model in two notable ways. First, the input pairs generated by random sampling for

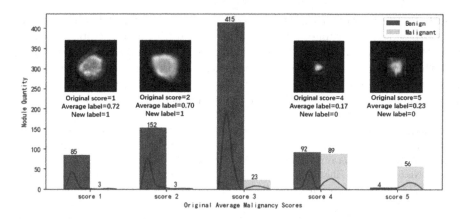

Fig. 4. Statistical result of LIDC re-labeling nodules (benign or malignant) in terms of original average malignancy scores, where the smooth curve describes the simplified frequency distribution histogram of average label outputs. For each average score of 1, 2, 4, and 5, one nodule re-labeling example with the opposite class (treat score 1 and 2 as benign; treat 4 and 5 as malignant) is provided.

metric learning provide a data augmentation effect to overcome overfitting with limited data. Second, under-labeled LIDC data take the average labels of top-ranked similarity nodules to increase the confidence of label propagation. These two points may explain why general supervised models (including fine-tuning models) perform worse than metric learning in re-labeling task. Unfortunately, after re-labeling, the class imbalance problem emerged (748 versus 174), while bringing up new limits in model training performance in the aforementioned experiments.

Moreover, due to the lack of pathological ground truth, the relabel outcomes of this study should always remain suspect until the LIDC clinical information is available. Considering a number of subsequent issues that LIDC may arise, sufficient evidence in this paper explores the motive for us to promote the ongoing collection work of a large pathological-proven nodule database, which is expected to become a powerful open-source database for the international medical imaging and clinical research community.

6   Conclusion and Future Work

The LIDC-IDRI database is currently the most popular public database of lung nodules with specific spatial coordinates and experts' annotations. However, because of the absence of clinical information, deep learning models trained based on this database have poor generalization capability in lung cancer prediction and downstream tasks. To challenge the low confidence labels of LIDC, an extra nodule dataset with pathological-proven labels was used to identify the annotation bias problems of LIDC and its label assignment difficulties. With the robust supervision of SCH-LND, we used a metric learning-based approach to re-label LIDC data according to the similar nodule retrieval. The empirical results show that with re-labeled LIDC data, improved performance is achieved along with the maximization of LIDC data utilization and the subsequent class imbalance problem. These conclusions provide a guideline for further collection of a large pathological-proven nodule database, which is beneficial to the community.

Acknowledgments. This work was partly supported by Medicine-Engineering Interdisciplinary Research Foundation of Shanghai Jiao Tong University (YG2021QN128), Shanghai Sailing Program (20YF1420800), National Nature Science Foundation of China (No.62003208), Shanghai Municipal of Science and Technology Project (Grant No. 20JC1419500), and Science and Technology Commission of Shanghai Municipality (Grant 20DZ2220400).

References

1. Armato, S.G., III., et al.: The lung image database consortium (LIDC) and image database resource initiative (IDRI): a completed reference database of lung nodules on CT scans. Med. Phys. **38**(2), 915–931 (2011)
2. Bellet, A., Habrard, A., Sebban, M.: Metric Learning. Synthesis Lectures on Artificial Intelligence and Machine Learning, vol. 9, no. 1, pp. 1–151 (2015)
3. Guo, Q., Feng, W., Zhou, C., Huang, R., Wan, L., Wang, S.: Learning dynamic siamese network for visual object tracking. In: Proceedings of the IEEE International Conference on Computer Vision, pp. 1763–1771 (2017)
4. Han, F., et al.: Texture feature analysis for computer-aided diagnosis on pulmonary nodules. J. Digit. Imaging **28**(1), 99–115 (2015)
5. He, K., Zhang, X., Ren, S., Sun, J.: Deep residual learning for image recognition. In: Proceedings of the IEEE Conference on Computer Vision and Pattern Recognition, pp. 770–778 (2016)
6. Hussein, S., Cao, K., Song, Q., Bagci, U.: Risk stratification of lung nodules using 3D CNN-based multi-task learning. In: Niethammer, M., et al. (eds.) IPMI 2017. LNCS, vol. 10265, pp. 249–260. Springer, Cham (2017). https://doi.org/10.1007/978-3-319-59050-9_20
7. Kaya, M., Bilge, H.Ş: Deep metric learning: a survey. Symmetry **11**(9), 1066 (2019)
8. Kingma, D.P., Ba, J.: Adam: a method for stochastic optimization. arXiv preprint arXiv:1412.6980 (2014)
9. Koch, G., Zemel, R., Salakhutdinov, R.: Siamese neural networks for one-shot image recognition. In: ICML Deep Learning Workshop, vol. 2. Lille (2015)
10. Kramer, B.S., Berg, C.D., Aberle, D.R., Prorok, P.C.: Lung cancer screening with low-dose helical CT: results from the national lung screening trial (NLST) (2011)
11. Liao, Z., Xie, Y., Hu, S., Xia, Y.: Learning from ambiguous labels for lung nodule malignancy prediction. arXiv preprint arXiv:2104.11436 (2021)
12. Liu, L., Dou, Q., Chen, H., Qin, J., Heng, P.A.: Multi-task deep model with margin ranking loss for lung nodule analysis. IEEE Trans. Med. Imaging **39**(3), 718–728 (2019)
13. McNitt-Gray, M.F., et al.: The lung image database consortium (LIDC) data collection process for nodule detection and annotation. Acad. Radiol. **14**(12), 1464–1474 (2007)

14. Setio, A.A.A., et al.: Validation, comparison, and combination of algorithms for automatic detection of pulmonary nodules in computed tomography images: the LUNA16 challenge. Med. Image Anal. **42**, 1–13 (2017)
15. Shen, W., et al.: Learning from experts: developing transferable deep features for patient-level lung cancer prediction. In: Ourselin, S., Joskowicz, L., Sabuncu, M.R., Unal, G., Wells, W. (eds.) MICCAI 2016. LNCS, vol. 9901, pp. 124–131. Springer, Cham (2016). https://doi.org/10.1007/978-3-319-46723-8_15
16. Shen, W., Zhou, M., Yang, F., Yang, C., Tian, J.: Multi-scale convolutional neural networks for lung nodule classification. In: Ourselin, S., Alexander, D.C., Westin, C.-F., Cardoso, M.J. (eds.) IPMI 2015. LNCS, vol. 9123, pp. 588–599. Springer, Cham (2015). https://doi.org/10.1007/978-3-319-19992-4_46
17. Shen, W., et al.: Multi-crop convolutional neural networks for lung nodule malignancy suspiciousness classification. Pattern Recogn. **61**, 663–673 (2017)
18. National Lung Screening Trial Research Team: The national lung screening trial: overview and study design. Radiology **258**(1), 243–253 (2011)
19. National Lung Screening Trial Research Team: Reduced lung-cancer mortality with low-dose computed tomographic screening. N. Engl. J. Med. **365**(5), 395–409 (2011)
20. Wu, B., Sun, X., Hu, L., Wang, Y.: Learning with unsure data for medical image diagnosis. In: Proceedings of the IEEE International Conference on Computer Vision, pp. 10590–10599 (2019)
21. Wu, B., Zhou, Z., Wang, J., Wang, Y.: Joint learning for pulmonary nodule segmentation, attributes and malignancy prediction. In: 2018 IEEE 15th International Symposium on Biomedical Imaging (ISBI 2018), pp. 1109–1113. IEEE (2018)
22. Wu, Y., He, K.: Group normalization. In: Proceedings of the European Conference on Computer Vision (ECCV), pp. 3–19 (2018)
23. Xie, Y., et al.: Knowledge-based collaborative deep learning for benign-malignant lung nodule classification on chest CT. IEEE Trans. Med. Imaging **38**(4), 991–1004 (2018)
24. Zhang, H., Gu, Y., Qin, Y., Yao, F., Yang, G.-Z.: Learning with sure data for nodule-level lung cancer prediction. In: Martel, A.L., et al. (eds.) MICCAI 2020. LNCS, vol. 12266, pp. 570–578. Springer, Cham (2020). https://doi.org/10.1007/978-3-030-59725-2_55

Weakly-Supervised, Self-supervised, and Contrastive Learning

Universal Lesion Detection and Classification Using Limited Data and Weakly-Supervised Self-training

Varun Naga[1], Tejas Sudharshan Mathai[1(✉)], Angshuman Paul[2], and Ronald M. Summers[1]

[1] Imaging Biomarkers and Computer-Aided Diagnosis Laboratory, Radiology and Imaging Sciences, Clinical Center, National Institutes of Health, Bethesda, MD, USA
`mathaits@nih.gov`
[2] Indian Institute of Technology, Jodhpur, Rajasthan, India

Abstract. Radiologists identify, measure, and classify clinically significant lesions routinely for cancer staging and tumor burden assessment. As these tasks are repetitive and cumbersome, only the largest lesion is identified leaving others of potential importance unmentioned. Automated deep learning-based methods for lesion detection have been proposed in literature to help relieve their tasks with the publicly available DeepLesion dataset (32,735 lesions, 32,120 CT slices, 10,594 studies, 4,427 patients, 8 body part labels). However, this dataset contains missing lesions, and displays a severe class imbalance in the labels. In our work, we use a subset of the DeepLesion dataset (boxes + tags) to train a state-of-the-art VFNet model to detect and classify suspicious lesions in CT volumes. Next, we predict on a larger data subset (containing only bounding boxes) and identify new lesion candidates for a weakly-supervised self-training scheme. The self-training is done across multiple rounds to improve the model's robustness against noise. Two experiments were conducted with static and variable thresholds during self-training, and we show that sensitivity improves from 72.5% without self-training to 76.4% with self-training. We also provide a structured reporting guideline through a "Lesions" subsection for entry into the "Findings" section of a radiology report. To our knowledge, we are the first to propose a weakly-supervised self-training approach for joint lesion detection and tagging in order to mine for underrepresented lesion classes in the DeepLesion dataset.

Keywords: CT · Detection · Classification · Deep learning · Self-training

---

Supplementary Information The online version contains supplementary material available at https://doi.org/10.1007/978-3-031-16760-7_6.

G. Zamzmi et al. (Eds.): MILLanD 2022, LNCS 13559, pp. 55–64, 2022.
https://doi.org/10.1007/978-3-031-16760-7_6

1 Introduction

Radiologists evaluate tumor burden and stage cancer in their clinical practice by detecting, measuring and classifying clinically significant lesions. Computed tomography (CT) and positron emission tomography (PET) studies are usually the preferred imaging modalities for lesion assessment [1]. In CT volumes acquired with or without contrast agents, lesions have diverse appearances and asymmetrical shapes. The lesion size is measured using its long and short axis diameters (LAD and SAD) according to the RECIST guidelines. Lesion size is a surrogate biomarker for malignancy and impacts the ensuing course of patient therapy. According to guidelines, lesions are clinically meaningful if their LAD ≥ 10 mm [2]. Assessment standardization is complicated by a number of factors, such as observer measurement variability, the variety of CT scanners, different contrast phases, and exam protocols. Moreover, a radiologist must identify the same lesion in a prior study and assess the treatment response (shrinkage, growth, unchanged) [1,2]. Another confounding factor is the chance of smaller metastatic lesions being missed during a busy clinical day.

To alleviate the radiologist's repetitive task of lesion assessment, many state-of-the-art automated approaches [3–7] have been developed to universally detect, classify, and segment lesions with high sensitivity on a publicly available dataset called DeepLesion [8]. DeepLesion contains eight (8) lesion-level tags for only the validation and test splits. As seen in Fig. 1(a), there is a profound lesion class imbalance in this dataset (validation and test) with large quantities of certain labels (lung, abdomen, mediastinum, and liver) in contrast to other under-represented classes (pelvis, soft tissue, kidney, bone). Since tags are unavailable for the DeepLesion training split, little research has been done on lesion classification [9,10] and these approaches are not easily reproduced due to the need for a sophisticated lesion ontology to generate multiple lesion tags (body part, type, and attributes). Moreover, DeepLesion is not fully annotated as only clinically significant lesions were measured while others remain unannotated [6–8]. These imbalances inhibit the development of efficient CT lesion detection and tagging algorithms. Approaches that use a limited dataset and exploit any unannotated or weakly-annotated data are desirable for clinical use cases, such as interval change detection (lesion tracking) [11–13] and structured report generation.

To that end, in this paper, we design a method that can use a limited DeepLesion subset (30% annotated split) consisting of lesion bounding boxes and body part labels to train a state-of-the-art VFNet model [14] for lesion detection and tagging. Our model subsequently utilizes a larger data subset (with only bounding boxes) through a weakly-supervised self-training process, in which the model learns from its own predictions and efficiently re-trains itself for lesion and tag prediction. The self-training process is performed over multiple rounds with each round designed to improve model robustness against noise through the inclusion of new data points (box + tags) predicted with high confidence along with the original annotated (box + tags) training data. The final model is used for detection and tagging of lesions, and we provide a clinical application of our work by describing a structured reporting guideline for creating a dedicated "Lesions"

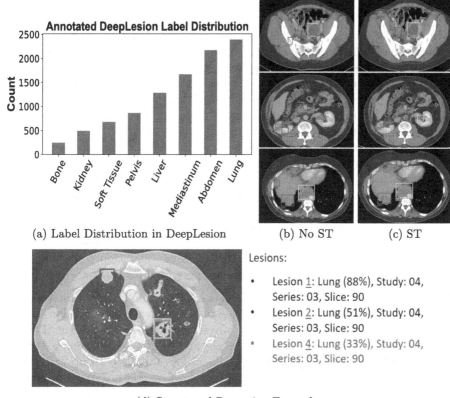

(a) Label Distribution in DeepLesion   (b) No ST   (c) ST

Lesions:

- Lesion 1: Lung (88%), Study: 04, Series: 03, Slice: 90
- Lesion 2: Lung (51%), Study: 04, Series: 03, Slice: 90
- Lesion 4: Lung (33%), Study: 04, Series: 03, Slice: 90

(d) Structured Reporting Example

Fig. 1. (a) Distribution of body part labels in the annotated DeepLesion dataset (30%, 9816 lesions, 9624 slices). (b) and (c) Model predictions before and after self-training (ST) respectively. Green boxes: ground truth, yellow: true positives, and red: false positives (FP). The top row shows a decrease in FP with ST. The middle row shows a "Kidney" lesion that was initially missed with no ST, but found after ST. The last row shows the predicted class corrected from "Lung" to "Mediastinum" after ST. (d) Four lung nodules were detected by the model. The top-3 lesion predictions, their labels, and confidence scores were entered into a structured "Lesions" list for inclusion in the "Findings" section of a radiology report. Lesions below a 50% confidence are shown in red. Lesion 2 was annotated in the original DeepLesion dataset, while Lesion 1 was not. Our model correctly detected lesion 1. but it was considered a FP. Lesion 3 had a lower confidence score than Lesion 4, and hence was not entered in the "Lesions" sub-section. (Color figure online)

sub-section for entry into the "Findings" section of a radiology report. The "Lesions" sub-section contains a structured list of detected lesions along with their body part tags, detection confidence, and series and slice numbers. To our knowledge, we are the first to present a joint lesion detection and tagging approach based on weakly-supervised self-training, such that under-represented classes in DeepLesion can be mined.

2   Methods

Data. The DeepLesion dataset [8] contains annotated keyslices with 2D bounding boxes that demarcate lesions present in that slice. Contextual information in the form of slices 30 mm above and below the keyslice were also provided, but these were not annotated. Annotations were done through RECIST measurements with long and short axis diameters (LAD and SAD) [8]. The dataset was divided into 70% train, 15% validation and 15% test splits. Eight (8) lesion-level tags (bone - 1, abdomen - 2, mediastinum - 3, liver - 4, lung - 5, kidney - 6, soft tissue - 7, and pelvis - 8) were available for only the validation and test splits. The lesion tags were obtained through a body part regressor [15], which provided a continuous score that represented the normalized position of the body part for a CT slice in a CT volume (e.g., liver, lung, kidney etc.). The body part label for the CT slice was assigned to any lesion annotated in that slice. In our work, we used the limited annotated 30% subset of the original dataset for model training. Figure 1(a) shows the labeled lesion distribution in the limited 30% data subset. This was then sub-divided into 70/15/15% training/validation/test splits. The test set was kept constant and all results are presented for this set.

Model. In this work, we used a state-of-the-art detection network called Varifocal Network (VFNet) [14] for the task of lesion detection and classification as seen in Fig. 2(a). VFNet combined a Fully Convolutional One-Stage Object (FCOS) detector [16] (without the centerness branch) and an Adaptive Training Sample Selection (ATSS) mechanism [17]. A Varifocal loss was used to up-weight the contribution of positive object candidates and down-weight negative candidates. Moreover, a star-shaped bounding box representation was utilized to extract contextual cues that reduced the misalignment between the ground truth and the predicted bounding boxes. VFNet was trained to predict a lesion's bounding box and body part label in the CT slice. We also conducted experiments with a Faster-RCNN model [18] for the overall task of lesion detection (without tagging). However, we noticed that Faster RCNN showed an inferior detection performance compared to VFNet (see supplementary material). Once a model had been trained, Weighted Boxes Fusion (WBF) [19] was used to combine the numerous predictions from multiple epochs of a single model run or from multiple runs of the same model. As these predictions clustered together in common image areas with many being false positives (FP) that decrease the overall precision and recall metrics, WBF amalgamated the clusters into one. Our aim was to improve VFNet's prediction capabilities for under-represented classes through the mining of data in DeepLesion.

Weakly Supervised Self Training. At this point, the VFNet model that was trained on limited DeepLesion data (30% annotated subset) was then used to iteratively mine new lesions in DeepLesion's original training split. This split contained only the annotated bounding boxes of a lesion in a CT slice *without* the lesion tags (body part labels), and only clinically significant lesions were measured leaving many others unannotated. These clinically meaningful bounding boxes served as weak supervision for our model. After the VFNet model was trained on the limited DeepLesion data, it generated predictions including the bounding boxes, class labels, and tag confidence scores for each lesion. Mined lesions were filtered, first by only considering mined lesions that had a 30% overlap with the originally annotated bounding boxes in the ground truth, and second by only using mined lesions that surpassed a tag confidence threshold (see Sect. 3). Once the mining procedure was complete, the lesions that met these two criteria were added back into the training data, effectively allowing the model to train on some of its own predictions. After lesion mining, the model was trained from scratch, and this procedure was repeated for four mining rounds. We also experimented with training VFNet from a previous mining round's checkpoint weights, but we noticed that the results were worse than training from scratch.

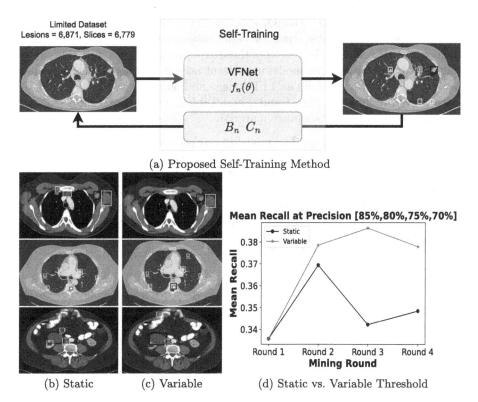

(a) Proposed Self-Training Method

(b) Static   (c) Variable   (d) Static vs. Variable Threshold

Fig. 2. (a) VFNet model in the self-training pipeline takes CT slices annotated with GT as inputs and predicts lesion bounding boxes (B_n), classes (C_n), and confidences at a mining round n. Lesions are filtered by their confidences and IoU overlap with GT, and then fed back to the model for re-training. (b)-(c) Comparison of a static threshold (T_S) vs variable threshold (T_V) used in self-training. Green boxes: GT, yellow: TP, and red: FP. The first row shows a "soft tissue" lesion detection with T_V showing fewer FP. The second row shows a "Bone" lesion that was missed by T_S, but identified with T_V. The third row reveals an incorrect "Abdomen" prediction with T_S that was subsequently corrected to "Kidney" by T_V. (d) Comparison of the mean recall at precisions [85,80,75,70]% for the experiments with static E_S and variable E_V thresholds respectively. (Color figure online)

3   Experiments and Results

Experimental Design. In the weakly-supervised self-training setting, we designed two experiments to detect and classify lesions with our limited dataset. In the first experiment E_S, we set a static lesion tagging confidence threshold (T_S) of 80% and a 30% box IoU overlap. Lesions that had predicted class confidences $\geq T_S$ and overlaps $\geq 30\%$ were incorporated into later mining rounds. Through this experiment, we hypothesized that only high quality mined lesions would be collected across the rounds that would directly lead to an efficient detector. In our second experiment E_V, a variable lesion tagging confidence threshold T_V was set along with a 30% box IoU overlap. A higher confidence threshold of 80% was set for the first mining round, and it was progressively lowered by 10% over the remaining rounds. The belief was that although good quality mined lesions would be found in the first round, larger lesion quantities would also be collected across the rounds with a reduced threshold. The results of these experiments were compared against an experiment E_N where the model underwent no self-training. Consistent with prior work [6,7,20], our results at 4 FP/image and 30% IoU overlap on the 15% test split are presented in Figs. 1 and 2 and Table 1. Implementation details for the model are in the supplementary material.

Results - No Self-training. The model in our no self-training experiment E_N achieved a mean sensitivity of 72.5% at 4FP with the lowest sensitivities for under-represented classes, such as "kidney" ($\sim$54%) and "Bone" ($\sim$56%) respectively, and the highest recalls for over-represented classes, such as "Lung" ($\sim$87%) and "Liver" ($\sim$83%). Generally, classes with more data (see Fig. 1) seemed to perform better with the exception of "Abdomen" class. We believe the "Abdomen" class performed relatively poorly as it was a "catch-all" term for all abdominal lesions that were not "Kidney" or "Liver" masses [8]. Anatomically however, the two

Table 1. VFNet sensitivities on the task of lesion detection and tagging. The recalls were calculated at 4FP and at 30% IoU overlap.

Mining round	Bone	Kidney	Soft tissue	Pelvis	Liver	Mediastinum	Abdomen	Lung	Mean (95% CI)
No self training									
No self-training	55.9	54.8	73.3	75.4	82.9	79.6	69.7	87.5	72.5 (71.8%-73.0%)
# Lesions used	179	353	476	612	912	1193	1506	1640	-
Static threshold of 80% across 4 rounds of self-training									
Round 1 (80%)	58.8	58.1	75.2	**79.0**	85.0	**85.5**	69.7	88.1	**74.9**
Round 2 (80%)	52.9	61.3	**75.2**	75.4	79.3	83.4	**73.0**	**88.9**	73.7
Round 3 (80%)	47.1	61.3	71.4	78.3	**85.0**	80.0	69.7	87.3	72.5
Round 4 (80%)	**58.8**	59.7	73.3	72.5	83.9	83.4	71.2	87.5	73.8 (73.3%-74.3%)
# Lesions mined	26	129	541	517	929	1049	708	2515	-
Variable threshold [80, 70, 60, 50%] across 4 rounds of self-training									
Round 1 (80%)	58.8	58.1	75.2	79.0	85.0	**85.5**	69.7	88.1	74.9
Round 2 (70%)	61.8	**66.1**	69.5	76.8	85.5	82.1	70.6	89.4	75.2
Round 3 (60%)	44.1	56.5	**75.2**	**78.3**	87.1	81.3	**73.9**	89.1	73.2
Round 4 (50%)	**61.8**	64.5	73.8	75.4	**89.6**	83.0	72.7	**90.5**	**76.4 (75.9%-76.9%)**
# Lesions mined	115	473	1187	1438	2089	2936	3003	4249	-

organs are in close proximity and axial slices often show cross-sections of both the kidney and liver within the same slice (c.f. Fig. 1(b) second row). A confusion matrix provided in the supplementary material confirmed our belief as it showed that the "Abdomen", "Liver" and "Kidney" lesions were most often confused with each other.

Results - Weakly Supervised Self-training. First, results from our static threshold experiment E_S are discussed. In contrast to E_N, sensitivities at round 4 either improved or were maintained for 7/8 classes except for the "Pelvis" class. The average sensitivity improved by 1.3% compared against E_N, and those of the individual classes improved by 1.4% on average. In rounds 2 and 3 of self-training, a drop in mean sensitivity was observed, but the performance recovered by round 4 to within 1.1% of the mean sensitivity from round 1. We also see a greater number of "Lung", "Mediastinum" and "Liver" lesions mined ($¿900$) in contrast to the "Bone" (26) and "Kidney" (129) lesions. Despite additional lesions being mined, we saw that only 3/8 classes ("Bone", "Kidney", "Abdomen") improved when the recalls at round 4 were compared against round 1.

From our variable threshold experiment E_V (commencing at 80% confidence), average recalls improved by 3.9% in contrast to E_N, and all 8/8 classes either improved or maintained their performance. As the "Kidney" class performed the worst in E_N, it saw the biggest increase of 9.7% in E_V. On average, the individual class sensitivities improved by $\sim 4\%$, which was bigger than that seen with E_S. An assessment over 4 rounds revealed a general trend of sensitivity improvement. While the recall dipped moving from round 2 to round 3 for certain classes, it recovered by round 4 and surpassed round 1 by 1.5%. Table 1 also shows that the number of mined lesions for "Bone" and "Kidney" classes are significantly lower in the dataset in contrast to the other classes, such as "Lung" and "Liver". The number of lesions mined after 4 rounds of self training is shown in Table 1. The supplementary material shows the number of lesions mined at each round.

For quantitative comparison of E_S and E_V results across rounds, we plotted the precision-recall curves for each mining round in Fig. 2(d). The model's mean recall at [85,80,75,70]% precision was evaluated to gauge the performance at higher True Positive (TP) rates, and we saw E_V outperforming E_S. By round 4, E_V had outperformed E_S by $\sim 3\%$. Additionally, the recall increased between mining rounds except for round 4, which saw a slight decrease by 1%. However, the overall performance had improved from round 1 by 4.2%, which suggested that additional rounds of self-training with a variable threshold T_V helped improve recall. Qualitative analysis in Figs. 1 and 2 showed that E_V improved recall by finding missed lesions, along with correct classification of lesion tags and a reduction in FP. We also saw improved performance on under-represented classes, such as "Kidney" and "Bone", as seen in Figs. 2(b) and 2(c).

4   Discussion and Conclusion

Discussion. As shown in Figs. 1 and 2, self-training improved model performance in lesion detection and tagging. We saw an improvement in sensitivities across classes for the variable threshold experiment E_V in comparison to the static threshold experiment E_S. We believe that E_V found a balance between data quality and quantity, making it ideal for the self-training procedure as the lowering of thresholds across rounds in E_V allowed the model to identify high-quality data initially while additional training data was progressively included over the remaining rounds to provide data variety. But as shown in Fig. 1(a) and Table 1 in the supplementary material, the model performance suffers from the under-representation of classes, such as "Bone" and "Kidney", in the dataset. For these classes, sensitivities varied without consistent improvements (c.f. Table 1) due to greater lesion quantities being mined for over-represented classes as opposed to the under-represented classes. Balancing the lesion quantities in these classes, which would drastically decrease the amount of training data, could shed some light on the performance of these low data quantity classes in self-training. Another solution involves a custom adjustment of loss weights for the under-represented classes in the VFNet loss function, which would penalize the model when it performs poorly on under-represented classes and mediate the class imbalance effect. Additionally, as evidenced by the confusion matrices in the supplementary material, it was evident that the model confused the "Abdomen", "Liver" and "Kidney" classes often. We believe that the "Abdomen" and "Soft Tissue" labels are ambiguous and non-specific labels that broadly encompass multiple regions in the abdomen. As these labels were generated using a body part regressor, future work involves the creation of fine-grained labels, and examining the performance of "Abdomen", "Kidney", and "Pelvis" classes. Furthermore, the DeepLesion dataset contains both contrast and non-contrast enhanced CT volumes, but the exact phase information is unavailable in the dataset description. Comparison against prior work [9,10] was not possible as MULAN [10] is the only existing approach to jointly detect and tag lesions in a CT slice. However, it used a Mask-RCNN model that needed segmentation labels, which we did not create in this work. Furthermore, MULAN also provided detailed tags, which would require a sophisticated ontology derived from reports to map them to the body part tags used in this work. To mitigate this issue, we tested our approach against Faster RCNN, but our VFNet model fared better at lesion detection (c.f. supplementary material). Prior to this study, limited research discussed the presentation of results from detection models in a clinical workflow. In Fig. 1(d), we present a structured reporting guideline with the creation of a "Lesions" sub-section for entry into the 'Findings' section of a radiology report. This sub-section contains a structured list of detected lesions along with their body part tags, confidences, and series and slice numbers.

Conclusion. In this work, we used a limited DeepLesion data subset (30% annotated data) containing lesion bounding boxes and body part labels to train a VFNet model for lesion detection and tagging. Subsequently, the model predicted lesion locations and tags on a larger data subset (boxes and no tags) through a weakly-supervised self-training process. The self-training process was done across multiple rounds, and two experiments were conducted that showed that sensitivity improved from 72.5% (no self-training) to 74.9% (static threshold) and 76.4% (variable threshold) respectively. In every round, new data points (boxes +

tags) predicted with high confidence were added to the original annotated (boxes + tags) training data, and the model was trained from scratch. We also provide a structured reporting guideline for the clinical workflow. A "Lesions" sub-section for entry into the "Findings" section of a radiology report was created, and it contained a structured list of detected lesions, body part tags, confidences, and series and slice numbers.

Acknowledgements. This work was supported by the Intramural Research Program of the National Institutes of Health (NIH) Clinical Center.

References

1. Eisenhauer, E., et al.: New response evaluation criteria in solid tumours: revised RECIST guideline (version 1.1). Eur. J. Cancer **45**(2), 228–247 (2009)
2. van Persijn van Meerten, E.L., et al.: RECIST revised: implications for the radiologist. A review article on the modified RECIST guideline. Eur. Radiol. **20**, 1456–1467 (2010)
3. Yang, J., et al.: *AlignShift*: bridging the gap of imaging thickness in 3D anisotropic volumes. In: Martel, A.L., et al. (eds.) MICCAI 2020. LNCS, vol. 12264, pp. 562–572. Springer, Cham (2020). https://doi.org/10.1007/978-3-030-59719-1_55
4. Yang, J., He, Y., Kuang, K., Lin, Z., Pfister, H., Ni, B.: Asymmetric 3D context fusion for universal lesion detection. In: de Bruijne, M., et al. (eds.) MICCAI 2021. LNCS, vol. 12905, pp. 571–580. Springer, Cham (2021). https://doi.org/10.1007/978-3-030-87240-3_55
5. Han, L., et al.: SATr: Slice Attention with Transformer for Universal Lesion Detection. arXiv (2022)
6. Yan, K., et al.: Learning from multiple datasets with heterogeneous and partial labels for universal lesion detection in CT. IEEE TMI **40**(10), 2759–2770 (2021)
7. Cai, J., et al.: Lesion harvester: iteratively mining unlabeled lesions and hard-negative examples at scale. IEEE TMI **40**(1), 59–70 (2021)
8. Yan, K., et al.: DeepLesion: automated mining of large-scale lesion annotations and universal lesion detection with deep learning. J. Med. Imaging **5**(3), 036501 (2018)
9. Yan, K., et al.: Holistic and comprehensive annotation of clinically significant findings on diverse CT images: learning from radiology reports and label ontology. In: IEEE CVPR (2019)
10. Yan, K., et al.: MULAN: multitask universal lesion analysis network for joint lesion detection, tagging, and segmentation. In: Shen, D., et al. (eds.) MICCAI 2019. LNCS, vol. 11769, pp. 194–202. Springer, Cham (2019). https://doi.org/10.1007/978-3-030-32226-7_22
11. Hering, A., et al.: Whole-body soft-tissue lesion tracking and segmentation in longitudinal CT imaging studies. In: PMLR, pp. 312–326 (2021)
12. Cai, J., et al.: Deep lesion tracker: monitoring lesions in 4D longitudinal imaging studies. In: IEEE CVPR, pp. 15159–15169 (2021)
13. Tang, W., et al.: Transformer Lesion Tracker. arXiv (2022)
14. Zhang, H., et al.: VarifocalNet: an IoU-aware dense object detector. In: IEEE CVPR, pp. 8514–8523 (2021)
15. Yan, K., et al.: Unsupervised body part regression via spatially self-ordering convolutional neural networks. In: IEEE ISBI, pp. 1022–1025 (2018)

16. Tian, Z., et al.: FCOS: fully convolutional one-stage object detection. In: IEEE ICCV, pp. 9627–9636 (2019)
17. Zhang, S, et al.: Bridging the gap between anchor-based and anchor-free detection via adaptive training sample selection. In: IEEE CVPR (2020)
18. Ren, S., et al.: Faster R-CNN: towards real-time object detection with region proposal networks. IEEE PAMI **39**(6), 1137–1149 (2017)
19. Solovyev, R., et al.: Weighted boxes fusion: ensembling boxes from different object detection models. Image Vis. Comput. **107**, 104117 (2021)
20. Mattikalli, T., et al.: Universal lesion detection in CT scans using neural network ensembles. In: SPIE Medical Imaging: Computer-Aided Diagnosis, vol. 12033 (2022)

BoxShrink: From Bounding Boxes to Segmentation Masks

Michael Gröger$^{(\boxtimes)}$ ⓘ, Vadim Borisov ⓘ, and Gjergji Kasneci ⓘ

University of Tübingen, Tübingen, Germany
`michael.groeger@posteo.net`

Abstract. One of the core challenges facing the medical image computing community is fast and efficient data sample labeling. Obtaining fine-grained labels for segmentation is particularly demanding since it is expensive, time-consuming, and requires sophisticated tools. On the contrary, applying bounding boxes is fast and takes significantly less time than fine-grained labeling, but does not produce detailed results. In response, we propose a novel framework for weakly-supervised tasks with the rapid and robust transformation of bounding boxes into segmentation masks without training any machine learning model, coined BoxShrink. The proposed framework comes in two variants – *rapid*-BoxShrink for fast label transformations, and *robust*-BoxShrink for more precise label transformations. An average of four percent improvement in IoU is found across several models when being trained using BoxShrink in a weakly-supervised setting, compared to using only bounding box annotations as inputs on a colonoscopy image data set. We open-sourced the code for the proposed framework and published it online.

Keywords: Weakly-supervised learning · Segmentation · Colonoscopy · Deep neural networks

1 Introduction

Convolutional neural networks (CNNs) have achieved remarkable results across image classification tasks of increasing complexity, from pure image classification to full panoptic segmentation, and have become, as a consequence, the standard method for these tasks in computer vision [19]. However, there are also certain drawbacks associated with these methods. One of them is that in order to achieve satisfactory results, a data set of an appropriate size and high-quality labels are needed [21]. The costs and time associated with labeling increase with the complexity of the task, with image classification being the cheapest and image segmentation being the most expensive one. All of these challenges especially

---

M. Gröger and V. Borisov—equal contribution.

Supplementary Information The online version contains supplementary material available at https://doi.org/10.1007/978-3-031-16760-7_7.

G. Zamzmi et al. (Eds.): MILLanD 2022, LNCS 13559, pp. 65–75, 2022.
https://doi.org/10.1007/978-3-031-16760-7_7

apply to medical artificial intelligence (MAI) applications since they depend on the input and feedback by expensive domain experts [22].

In this work, we present a novel approach for fast segmentation label prepossessing, *which is decoupled from any particular artificial neural network architecture*. The proposed algorithmic framework can serve as a first approach for practitioners to transform a data set with only bounding box annotations into a prelabeled (i.e., semantically segmented) version of the data set. Our framework consists of independent components such as superpixels [23], fully-connected conditional random fields [14] and embeddings. This makes it easy to add our framework to an existing machine learning pipeline.

To evaluate the proposed framework, we select an endoscopic colonoscopy data set [4]. Multiple experiments show that our framework helps to considerably reduce the gap between the segmentation performance and efficiency of a neural network that is trained only on bounding boxes and one trained on fully segmented segmentation masks.

The main contributions of this work are:

– We propose the BoxShrink framework consisting of two methods. One for a time-efficient and one for a more robust transformation of bounding-boxes into segmentation masks. In both methods there is no need to train a model.
– We publish our bounding-box labels for the CVC-Clinic data set for future research in the area of weakly-supervised learning.
– We open-source our code and publish it online.[1]

2   Related Work

In this Section, we further define weakly-supervised learning and separate it from other approaches such as semi-supervised learning. Also, we localize our work among those which use similar components.

To reduce the need for resources such as time and money, various learning methodologies were introduced such as semi-supervised and weakly-supervised learning [30]. Semi-supervised learning leverages labeled data, e.g. for segmentation tasks correctly and fully segmented images and the availability of a larger amount of unlabeled data [16]. Weakly-supervised learning on the other hand, exploits noisy labels as a weak supervisory signal to generate segmentation masks. These labels can be provided in different forms such as points [3], or image-level labels [27], being the more simpler ones, or more complex ones such as scribbles [15,24], or bounding boxes [6,11]. A similar work [29] to ours also utilizes superpixel embeddings and CRFs, but their method requires an additional construction of a graph of superpixels and a custom deep neural network architecture. Our method, on the other hand, is easier to integrate into existing pipelines. Also, in contrast to many other weakly-supervised approaches [10,28], we do not apply CRFs as a postprocessing step on the output of the model but as a preprocessing step on the input, hence, we leave the downstream model untouched. Furthermore, the proposed framework does not require special hardware such as GPU or TPU for the label preprocessing step.

---

[1] https://github.com/michaelgroeger/boxshrink.

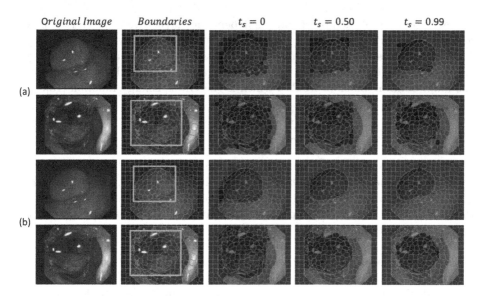

Fig. 1. The impact of varying the threshold t_s, i.e., a hyperparameter of the BoxShrink framework for tuning the final segmentation quality, where (a) shows two data samples from the data set after the superpixel assignment step (Sect. 3.2), and (b) demonstrates pseudo-masks after the FCRF postprocessing. As seen from this experiment, having a higher threshold might generate better masks but increases the risk of losing correct foreground pixels.

3   Boxshrink Framework

This section presents our proposed BoxShrink framework. First, we define its main components: superpixel segmentation, fully-connected conditional random fields, and the embedding step. We then explain two different settings of the framework, both having the same goal: to reduce the number of background pixels labeled as foreground contained in the bounding box mask.

3.1   Main Components

Superpixels aim to group pixels into bigger patches based on their color similarity or other characteristics [23]. In our implementation, we utilize the SLIC algorithm proposed by [1] which is a k-means-based algorithm grouping pixels based on their proximity in a 5D space. A crucial hyperparameter of SLIC is the number of segments to be generated which is a upper bound for the algorithm on how many superpixels should be returned for the given image. The relationship between the output of SLIC and the maximum number of segments can be seen in the supplementary material.

Fully-connected-CRFs are an advanced version of conditional random fields (CRFs) which represent pixels as a graph structure. CRFs take into account a unary potential of each pixel and the dependency structure between that pixel and its neighboring ones using pairwise potentials [25]. Fully-connected-CRFs (FCRFs) address some of the limitations of classic CRFs, such as the lack of capturing long-range dependencies by connecting all pixel pairs. Equation 1 shows the main building block of FCRFs which is the Gibbs-Energy function [13].

$$E(x) = \sum_{i=1}^{N} \psi_u(x_i) + \sum_{i<j}^{N} \psi_p(x_i, x_j), \tag{1}$$

where the first term $\psi_u(x_i)$ measures the unary potential, that is, the cost if the assigned label disagrees with that of the initial classifier, the second term $\psi_p(x_i, x_j)$ measures the pairwise potential, which is the cost if two similar pixels disagree on their label x. The input is over all pixels N. We use FCRFs to smooth the output pseudo-mask.

Superpixel Embeddings are a key component of the *robust*-BoxShrink variant. The embedding function M produces a numerical representation of every superpixel $k_i \in K$ by returning an embedding vector. Formally, this operation can be depicted $M : \mathbb{R}^m \to \mathbb{R}^n$. Practically, this can be done by feeding each superpixel k_i separately into a CNN model, such as a Resnet-50 [9] pretrained on ImageNet [7]. By doing so, we obtain a 2048-dimensional vector representation for every superpixel. It allows us to get an aggregated representation of the foreground and background, by computing the mean embedding of all foreground and background superpixels in the training data set. These mean vectors are then used to assign superpixels either to the foreground or background class based on their cosine similarity.

3.2   *rapid*-BoxShrink

We first split each image into superpixels using the SLIC algorithm for the *rapid*-BoxShrink strategy. We overlap the superpixels with the provided bounding box mask and build a new mask based on those superpixels, which overlap the bounding box mask to a certain threshold. This approach is based on the assumption that the object of interest is always fully contained in the bounding box. The results depend on the number of segments generated which can be seen in the supplementary materials and the chosen threshold shown in Fig. 1. To this end, as shown in the supplementary material in Algorithm 1, to make the final pseudo-mask more smooth, we run a FCRF as described in Sect. 3.1 on the thresholded superpixel mask.

3.3   *robust*-BoxShrink

Leveraging the availability of superpixels, we also explore the use of embeddings to shrink the number of background pixels in the pseudo-mask. We segmented each image in the training data set into superpixels and then assigned them either to the foreground or background group by applying the thresholding approach as we have done it in the *rapid*-BoxShrink variant (Sect. 3.2). To

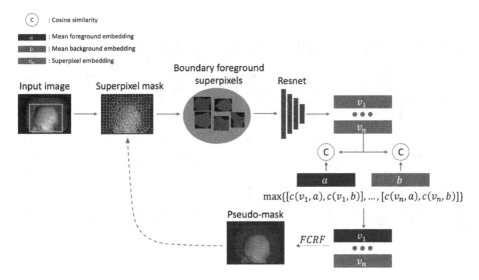

Fig. 2. Overview of the *robust*-BoxShrink method assuming the mean embedding vectors are given. First, we generate a superpixel mask based on the *rapid*-BoxShrink approach but without utilizing the FCRF. Then, we extract each foreground superpixel on the boundary between foreground and background. Feeding each superpixel into a pretrained ResNet model yields one 2048-dimensional embedding vector per superpixel. Next, we calculate the cosine similarity score of each embedding and the mean background and foreground embedding. Based on the highest score we either keep the superpixel as foreground or assign it to the background class. Finally, we apply a FCRF on the resulting superpixel mask. The dashed line indicates that this approach can be run iteratively.

generate the pseudo-masks, we start with the bounding box mask and segment the image using again the thresholding technique. This yields $\mathcal{F}$ superpixels for the foreground and $\mathcal{B}$ superpixels for the background. Then we go along the boundary foreground superpixels $\mathcal{F}_o$ and assign them either to the background or foreground class, depending on their cosine similarity score to the mean background and foreground embedding. The whole process can be seen in Fig. 2. The Algorithm 2, which can be found in the supplementary materials, summarizes the main steps of the *robust*-BoxShrink method.

4 Experiments

This Section presents qualitative and quantitative experiments for both versions of the BoxShrink framework.

Data Set. For all our experiments we utilize the endoscopic colonoscopy frames for polyp detection data set (CVC-Clinic DB) [4], it consists of 612 endoscopy images, each having a size of $288 \times 384 \times 3$. The data set comes along with binary ground truth segmentation masks, which we utilize for the evaluation of

U-Net (VGG-16) Outputs for different settings

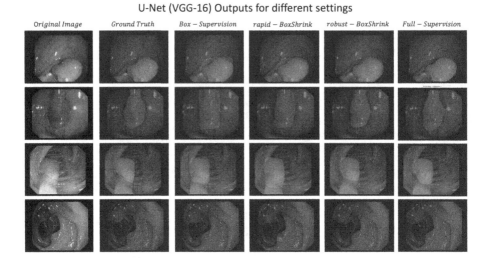

Fig. 3. Qualitative model prediction masks on four random samples from the CVC-Clinic test set. The setting on which the model was trained on is indicated on top.

our weakly-supervised framework and to infer the bounding boxes. This data set was featured in multiple studies [2,8].

4.1   Qualitative and Quantitative Experiments

For our experiments, we utilize two popular deep learning architectures for segmentation tasks - U-Net [20] and DeepLabV3+ [5].

Settings. We have four settings, using: (1) Bounding boxes as labels which serves as our lower baseline, (2) labels generated with the *rapid*-BoxShrink label transformation strategy, (3) labels generated with the *robust*-BoxShrink label transformation strategy, and (4) a fully-supervised upper baseline with segmentation masks as labels.

Quality Measure. We use the Intersection over Union (IoU) score as an evaluation measure. The IoU, also called Jaccard similarity J between two sets $\boldsymbol{A}$ and $\boldsymbol{B}$, is a commonly used measure of how well the prediction aligns with the ground truth in image segmentation [18]. As the equation below shows, the IoU is computed by dividing the intersection of two masks by their union.

$$J(\boldsymbol{A}, \boldsymbol{B}) = \frac{|\boldsymbol{A} \cap \boldsymbol{B}|}{|\boldsymbol{A} \cup \boldsymbol{B}|}. \tag{2}$$

Results. We present the quantitative results in Table 1. In line with other publications, we also share situations where our presented Framework fails. Figure 5, which can be found in the supplementary materials shows some examples.

Figure 3 shows some good prediction masks from the test set made by models trained on the aforementioned four different settings.

4.2 Reproducibility Details

We split the CVC-Clinic DB data set into 80% training data, 10% validation data and 10% test data. For splitting, we use the implementation from sklearn [17] with a random state of 1. To generate the superpixel masks, we set the maximum number of segments s to 200, a threshold t_s of 0.6 for all training images and use the implementation from skimage [26]. To get the embeddings, we use a maximum number s of 250 segments and a threshold t_s of 0.1 to not loose too much of the foreground. To smooth the superpixel masks we use the FCRF implementation provided by the pydensecrf package.[2] Note that we do not train the FCRF (similar to [10]) and set the FCRF hyperparmeters of the x/y-standard deviation for the pairwise Gaussian to 5 and for the pairwise bilateral to 25. We set the rgb-standard deviation to 10. To determine the best performing model, we use the intersection over union (IoU) during training on the validation set. After the training, the best performing model is kept and evaluated once on the test set. Both, the test and validation set consist of ground truth masks. We generate all models using the segmentation-models PyTorch library.[3]

For our experiments we select ResNet-18, ResNet-50, and VGG-16 backbones pretrained on the ImageNet data set paired with U-Net and DeepLabV3+ as a decoder. We use the Sigmoid function as an activation function and the Adam [12] optimizer with a learning rate of 0.0001. As the loss function we utilize the Cross-Entropy Loss. During training, we apply step-wise learning rate scheduling where we decay the learning rate by 0.5 each 5 epochs. We train the ResNet-18 & VGG-16 architecture for 25 epochs and the ResNet-50 architecture for 15 epochs. The training is being done on a 16 GB Nvidia Tesla P-100. We use a batch size of 64 when using the ResNet-18, 32 for the VGG-16 architecture and 16 when using ResNet-50. For both methods, *rapid*-BoxShrink and *robust*-BoxShrink, we return the initial bounding box mask if the total mask occupancy, that is the ratio of the bounding box and the total image is less than 0.1 or the IoU between the pseudo mask and the bounding box mask is less than 0.1.

5 Discussion

In this Section, we further discuss the application and future work of the proposed weakly-supervised framework.

The choice between *rapid*-BoxShrink and *robust*-BoxShrink depends on multiple factors - the time budget and expected label transformation quality. In our experiments, we observe that *rapid*-BoxShrink takes on average only 0.5 seconds to transform the labels for a singe data sample, where *robust*-BoxShrink

---

[2] https://github.com/lucasb-eyer/pydensecrf.
[3] https://github.com/qubvel/segmentation_models.pytorch.

Table 1. Experimental results on the CVC-Clinic data set. All models are evaluated on the *ground truth segmentation mask* in the validation and test set. The label format indicates the initial input label on which the model was either trained or our proposed frameworks were applied to. The results are averages of six runs; we also report the corresponding standard deviation for each setting. This is being done to deliver a more consistent picture because of the random initialization of the decoder part and the stochasticity of the optimizer. The best performing results for our proposed methods are marked in bold. Higher IoU is better.

Segmentation model	Label format	Backbone	Validation (IoU)	Test (IoU)
U-Net	Bounding Boxes	VGG-16	0.749 ± 0.023	0.772 ± 0.030
U-Net (*rapid*-BoxShrink)	Bounding Boxes	VGG-16	0.769 ± 0.026	0.807 ± 0.028
U-Net (*robust*-BoxShrink)	Bounding Boxes	VGG-16	$\mathbf{0.775 \pm 0.013}$	$\mathbf{0.824 \pm 0.010}$
U-Net	Segment. Masks	VGG-16	0.796 ± 0.025	0.829 ± 0.025
U-Net	Bounding Boxes	ResNet-18	0.691 ± 0.051	0.729 ± 0.060
U-Net (*rapid*-BoxShrink)	Bounding Boxes	ResNet-18	0.730 ± 0.021	0.781 ± 0.024
U-Net (*robust*-BoxShrink)	Bounding Boxes	ResNet-18	$\mathbf{0.755 \pm 0.021}$	$\mathbf{0.808 \pm 0.021}$
U-Net	Segment. Masks	ResNet-18	0.800 ± 0.032	0.859 ± 0.044
U-Net	Bounding Boxes	ResNet-50	0.785 ± 0.010	0.810 ± 0.010
U-Net (*rapid*-BoxShrink)	Bounding Boxes	ResNet-50	0.807 ± 0.018	0.851 ± 0.019
U-Net (*robust*-BoxShrink)	Bounding Boxes	ResNet-50	$\mathbf{0.813 \pm 0.015}$	$\mathbf{0.852 \pm 0.012}$
U-Net	Segment. Masks	ResNet-50	0.889 ± 0.012	0.920 ± 0.016
DeepLabV3+	Bounding Boxes	VGG-16	0.746 ± 0.033	0.766 ± 0.034
DeepLabV3+ (*rapid*-BoxShrink)	Bounding Boxes	VGG-16	$\mathbf{0.779 \pm 0.023}$	$\mathbf{0.817 \pm 0.0201}$
DeepLabV3+ (*robust*-BoxShrink)	Bounding Boxes	VGG-16	0.767 ± 0.0187	0.809 ± 0.024
DeepLabV3+	Segment. Masks	VGG-16	0.832 ± 0.049	0.858 ± 0.051
DeepLabV3+	Bounding Boxes	ResNet-18	0.723 ± 0.025	0.758 ± 0.021
DeepLabV3+ (*rapid*-BoxShrink)	Bounding Boxes	ResNet-18	0.743 ± 0.021	0.787 ± 0.026
DeepLabV3+ (*robust*-BoxShrink)	Bounding Boxes	ResNet-18	$\mathbf{0.759 \pm 0.005}$	$\mathbf{0.806 \pm 0.002}$
DeepLabV3+	Segment. Masks	ResNet-18	0.808 ± 0.010	0.844 ± 0.012

needs on average 3 seconds to complete the label transformation, the processing time can be further optimized in future versions. However, from our extensive experiments (Sect. 4.1), we can conclude that *robust*-BoxShrink tends to outperform *rapid*-BoxShrink in the weakly-supervised setting. The difference between the two variants is smaller for bigger models with *rapid*-BoxShrink being once better than *robust*-BoxShrink for the VGG-16 architecture. One explanation could be that bigger models are more robust to the label noise than smaller ones. We want to point out however, that the margin between the two is still overlapped by the standard deviations of both methods.

Future Work. We want to further integrate the framework into the training pipeline by, e.g., adjusting the mean foreground and background embeddings as the model gets better. Also, we have evaluated our approach on a medium-sized data set with binary class segmentation. For a more detailed quality evaluation, an analysis of BoxShrink's performance on multi-class problems and bigger data sets is required. Lastly, starting with BoxShrink pseudo-masks instead of bounding box annotations directly could also improve existing state-of-the-art weakly-supervised learning algorithms.

6   Conclusion

In this work, we presented BoxShrink, a weakly-supervised learning framework for segmentation tasks. We successfully demonstrate the effectiveness of the BoxShrink framework in the weakly-supervised setting on a colonoscopy medical image data set, where we employ bounding-box labeling and output the segmentation masks. Compared to the fully-supervised setting, our weakly-supervised framework shows nearly the same results. Finally, we open-sourced and published the code and bounding boxes for the CVC-Clinic data set .

References

1. Achanta, R., Shaji, A., Smith, K., Lucchi, A., Fua, P., Süsstrunk, S.: SLIC superpixels compared to state-of-the-art superpixel methods. IEEE Trans. Pattern Anal. Mach. Intell. **34**(11), 2274–2282 (2012)
2. Akbari, M., et al.: Polyp segmentation in colonoscopy images using fully convolutional network. In: 2018 40th Annual International Conference of the IEEE Engineering in Medicine and Biology Society (EMBC), pp. 69–72. IEEE (2018)
3. Bearman, A., Russakovsky, O., Ferrari, V., Fei-Fei, L.: What's the point: semantic segmentation with point supervision. In: Leibe, B., Matas, J., Sebe, N., Welling, M. (eds.) ECCV 2016. LNCS, vol. 9911, pp. 549–565. Springer, Cham (2016). https://doi.org/10.1007/978-3-319-46478-7_34
4. Bernal, J., et al.: Comparative validation of polyp detection methods in video colonoscopy: results from the MICCAI 2015 endoscopic vision challenge. IEEE Trans. Med. Imaging **36**(6), 1231–1249 (2017)
5. Chen, L.C., Zhu, Y., Papandreou, G., Schroff, F., Adam, H.: Encoder-decoder with atrous separable convolution for semantic image segmentation. In: Proceedings of the European Conference on Computer Vision (ECCV), pp. 801–818 (2018)
6. Dai, J., He, K., Sun, J.: BoxSup: exploiting bounding boxes to supervise convolutional networks for semantic segmentation. In: Proceedings of the IEEE International Conference on Computer Vision, pp. 1635–1643 (2015)
7. Deng, J., Dong, W., Socher, R., Li, L.J., Li, K., Fei-Fei, L.: ImageNet: a large-scale hierarchical image database. In: 2009 IEEE Conference on Computer Vision and Pattern Recognition, pp. 248–255. IEEE (2009)
8. Fan, D.-P., Ji, G.-P., Zhou, T., Chen, G., Fu, H., Shen, J., Shao, L.: PraNet: parallel reverse attention network for polyp segmentation. In: Martel, A.L., Abolmaesumi, P., Stoyanov, D., Mateus, D., Zuluaga, M.A., Zhou, S.K., Racoceanu, D., Joskowicz, L. (eds.) MICCAI 2020. LNCS, vol. 12266, pp. 263–273. Springer, Cham (2020). https://doi.org/10.1007/978-3-030-59725-2_26
9. He, K., Zhang, X., Ren, S., Sun, J.: Deep residual learning for image recognition. In: Proceedings of the IEEE Conference on Computer Vision and Pattern Recognition, pp. 770–778 (2016)

10. Huang, Z., Wang, X., Wang, J., Liu, W., Wang, J.: Weakly-supervised semantic segmentation network with deep seeded region growing. In: Proceedings of the IEEE Conference on Computer Vision and Pattern Recognition, pp. 7014–7023 (2018)
11. Khoreva, A., Benenson, R., Hosang, J., Hein, M., Schiele, B.: Simple does it: weakly supervised instance and semantic segmentation. In: Proceedings of the IEEE Conference on Computer Vision and Pattern Recognition, pp. 876–885 (2017)
12. Kingma, D.P., Ba, J.: Adam: A method for stochastic optimization. arXiv preprint arXiv:1412.6980 (2014)
13. Krähenbühl, P., Koltun, V.: Efficient inference in fully connected CRFs with Gaussian edge potentials. In: Advances in neural Information Processing Systems, vol. 24 (2011)
14. Krähenbühl, P., Koltun, V.: Parameter learning and convergent inference for dense random fields. In: International Conference on Machine Learning, pp. 513–521. PMLR (2013)
15. Lin, D., Dai, J., Jia, J., He, K., Sun, J.: Scribblesup: Scribble-supervised convolutional networks for semantic segmentation. In: Proceedings of the IEEE Conference on Computer Vision and Pattern Recognition, pp. 3159–3167 (2016)
16. Ouali, Y., Hudelot, C., Tami, M.: Semi-supervised semantic segmentation with cross-consistency training. In: Proceedings of the IEEE/CVF Conference on Computer Vision and Pattern Recognition, pp. 12674–12684 (2020)
17. Pedregosa, F., et al.: Scikit-learn: Machine learning in Python. J. Mach. Learn. Res. **12**, 2825–2830 (2011)
18. Rahman, M.A., Wang, Y.: Optimizing intersection-over-union in deep neural networks for image segmentation. In: Bebis, B., et al. (eds.) ISVC 2016. LNCS, vol. 10072, pp. 234–244. Springer, Cham (2016). https://doi.org/10.1007/978-3-319-50835-1_22
19. Rawat, W., Wang, Z.: Deep convolutional neural networks for image classification: a comprehensive review. Neural Comput. **29**(9), 2352–2449 (2017)
20. Ronneberger, O., Fischer, P., Brox, T.: U-Net: convolutional networks for biomedical image segmentation. In: Navab, N., Hornegger, J., Wells, W.M., Frangi, A.F. (eds.) MICCAI 2015. LNCS, vol. 9351, pp. 234–241. Springer, Cham (2015). https://doi.org/10.1007/978-3-319-24574-4_28
21. Song, H., Kim, M., Park, D., Shin, Y., Lee, J.G.: Learning from noisy labels with deep neural networks: a survey. IEEE Trans. Neural Netw. Learn. Syst. (2022)
22. Sourati, J., Gholipour, A., Dy, J.G., Tomas-Fernandez, X., Kurugol, S., Warfield, S.K.: Intelligent labeling based on fisher information for medical image segmentation using deep learning. IEEE Trans. Med. Imag. **38**(11), 2642–2653 (2019)
23. Stutz, D., Hermans, A., Leibe, B.: Superpixels: an evaluation of the state-of-the-art. Comput. Vis. Image Underst. **166**, 1–27 (2018)
24. Tang, M., Djelouah, A., Perazzi, F., Boykov, Y., Schroers, C.: Normalized cut loss for weakly-supervised CNN segmentation. In: Proceedings of the IEEE Conference on Computer Vision and Pattern Recognition, pp. 1818–1827 (2018)
25. Triggs, B., Verbeek, J.: Scene segmentation with CRFs learned from partially labeled images. In: Advances in Neural Information Processing Systems, vol. 20 (2007)
26. Van der Walt, S., et al.: scikit-image: image processing in python. PeerJ **2**, e453 (2014)
27. Wang, W., Lai, Q., Fu, H., Shen, J., Ling, H., Yang, R.: Salient object detection in the deep learning era: An in-depth survey. IEEE Trans. Pattern Anal. Mach. Intell. (2021)

28. Wei, Y., Feng, J., Liang, X., Cheng, M.M., Zhao, Y., Yan, S.: Object region mining with adversarial erasing: a simple classification to semantic segmentation approach. In: Proceedings of the IEEE Conference on Computer Vision and Pattern Recognition, pp. 1568–1576 (2017)
29. Xing, F.Z., Cambria, E., Huang, W.B., Xu, Y.: Weakly supervised semantic segmentation with superpixel embedding. In: 2016 IEEE International Conference on Image Processing (ICIP), pp. 1269–1273. IEEE (2016)
30. Yang, X., Song, Z., King, I., Xu, Z.: A survey on deep semi-supervised learning. arXiv preprint arXiv:2103.00550 (2021)

Multi-Feature Vision Transformer via Self-Supervised Representation Learning for Improvement of COVID-19 Diagnosis

Xiao Qi[1(✉)], David J. Foran[4], John L. Nosher[2], and Ilker Hacihaliloglu[2,3]

[1] Department of Electrical and Computer Engineering, Rutgers University,
New Brunswick, NJ, USA
xiao.qi@rutgers.edu
[2] Department of Radiology, The University of British Columbia,
Vancouver, BC, Canada
[3] Department of Medicine, The University of British Columbia,
Vancouver, BC, Canada
[4] Rutgers Cancer Institute of New Jersey, New Brunswick, NJ, USA

Abstract. The role of chest X-ray (CXR) imaging, due to being more cost-effective, widely available, and having a faster acquisition time compared to CT, has evolved during the COVID-19 pandemic. To improve the diagnostic performance of CXR imaging a growing number of studies have investigated whether supervised deep learning methods can provide additional support. However, supervised methods rely on a large number of labeled radiology images, which is a time-consuming and complex procedure requiring expert clinician input. Due to the relative scarcity of COVID-19 patient data and the costly labeling process, self-supervised learning methods have gained momentum and has been proposed achieving comparable results to fully supervised learning approaches. In this work, we study the effectiveness of self-supervised learning in the context of diagnosing COVID-19 disease from CXR images. We propose a multi-feature Vision Transformer (ViT) guided architecture where we deploy a cross-attention mechanism to learn information from both original CXR images and corresponding enhanced local phase CXR images. By using 10% labeled CXR scans, the proposed model achieves 91.10% and 96.21% overall accuracy tested on total 35,483 CXR images of healthy (8,851), regular pneumonia (6,045), and COVID-19 (18,159) scans and shows significant improvement over state-of-the-art techniques. Code is available https://github.com/endiqq/Multi-Feature-ViT.

Keywords: Self-supervised learning · Vision transformer · Cross-attention · COVID-19 · Chest X-ray

1 Introduction

The rapid spread of COVID-19 outbreak caused a surge of patients to emergency departments and hospitalization. Compared to CT, chest X-ray (CXR) has

G. Zamzmi et al. (Eds.): MILLanD 2022, LNCS 13559, pp. 76–85, 2022.
https://doi.org/10.1007/978-3-031-16760-7_8

several advantages such as its wide availability, exposure to less radiation, and faster image acquisition times. Due to this CXR has become the primary diagnostic tool for improved management of COVID-19. However, the interpretation of CXR images, compared to CT, is more challenging due to low image resolution and COVID-19 image features being similar to regular pneumonia. Computeraided diagnosis via deep learning has been investigated to help mitigate these problems and help clinicians during the decision-making process [20,21,24]. Most supervised deep learning methods rely on a large number of labeled radiology images. Medical image labeling is a time-consuming and complex procedure requiring expert clinician input.

Semi-supervised learning methods have been proposed to provide a solution to scarcity of data in the context of COVID-19 diagnosis. [22] proposed a multi-feature guided teacher-student distillation approach. Most recently selfsupervised learning methods, which utilize all the unlabeled data during learning, have been investigated for COVID-19 diagnosis [8,9,19]. [8] achieved 79.5% accuracy and 86.6% area under the receiver operating characteristic curve (AUC) on 426 COVID-19 scans while using 1% of the labeled data for the pretext task. [9] reported a mean average precision of 41.6% for 1,214 COVID-10 test data. [19] reported 99.5% accuracy using 607 COVID-19 scans. While these initial results on self-supervised learning are promising most of the prior work was evaluated on limited COVID-19 scans.

In order to break the challenges associated with scarcity of training data and to boost classification performance, we propose a new self-supervised learning approach where the proposed framework exploits local phase enhanced CXR image features to significantly improve the learning performance, specially when the data is limited. Our contributions and findings include the following: 1) We developed MoCo-COVID, a Vision Transformer(ViT) with modified Momentum Contrast (MoCo) pretraining on CXR images for self-supervised learning. This is the first study pretraining a ViT using MoCo for COVID-19 diagnosis from CXR images. 2) We demonstrated the performance of MoCo-COVID can be significantly improved by leveraging the local phase-based enhanced CXR scans specially in low data regime. 80.27% and 93.24% overall accuracy were achieved tested on 799 and 14,123 COVID-19 scans while using 1% of the labeled local phase-based enhanced data for the training. 3) A novel objective function was proposed using knowledge distillation to provide better generalization. 4) We developed a multi-feature ViT architecture based on cross-attention mechanism (MF-ViT CA) to further improve accuracy. The proposed MF-ViT CA achieves 95.03% and 97.35% mean accuracy on two large-scale test datasets including 14,922 COVID-19 scans and outperforms state-of-the-art semi-supervised learning and self-supervised learning methods.

2   Methods

Datasets: All images were collected from six public data repositories, which are BIMCV [12], COVIDx [30], COVID-19-AR [6], MIDRC-RICORD-1c [28],

COVID-19 Image Repository [31] and COVID-19-NY-SBU [5]. Our dataset consists of a total of 33,055 CXR scans from 18,252 patients with three classes: normal, pneumonia, and COVID-19. These images were split into two datasets: **1) Dataset-1:** A subset containing 12,108 CXR scans with a balanced distribution of classes (Fig. 1(b)). Dataset-1 was split into 60% training, 20% as validation, and 20% as testing dataset. No subject overlaps among train, validation, and test datasets. The test data in this dataset is referred to as *Test-1*. **2) Dataset-2:** Includes 20,947 CXR scans from 8,181 patients and has a larger number of scans in COVID-19 class. Dataset-2 only serves as an additional test dataset, referred to as *Test-2*, for evaluating the robustness of the proposed methods.

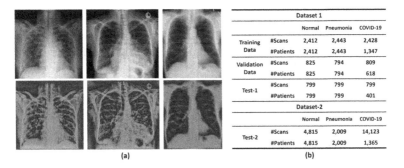

(a)   (b)

Fig. 1. (a) Top row original CXR images. Bottom row $MF(x,y)$ images. The first two columns are from subjects who are diagnosed with COVID-19. The last column is from a healthy subject. (b) Class distribution of the evaluation datasets.

Image Enhancement: Local phase-based image analysis methods are more robust to intensity variations, usually arising from patient characteristics or image acquisition settings, and have been incorporated into various medical image processing tasks [1,15,32]. The enhanced local phase CXR image, denoted as $MF(x,y)$, is obtained by combining three different local phase image features: 1-Local weighted mean phase angle ($LwPA(x,y)$), 2-Weighted local phase energy ($LPE(x,y)$), and 3-Enhanced local energy attenuation image ($ELEA(x,y)$). $LPE(x,y)$ and $LwPA(x,y)$ image features are extracted by filtering the CXR image in frequency domain using monogenic filter and α-scale space derivative (ASSD) bandpass quadrature filters [21]. $ELEA(x,y)$ image is extracted, processing the $LPE(x,y)$ image, by modeling the scattering and attenuation effects of lung tissue inside a local region using L1 norm-based contextual regularization method [21]. We have used the filter parameters reported in [21] for enhancing all the CXR images. Investigating Fig. 1(a) we can see that structural features inside the lung tissue are more dominant for COVID-19 CXR images compared to healthy lung (last column Fig. 1(a)). The enhanced local phase CXR images ($MF(x,y)$) and the original CXR images are used to train proposed self-supervised learning methods explained in the next sections.

MoCo-COVID-Self-Supervised Pretraining Using MoCo: We introduce a MoCo-COVID framework (Fig. 2(c)). During the self-supervised training, a CXR image is first transformed via two random augmentations(Aug.1 and Aug.2) into images x_q and x_k. x_q is passed through an encoder network, while x_k is passed through a momentum encoder network. We choose ViT-Small (ViT-S) [7] with 6 heads as the backbone, instead of 12 heads used by MoCo v3, to have a lower parameter count, and a faster throughput [3]. Sine-cosine variant [29] is added to the sequence as positional embedding. The representations generated by each network are then passed into the projection head followed by a prediction head. The projection head has three layers and the prediction head has two layers. Each layer follows with batch normalization (BN) and a rectified linear unit (ReLU) except the last layer of both projection head and prediction head. Then the InfoNCE contrastive loss function [18] is adopted to promote the similarity between the representations r_q and r_k:

$$L(r_q, r_k) = -log\frac{\exp(r_q.r_k + /\tau)}{\sum_{i=1}^{K} \exp(r_q.r_k, i/\tau)},\tag{1}$$

where τ is a temperature hyperparameter and K is the number of currently stored representations. The momentum coefficient follows a cosine schedule changing from 0.9 to 0.999 during the MoCo-COVID pretraining.

Multi-Feature Fusion Vision Transformer via Cross Attention: Figure 2-(a) illustrates the architecture of our proposed Multi-Feature Vision Transformer with cross-attention (CA) block (MF-ViT CA), which consists of two branches and a CA block. *CXR-branch* is used for processing the original CXR image, *Enh-branch* is used for processing the enhanced local phase CXR image ($MF(x,y)$), and CA block for extracting information from both branches. During the forward pass, an original CXR image and corresponding $MF(x,y)$ image is first passed to the pretrained MoCo encoder in parallel to obtain a tensor of dimension 197×384 for each image. These two tensors are then fed as inputs to our CA block. In the CA block, the CLS token of one branch fuses with patch tokens of the other branch using CA mechanism, and after fusion the CLS token concatenates with its own patch tokens again to produce an output in the same dimension of input tensor for each branch, described more details in below. The outputs of cross-attention and MoCo encoder are then combined via element-wise summation for each branch. The CLS token of dimension 1×384 from each branch as a compact representation, which encodes the information from both the original CXR image and $MF(x,y)$ image, is fed into a linear projection layer with three units. After that, the outputs of the two projection functions are fused using an element-wise summation.

Loss Function: We used hard-label distillation, which is a variation of distillation introduced by [27], for training CA block. In our study, *CXR-branch* and *Enh-branch*, which are obtained with the MoCo-COVID-pretrained ViT-S by using original and enhanced CXR scans (denoted as *cxr* and *enh* in Eq. 2), are considered as the teacher models. The CA block is considered as the student model. The objective function with this hard-label distillation is:

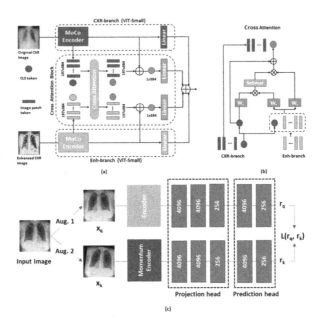

Fig. 2. (a) Proposed multi-feature fusion ViT architecture using the cross attention block which is shown in (b). (c) The proposed MoCo-COVID architecture.

$$L_{\text{global}}^{\text{hardDistill}} = \frac{1}{3}L_{\text{CE}}(\psi(Z_s), y) + \frac{1}{3}L_{\text{CE}}(\psi(Z_s), y_{t_{cxr}}) + \frac{1}{3}L_{\text{CE}}(\psi(Z_s), y_{t_{enh}}). \quad (2)$$

where Z_s is the logits of the student model and ψ is the softmax function. The idea is to use both the real target y and the target generated by the teachers $y_t = \text{argmax}_c Z_t(c)$, where Z_t is the logits of the teacher models. For a given image, the predicated label associated with the teacher may change due to data augmentation during the forward pass. Thus, the teacher model is aiming at producing predicted labels that are similar but not identical to true label.

The major benefit of the proposed hard label distillation is being parameter-free compared to soft distillation in [11]. In our study, the probability distribution has the correct class at a very high probability, with all other class probabilities close to 0. The problem with these weak probabilities is they do not capture desirable information for the student model to learn effectively. To address this issue, we proposed this hard label distillation loss function by adding two distillation losses, which are losses between the predicted label of teacher model and logits of student model. Distillation loss would soften the distributions predicted by the teacher model so that the student model can learn more information, and this is especially useful when dealing with small datasets [11]. And the proposed objective function ensures the student model inherits better quality from the teacher model and mitigates the over-confidence issue of neural networks by improving the generalization.

Cross-Attention (CA) Mechanism: The proposed CA mechanism is inspired by [2], which is designed for fusing multi-scale features from two branches. In our study, we intend to extract information from two types of images via cross-attention, and thus we removed projection function used in [2] for changing the dimension of feature maps. Figure 2(b) presents the structure of our proposed cross-attention. Similar to [2], we utilize the CLS token at each branch to fuse with patch tokens from the other branch and then project it back to its own branch in order to exchange information among the patch tokens from the other branch. Since the CLS token already learns the extracted information from all patch tokens in its own branch, interacting with the patch tokens from the other branch helps to include information from different feature inputs. In the following section, we provide a detailed explanation about the CA mechanism for the *CXR-branch*. *Enh-branch* follows the same process.

CXR-Branch-CA: An illustration of CA for *CXR-branch* is presented in the Fig. 2(b). Firstly, the CLS tokens from *CXR-branch*, denoted as *cxr*, concatenates the patch tokens from the *Enh-branch* to form x'^{cxr} shown as Eq. 3.

$$x'^{cxr} = [\ x_{cls}^{cxr} \ \|\ x_{patch}^{enh}\ ] \tag{3}$$

Then, the CA is performed between x_{cls}^{cxr} and x'^{cxr} using linear projections to computer queries, keys and values ($\mathbf{Q}$, $\mathbf{K}$ and $\mathbf{V}$), where CLS token is the only information used in query. And it uses the scaled dot product for calculating the attention weights between $\mathbf{Q}$ and $\mathbf{K}$ and then aggregates $\mathbf{V}$. The CA can be expressed as below:

$$\mathbf{Q} = x_{cls}^{cxr}\mathbf{W}_q,\ \mathbf{K} = x'^{cxr}\mathbf{W}_k,\ \mathbf{V} = x'^{cxr}\mathbf{W}_v,$$
$$\mathbf{CA} = \text{softmax}(\mathbf{QK}^T/\sqrt{D/h})\mathbf{V}, \tag{4}$$

In the Eq. 4, $\mathbf{W}_q$, $\mathbf{W}_k, \mathbf{W}_v \in \mathbb{R}^{C\times(C/h)}$ are learnable parameters, where C and h are the embedding dimension and number of heads. We use the three heads in the cross attention in this study. In the end, the new CLS token of *CXR-branch*, which is obtained by cross attention and residual shortcut, concatenates with patch tokens from *CXR-branch* as the output of *CXR-branch* shown as below:

$$y_{cls}^{cxr} = x_{cls}^{cxr} + \mathbf{CA},\ z^{cxr} = [\ y_{cls}^{cxr} \ \|\ x_{patch}^{cxr}\ ] \tag{5}$$

3 Experiments and Results

MoCo-COVID Pretraining: We pretrained our MoCo-COVID end-to-end for both original CXR image (denoted as CXR-ViT-S) and $MF(x, y)$ (denoted as Enh-ViT-S), on all training dataset without label information. MoCo-COVID pretraining initialization was performed using the weights obtained on ImageNet-initialized models for a faster convergence [23]. Data augmentation included resizing to a 224 × 224 gird, random rotation (10 °C), and horizontal flipping similar to [25]. We maintained hyperparameters related to momentum, weight decay, and feature dimension from MoCo v3 [3]. To be specific, the model was optimized by AdamW [17], a weight decay parameter of 0.1 and batch size of 16 on 2 NVIDIA GTX 1080 using PyTorch's DistributedDataParallel framework [14]. We pretrained for 300 epochs (40 warm-up epochs) with a cosine linear-rate scheduler and set the initial learning rate as $lr \times$ BatchSize/4 , where lr is $1.5e^{-4}$.

We fine-tuned models with different fractions of labeled data. Label fraction represents the percentage of labeled data retained during fine-tuning. For example, a model fine-tuned with 1% label fraction meaning the model will only have access to 1% of the training dataset as labeled dataset, and the remaining 99% are hidden from the model as unseen data. The label fractions of training dataset are 0.25% (18 scans), 1% (72 scans), 10% (728 scans), 30% (2184 scans), and 100%. Fine-tuning was repeated five times for each label fraction. Label fractions less than 100% are random samples from the training dataset.

We conducted two fine-tuning ablations, which are linear probing (LP) and end-to-end fine-tuning (FT). LP means the pretrained weight values of the MoCo-COVID encoder were frozen and, after removing the projection and prediction heads, a new linear classifier with randomly reinitialized weights was added and fine-tuned using labeled data. FT allowed the entire model including MoCo-COVID encoder to fine-tune not just the newly added classifier. The models were fine-tuned using 90 epochs. All fine-tunings used the cosine annealing learning rate decay [16] and SGD [13] optimizer.

Ablations of Multi-Feature ViT Using Cross-Attention Mechanism (MF-ViT CA): The weights of the *CXR-branch* and *Enh-branch* are initialized to the MoCo-COVID pretrained weight values of CXR-ViT-S FT and Enh-ViT-S FT respectively, and the weights of the CA block are randomly reinitialized with a uniform distribution [10]. The CA block was fine-tuned using labeled data with hard-label distillation. We compared the proposed MF-ViT CA with a model, where it also has two MoCo-COVID pretrained branches (*CXR branch* and *Enh branch*) without using cross-attention block, denoted as MF-ViT LP. During the fine-tuning, we only fine-tuned the linear layers of *CXR-branch* and *Enh-branch*.

Baselines: As baseline comparison we report results from MoCo-CXR [25], which uses MoCo v2 pretrained Dense121, when trained using original CXR and enhanced local phase CXR images ($MF(x,y)$). We report end-to-end fine-tuning protocol (FT) results for MoCo-CXR [25] and the network architecture was optimized to achieve the best results using our dataset to provide a fair comparison. Finally, we also compare our results against [22] semi-supervised, and fully supervised methods where $MF(x,y)$ were used.

Quantitative Results: Quantitative results are displayed in Table 1. The proposed MF-ViT CA architecture achieved the best accuracy compared to the rest of the self-supervised learning models when label fractions were more than 1%. MF-ViT CA performed significantly better (paired t-test $p < 0.05$) when tested on *Test-2* data compared to *Test-1* data proving the robustness of the method when tested on large scale COVID-19 data (14,123 images). The proposed Enh-ViT-S FT model had the highest accuracy for label fraction less than 10%. We can also observe that end-to-end fine-tuning protocol (FT) results are significant improvements over linear probing (LP) protocol in the proposed MoCo-COVID model. The accuracy of the baseline architecture MoCo-CXR [25] and all the proposed architectures improve when enhanced local phase CXR images ($MF(x, y)$) were used as an input. Finally, we have also observed that the CA mechanism significantly improves the results of the proposed MF-ViT LP model (paired t-text $p < 0.05$) (Table 1). From the results, we observe that the MF-ViT CA yields a statistically significant gain (paired t-text $p < 0.05$) compared to MF-TS [22] at 0.25% (18 scans) and 1% label fractions (72 scans). This indicates that the proposed models provide high-quality representations, better generalization capability, and transferable initialization for COVID-19 interpretation for minimal label fractions and when evaluated on large test data.

Table 1. Accuracy results obtained from *Test-1* and *Test-2* data. Green shaded region corresponds to the highest scores obtained. * indicates statistical improvement compared with second best self-supervised learning method ($p < 0.05$) using paired t-test.

Method	0.25%		1%		10%		30%		100%	
	Test1	Test2	Test1	Test2	Test1	Test2	Test1	Test2	Test1	Test2
MoCo-CXR[25]-pretrained end-to-end Dense121										
FT CXR	65.16	73.85	78.85	77.52	90.23	84.57	92.86	90.62	94.74	93.70
FT Enh	73.60	81.85	83.12	90.87	90.40	95.84	91.57	95.95	93.73	96.50
MoCo-COVID Pretrained (ours)										
CXR-ViT-S LP	72.64	74.18	77.35	78.33	83.76	81.71	85.10	83.88	86.93	86.15
Enh-ViT-S LP	79.97	91.71	84.06	94.00	87.81	94.87	89.10	95.85	90.51	94.14
CXR-ViT-S FT	73.00	73.37	78.23	81.13	88.59	85.94	91.66	89.48	93.26	92.19
Enh-ViT-S FT	**80.27**	**93.24***	**84.10**	**94.00**	89.09	95.33	91.43	96.23	92.62	96.57
Multi-Feature Model (ours)										
MF-ViT LP	69.01	65.22	67.20	69.72	86.72	85.20	91.06	92.02	92.53	95.01
MF-ViT CA	79.88	89.91	82.72	92.57	**91.10***	**96.21**	**93.27**	**96.84***	**95.03**	**97.35***
Semi-Supervised Learning										
MF-TS[22]	77.13	80.93	82.27	86.57	90.73	95.65	92.68	96.35	-	-
Fully-Supervised Learning										
XNet[4]	-	-	-	-	-	-	-	-	94.38	89.20
InceptionV4[26]	-	-	-	-	-	-	-	-	93.98	88.92

4   Conclusion

Our large quantitative evaluation results obtained using the largest COVID-19 data collected from different sites, show the significant improvements achieved using the local phase image features for self-supervised learning. Although we did not have access to the CXR machine type and non-image patient information (BMI, age, sex) we believe the large data used in this work represents images with varying image acquisition settings and intensity variations. Our quantitative results show significantly improved accuracy values over the investigated baselines proving the robustness of our proposed methods. Future work will include the extension of the method for diagnosing different lung diseases from CXR images.

References

1. Alessandrini, M., Basarab, A., Liebgott, H., Bernard, O.: Myocardial motion estimation from medical images using the monogenic signal. IEEE Trans. Image Process. **22**(3), 1084–1095 (2012)
2. Chen, C.F.R., Fan, Q., Panda, R.: CrossViT: cross-attention multi-scale vision transformer for image classification. In: Proceedings of the IEEE/CVF International Conference on Computer Vision, pp. 357–366 (2021)
3. Chen, X., Xie, S., He, K.: An empirical study of training self-supervised vision transformers. CoRR abs/2104.02057 (2021). https://arxiv.org/abs/2104.02057
4. Chollet, F.: Xception: Deep learning with depthwise separable convolutions. In: Proceedings of the IEEE Conference on Computer Vision and Pattern Recognition, pp. 1251–1258 (2017)
5. Clark, K., et al.: The cancer imaging archive (TCIA): maintaining and operating a public information repository. J. Digital Imaging **26**(6), 1045–1057 (2013). https://doi.org/10.1007/s10278-013-9622-7
6. Desai, S., et al.: Chest imaging representing a COVID-19 positive rural U.S. population. Sci. Data **7**, 1–6 (2020). https://doi.org/10.1038/s41597-020-00741-6
7. Dosovitskiy, A., et al.: An image is worth 16×16 words: transformers for image recognition at scale. arXiv preprint arXiv:2010.11929 (2020)
8. Gazda, M., Plavka, J., Gazda, J., Drotar, P.: Self-supervised deep convolutional neural network for chest x-ray classification. IEEE Access **9**, 151972–151982 (2021)
9. Hao, Y., Wang, Y., Wang, X.: Self-supervised pretraining for COVID-19 and other pneumonia detection from chest X-ray images. In: Xie, Q., Zhao, L., Li, K., Yadav, A., Wang, L. (eds.) ICNC-FSKD 2021. LNDECT, vol. 89, pp. 1000–1007. Springer, Cham (2022). https://doi.org/10.1007/978-3-030-89698-0_102
10. He, K., Zhang, X., Ren, S., Sun, J.: Delving deep into rectifiers: surpassing human-level performance on ImageNet classification. CoRR abs/1502.01852 (2015). http://arxiv.org/abs/1502.01852
11. Hinton, G., Vinyals, O., Dean, J.: Distilling the knowledge in a neural network (2015). https://doi.org/10.48550/ARXIV.1503.02531, https://arxiv.org/abs/1503.02531
12. de la Iglesia Vayá, M., et al.: BIMCV COVID-19+: a large annotated dataset of RX and CT images from COVID-19 patients. arXiv preprint arXiv:2006.01174 (2020)
13. Kingma, D.P., Ba, J.: Adam: a method for stochastic optimization (2017)
14. Li, S., et al.: Pytorch distributed: experiences on accelerating data parallel training. CoRR abs/2006.15704 (2020). https://arxiv.org/abs/2006.15704

15. Li, Z., van Vliet, L.J., Stoker, J., Vos, F.M.: A hybrid optimization strategy for registering images with large local deformations and intensity variations. Int. J. Comput. Assist. Radiol. Surg. **13**(3), 343–351 (2017). https://doi.org/10.1007/s11548-017-1697-z

16. Loshchilov, I., Hutter, F.: SGDR: stochastic gradient descent with restarts. CoRR abs/1608.03983 (2016). http://arxiv.org/abs/1608.03983

17. Loshchilov, I., Hutter, F.: Fixing weight decay regularization in Adam. CoRR abs/1711.05101 (2017). http://arxiv.org/abs/1711.05101

18. Van den Oord, A., Li, Y., Vinyals, O.: Representation learning with contrastive predictive coding. arXiv e-prints. arXiv-1807 (2018)

19. Park, J., Kwak, I.Y., Lim, C.: A deep learning model with self-supervised learning and attention mechanism for COVID-19 diagnosis using chest X-ray images. Electronics **10**(16), 1996 (2021)

20. Park, S., et al.: Multi-task vision transformer using low-level chest X-ray feature corpus for COVID-19 diagnosis and severity quantification. Med. Image Anal. **75**, 102299 (2022)

21. Qi, X., Brown, L.G., Foran, D.J., Nosher, J., Hacihaliloglu, I.: Chest X-ray image phase features for improved diagnosis of COVID-19 using convolutional neural network. Int. J. Comput. Assist. Radiol. Surg. **19**, 1–10 (2020)

22. Qi, X., Foran, D.J., Nosher, J.L., Hacihaliloglu, I.: Multi-feature semi-supervised learning for COVID-19 diagnosis from chest X-ray images. In: Lian, C., Cao, X., Rekik, I., Xu, X., Yan, P. (eds.) MLMI 2021. LNCS, vol. 12966, pp. 151–160. Springer, Cham (2021). https://doi.org/10.1007/978-3-030-87589-3_16

23. Raghu, M., Zhang, C., Kleinberg, J.M., Bengio, S.: Transfusion: understanding transfer learning with applications to medical imaging. CoRR abs/1902.07208 (2019). http://arxiv.org/abs/1902.07208

24. Serena Low, W.C., et al.: An overview of deep learning techniques on chest X-ray and CT scan identification of COVID-19. In: Computational and Mathematical Methods in Medicine 2021 (2021)

25. Sowrirajan, H., Yang, J., Ng, A.Y., Rajpurkar, P.: MOCO pretraining improves representation and transferability of chest X-ray models. CoRR abs/2010.05352 (2020). https://arxiv.org/abs/2010.05352

26. Szegedy, C., Ioffe, S., Vanhoucke, V., Alemi, A.: Inception-v4, inception-resnet and the impact of residual connections on learning (2016)

27. Touvron, H., Cord, M., Douze, M., Massa, F., Sablayrolles, A., Jégou, H.: Training data-efficient image transformers & distillation through attention. CoRR abs/2012.12877 (2020). https://arxiv.org/abs/2012.12877

28. Tsai, E.B., et al.: The RSNA international COVID-19 open annotated radiology database (RICORD). Radiology. **299**, E204 (2021). https://doi.org/10.1148/radiol.2021203957, PMID: 33399506

29. Vaswani, A., et al.: Attention is all you need. CoRR abs/1706.03762 (2017). http://arxiv.org/abs/1706.03762

30. Wang, L., Lin, Z.Q., Wong, A.: COVID-net: a tailored deep convolutional neural network design for detection of COVID-19 cases from chest X-ray images. Sci. Rep. **10**(1), 19549 (2020). https://doi.org/10.1038/s41598-020-76550-z

31. Winther, H.B., et al.: COVID-19 image repository (2020). https://doi.org/10.6084/m9.figshare.12275009.v1

32. Zhao, Y., Liu, Y., Wu, X., Harding, S.P., Zheng, Y.: Retinal vessel segmentation: an efficient graph cut approach with Retinex and local phase. PLoS ONE **10**(4), e0122332 (2015)

SB-SSL: Slice-Based Self-supervised Transformers for Knee Abnormality Classification from MRI

Sara Atito[1], Syed Muhammad Anwar[2]([envelope]), Muhammad Awais[1,3],
and Josef Kittler[1]

[1] Centre for Vision, Speech and Signal Processing (CVSSP),
University of Surrey, Guildford, UK
[2] Children's National Hospital, Washington, DC, USA
sanwar@childrensnational.org
[3] Surrey Institute for People-Centred AI, Guildford, UK

Abstract. The availability of large scale data with high quality ground truth labels is a challenge when developing supervised machine learning solutions for healthcare domain. Although, the amount of digital data in clinical workflows is increasing, most of this data is distributed on clinical sites and protected to ensure patient privacy. Radiological readings and dealing with large-scale clinical data puts a significant burden on the available resources, and this is where machine learning and artificial intelligence play a pivotal role. Magnetic Resonance Imaging (MRI) for musculoskeletal (MSK) diagnosis is one example where the scans have a wealth of information, but require a significant amount of time for reading and labeling. Self-supervised learning (SSL) can be a solution for handling the lack of availability of ground truth labels, but generally requires a large amount of training data during the pretraining stage. Herein, we propose a slice-based self-supervised deep learning framework (SB-SSL), a novel slice-based paradigm for classifying abnormality using knee MRI scans. We show that for a limited number of cases (<1000), our proposed framework is capable to identify anterior cruciate ligament tear with an accuracy of 89.17% and an AUC of 0.954, outperforming state-of-the-art without usage of external data during pretraining. This demonstrates that our proposed framework is suited for SSL in the limited data regime.

Keywords: Self-supervised learning · Group masked model learning · Masked autoencoders · Knee abnormality · Transformers · MRI

1 Introduction

Knee abnormality can arise from a variety of factors including aging, physical injury, and joint disease. MRI is the standard-of-care for diagnosis of knee abnormalities [21], where the image contains a wealth of information and the scanning

S. Atito and S. M. Anwar—Contributed equally to this article.

G. Zamzmi et al. (Eds.): MILLanD 2022, LNCS 13559, pp. 86–95, 2022.
https://doi.org/10.1007/978-3-031-16760-7_9

protocols are safe from a clinical perspective. Knee MRI exams are among the most widely performed scans in MSK radiology [14]. MSK conditions arise from a variety of reasons (including sports injury and lifestyle choices) effecting adults and pediatrics. Both the amount of information within a knee MRI scan, and the number of such scans performed on a daily basis put a huge burden on the radiologist and the clinical workforce dealing with MSK related conditions and knee abnormalities In recent years, machine learning is the technology of choice in radiology for automated image analysis and abnormality identification [2]. However, the clinical translation of this technology is facing challenges such as lack of adequate annotations and training data. In particular, manual segmentation and data labeling is a labor intensive and tedious task, which is also effected by inter-rater variability. The probability of error, accounting for the day-to-day workload on radiologists, is high and this is where machine learning can benefit the most by identifying the most critical cases needing immediate attention.

In contrast to Convolutional Neural Networks (CNNs), transformer-based deep learning models have shown to perform better due to an inherent design incorporating attention and parallel computing [17]. The success of transformer based networks in the field of natural language processing (NLP) is phenomenal and became the default choice in most recent NLP applications. The recent introduction of vision transformer [10], has resulted in the translation of some of this success to vision tasks. Training self-supervised vision transformers for medical applications could alleviate some of the problems associated with acquiring high quality ground truth labels and hence, accelerate the research in computer aided diagnosis. However, such networks require a large training data. Therefore, in Computer Vision (CV) problems, the default practice is to use a pretrained model on a large supervised data like ImageNet-1K, before fine tuning for a specific downstream task with limited data [4].

Recently, self-supervised pretraining of deep neural networks without using any labels has outperformed supervised pretraining in CV [3,5]. This phenomenal shift in CV is less investigated in medical image analysis domain. We argue that recent SSL approaches are ideally suited for medical image analysis, since medical data are an order of magnitude smaller than natural images due to several reasons, including privacy concerns, expensive annotation, rarity of certain diseases, etc. Hence for medical applications, SSL can lead the way for a wider adoption of such techniques in domains where labels are not available or are difficult to acquire [1]. Therefore, the purpose of this study is to investigate: 1) is ImageNet-1K pretraining needed for medical imaging? 2) can we perform self-supervised pretraining on a small medical data and outperform large scale out of distribution supervised pretraining? If successful this will form the basis for SSL for medical imaging in limited data regimes. Towards this, we propose a slice-based self-supervised deep learning framework (SB-SSL) for abnormality classification using knee MRI, where our main contributions are:

– We propose a novel slice based self-supervised transformer model (SB-SSL) for knee abnormality classification using magnetic resonance imaging data.

– The model is pretrained from scratch on limited data without labels and fine tuned for the downstream knee abnormality classification task with state-of-the-art performance.
– Our experimental results show that, when trained using the group masked model learning (GMML) paradigm, SSL can be successfully applied for medical image analysis with limited data/label.

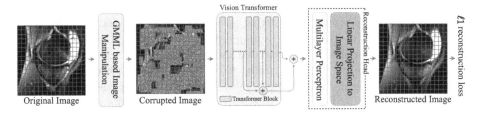

Fig. 1. Proposed self-supervised learning approach.

2   Related Works

In [6], a deep learning based method was presented for the detection of abnormalities in knee MRI. The publicly available MRNet data was presented, along with an AlexNet [16] based model for classifying abnormalities, meniscal tear, and anterior cruciate ligament (ACL) tear. This was among the first approaches where deep learning was applied to this task, and since then has been used in multiple studies to further improve the classification performance [11,13,20,24].

A CNN based self supervised training paradigm was developed, where solving the jigsaw puzzle was used as the pre-text task [20]. In the downstream task, ACL tear was classified with an accuracy of 76.62% and an area under the curve (AUC) of 0.848 using the sagittal plane. In [24], efficiently-layered network (ELNet) was proposed where the model reduced the number of parameters compared to AlexNet, and utilized individual slice views for classification of meniscus (coronal) and ACL (axial) tears. An accuracy of 0.904 with an AUC of 0.960 was achieved in detecting the ACL tear. This performance was improved by adding a feature pyramid network and pyramidal detail pooling to ELNet [11]. An AUC of 0.976 and an accuracy of 0.886 was achieved in ACL tear classification task. However, both these methods are based on supervised training. Meniscus tears were identified using a deep learning model and compared with manual evaluation [13]. An accuracy of 95.8% was achieved for an internal validation set, however the model was not evaluated on any of the publicly available data.

In general, it should be noted that for methods that report higher performance, training is based on the availability of ground truth labels. Whereas for self supervised training, which could alleviate this burden, the model performance drops. We propose, for the first time, a transformer based self-supervised framework for knee abnormality classification using MRI. Our innovative training paradigm use self-supervised training and shows that such a framework can be effectively used even when the size of training data is relatively small.

3   Methodology

In this work, we introduce a general slice-based self-supervised vision transformer for knee MRI medical records. The system diagram of the proposed approach is shown in Fig. 1. Transformers [25] have shown great success in various NLP and CV tasks [3–5,7–9,22,27] and are the basis of our proposed framework.

3.1   Vision Transformer

Vision transformer [10] receives, as input, a feature map from the output of a convolutional block/layer with K kernels of size $p \times p$ and stride $p \times p$. The convolutional block takes an input image $\mathbf{x} \in \mathcal{R}^{C \times H \times W}$ and converts it to feature maps of size $\sqrt{n} \times \sqrt{n} \times K$, where C, H, and W are the number of channels, height, and width, of the input image, $(p \times p)$ is the patch size, and n is the number of patches, i.e., $n = \frac{H}{p} \times \frac{W}{p}$. Learnable position embeddings are added to the patch embeddings as an input to the transformer encoder to retain the relative spatial relation between the patches.

The transformer encoder consists of L consecutive Multi-head Self-Attention (MSA) and Multi-Layer Perceptron (MLP) blocks. The MSA block is defined by h self-attention heads, where each head outputs a sequence of size $n \times d$. The self attention mechanism is based on a trainable triplet (query, key, and value). Each query vector in $\mathbf{Q} \in \mathcal{R}^{n \times d}$ for a given head is matched against a set of key vectors $\mathbf{K} \in \mathcal{R}^{n \times d}$, scaled by the square root of d to have more stable gradients as the dot product of q and k tend to grow large in magnitude, resulting in vanishing gradients and a slowdown of learning. After applying softmax, the output is then multiplied by a set of values $\mathbf{V} \in \mathcal{R}^{n \times d}$. Thus, the output of the self-attention block is the weighted sum of $\mathbf{V}$ as shown in Eq. 1. The output sequences across heads are then concatenated into $n \times (d \times h)$, and projected by a linear layer to a $n \times K$ sequence. The MLP block consists of two point-wise convolution layers with GeLU [12] non-linearity.

$$\text{SelfAttention}(\mathbf{Q}, \mathbf{K}, \mathbf{V}) = \text{Softmax}(\frac{\mathbf{Q}\mathbf{K}^T}{\sqrt{d}})\mathbf{V}. \tag{1}$$

3.2   Self-supervised Pretraining

We leverage the strength of the transformers and train it as an autoencoder with a light decoder employing GMML [4,5]. Starting with the vanilla transformer autoencoder, the model is pretrained as an autoencoder to reconstruct the input image, i.e., $D(E(\mathbf{x})) = \mathbf{x}$, where $\mathbf{x}$ is the input image, E is the encoder which is vision transformer in our case, and D is a light reconstruction decoder. Due to the strength of transformers, it is expected that the model will perfectly reconstruct the input image after a few training epochs. Indeed, this is attributed to the fact that without a proper choice of constraints, autoencoders are capable of learning identity mapping, i.e., memorizing the input without learning any useful discriminative features.

To promote the learning of context and learn better semantic representations of the input images from the transformer-based autoencoder, we apply several transformations to local patches of the image. The aim is to recover these masked local parts at the output of the light decoder. In doing so, especially with a high percentage of corruption (up to 70%), the model implicitly learns the semantic concepts in the image and the underline structure of the data in order to be able to recover the image back. Image in-painting is a simple but effective pre-text task for self-supervision, which proceeds by training a network to predict arbitrary transformed regions based on the context.

The objective of image reconstruction is to restore the original image from the corrupted image. For this task, we use the $\ell1$-loss between the reconstructed image and the original image in an end-to-end self-supervised trainable system as shown in Eq. 2. Although, $\ell2$-loss generally converges faster than $\ell1$-loss, it is prone to over-smooth the edges for image restoration [26]. Therefore, $\ell1$-loss is more commonly used for image-to-image processing.

$$\mathcal{L}(\mathbf{W}) = \sum_{k}^{b} \left(\sum_{i}^{H} \sum_{j}^{W} \mathbb{1}_{[\mathbf{M}_{i,j}^{k}=1]} |\mathbf{x}_{i,j}^{k} - \bar{\mathbf{x}}_{i,j}^{k}| \right), \tag{2}$$

where $\mathbf{W}$ denotes the parameters to be learned during training, b is the batch size, $\mathbf{M}$ is a binary mask with 1 indicating the manipulated pixels, and $\bar{\mathbf{x}}$ is the reconstructed image. To further improve the performance of the autoencoder, we introduced skip connections from several intermediate transformer blocks to the decoder. These additional connections can directly send the feature maps from the earlier layers of the transformers to the decoder which helps to use fine-grained details learned in the early layers to construct the image. Besides, skip connections in general make the loss landscape smoother which leads to faster convergence. Further, the reconstructed image $\bar{\mathbf{x}}$ is obtained by averaging the output features from the intermediate blocks from the transformer encoder ($E(.)$) and feeding the output to a light decoder ($D(.)$) represented mathematically as $\bar{\mathbf{x}} = D \left(\sum_{i \in \mathcal{B}} E_i(\hat{\mathbf{x}}) \right)$, where $E_i(.)$ is the output features from block i and $\mathcal{B}$ is a pre-defined index set of transformer blocks that are included in the decoding process. Herein, we set $\mathcal{B}$ to $\{6, 8, 10, 12\}$.

As for the decoder, unlike CNN-based autoencoders which require expensive decoders consisting of convolutional and transposed convolution layers, the decoder in the transformer autoencoder can be implemented using a light decoder design. Specifically, our decoder consisted of two point-wise convolutional layers with GeLU non-linearity and a transposed convolutional layer to return back to the image space. Since the backbone, i.e., vision transformer, and the light decoder are isotropic, some of the transformer blocks may act as decoder and hence, heavy and computationally expensive type of decoders are not required.

4 Experimental Results

To demonstrate the effectiveness of our proposed self-supervised vision transformer on medical images, we employed the MRNet dataset [6]. The dataset consists of 1,370 knee MRI records, split into a training set of 1,130 records of 1,088 patients and a validation set of 120 records of 111 patients. Each MRI is labeled according to the presence/absence of meniscus tear, ACL tear, or any other abnormality in the knee. In this work, we tackled the ACL tear identification problem using the Sagittal plane. The dataset is highly imbalanced with only 208 MRIs representing ACL tear.

4.1 Implementation Details

In our work, we employed the ViT Small (ViT-S) variant of the transformer [23] with 256×256 input image size. For optimization of the transformer parameters during self-supervised pre-training, we used the Adam optimizer [19] with a momentum of 0.9. The weight decay follows a cosine schedule [18] from 0.04 to 0.4, and a base learning rate of $5e^{-4}$. All models were pre-trained employing 4 Nvidia Tesla V100 32 GB GPU cards with 64 batch size per GPU.

Simple data augmentation techniques were applied like random cropping, random horizontal flipping, random Gaussian blurring, and random adjusting of the sharpness, contrast, saturation, and the hue of the image. The augmented image was further corrupted by randomly replacing patches from the image with zeros, with a replacement rate of up to 70% of the image pixels.

For fine-tuning, we drop the light decoder and fine tune the pre-trained model by passing the volume, slice by slice, to the transformer encoder. The outputs of the class tokens corresponding to each slice are then concatenated to obtain $y \in \mathcal{R}^{f \times K}$, where f is the number of slices. After that, the features y are fed to a fully connected layer with K nodes followed by GeLU non-linearity, followed by a linear layer with 2 nodes corresponding to the presence/absence of the ACL tear. As the dataset is highly imbalanced, we used oversampling on the training set to balance the dataset. Specifically, we over-sample the minority class, i.e., presence of ACL tear, to match the number of the majority class. Finally, we applied the same optimization parameters and data augmentations used for the self-supervised training.

Further, we employed ensemble learning [15]. Generally, neural networks have high variance due to the stochastic training approach that makes them sensitive to the nature of the training data. The models may find a different set of weights each time they are trained, which in turn may produce different predictions. To mitigate this issue, for each experiment, we trained 5 models with different weight initialization and combined the predictions from these models. Not only this approach reduced the variance of the predictions, but also resulted in predictions that were better than any single model.

4.2 Results

It is well known that transformers are data-hungry which make them hard to train, mostly, due to the lack of the typical inductive bias of convolution operations. Consequently, the common protocol for self-supervised learning with transformers is to pretrain the model on a large scale dataset, such as ImageNet or even larger datasets. We compare our proposed approach with the state-of-the-art SSL methods when the pretraining and the fine-tuning are performed only on the MRNet dataset. Table 1 shows that our method outperforms the state-of-the-art with a large margin with an improvement of 12.6% top-1 validation accuracy on the ACL tears classification task employing the sagittal plane. Most importantly, without using any external data, our proposed approach outperforms the competitors that are pre-trained with ImageNet-1K marking a milestone for the medical domain. The receiver operating characteristic (ROC) curve for three transformer variants, ViT-Tiny, ViT-Small, and ViT-Base are shown in Fig. 2, where ViT-T performs the best.

Table 1. Comparison with SOTA on ACL tears classification employing sagittal plane.

Method	Backbone	# params	ACL Tear (Sagittal plane) Accuracy (%)	AUC
Training using only the given dataset				
Random Init	CNN	77M	71.67	0.754
Random Init	ViT-S	21M	70.00	0.721
[20]	CNN	77M	76.62	0.848
[20] + noise	CNN	77M	75.83	0.817
SB-SSL (Ours)	ViT-T	5M	85.83	0.952
SB-SSL (Ours)	ViT-S	21M	88.33	0.954
SB-SSL (Ours)	ViT-B	86M	89.17	0.954
Transfer learning from ImageNet-1K dataset				
MRNet [6]	AlexNet	61M	86.63	0.963

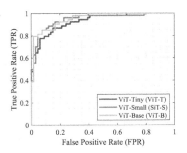

Fig. 2. ROC curves of the classification of ACL tears employing different vision transformer architectures.

4.3   Ablation Studies

In this section, we investigate the effect of different recipes of the proposed approach, such as the effect of longer pretraining, the size of the model, and the type of image corruption during the pretraining stage. Further, we show the interpretability of the system by visualizing the attention of the trained models.

Effects of Longer Pretraining and Model Size. In Fig. 3, we show the performance of the proposed approach when pretrained for longer duration across different vision transformer architectures. The x-axis represents the number of self-supervised pretraining epochs, with zero indicating that the model was not pretrained, i.e., training from scratch. From the reported results, it is evident that the training from random initialization has produced a lower accuracy as the amount of data available is insufficient to train the transformer. The results significantly improved when the models were pretrained without any external data by 25.8%, 18.3%, and 13.3% employing ViT-T, ViT-S, and ViT-B, respectively, compared to training from scratch. Another observation is that pre-training the self-supervised for longer and employing bigger transformer architectures contribute positively to the performance of the proposed approach.

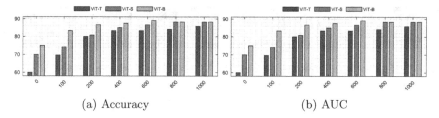

(a) Accuracy   (b) AUC

Fig. 3. Top-1 validation accuracies and AUC of the MRNet validation set across different vision transformer architectures. The x-axis represents number of epochs used for pretraining.

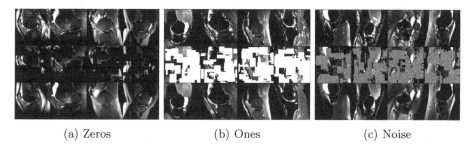

(a) Zeros   (b) Ones   (c) Noise

Fig. 4. Samples of different types of corruption. The rows represent the original images, corrupted images, and the reconstructed images after the pretraining stage, respectively.

The Effects of Different Types of Corruption: We first investigate the effect of training a vanilla transformer autoencoder, where the model is pretrained as an autoencoder to reconstruct the input image. As expected, after finetuning, the performance was similar to the performance of the model trained from scratch. Following, we investigate the effect of applying different types of image inpainting including: random masking by replacing a group of connected patches from the image with zeros, ones, or noise. Samples of the different types of corruption are shown in Fig. 4 along with the reconstructed images after the pretraining stage. The performance when pretraining the models with different types of corruption is on par, with noise being marginally better than others.

Attention Visualization. To verify that the model is learning pertinent features, in Fig. 5, we provide visualizations of the self-attention corresponding to the class token of the 10th layer of the vision transformer. To generate the attention for an image, we compute the normalized average over the self-attention heads to obtain a 16×16 tokens. The tokens are then mapped to a color scheme, up-sampled to 256×256 pixels, and overlaid with the original input image. For visualization, we selected the mid slice of randomly selected MRI volumes from the MRNet validation set. We observe that the attention is clearly focusing on the area of interest, corresponding to the main part of the MRI slice on which the detection of ACL tears is performed.

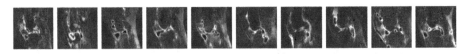

Fig. 5. Self-attention visualizations from the ViT-S model finetuned on the ACL tears task employing the sagittal plane.

5   Conclusion

We proposed a novel framework SB-SSL, pre-trained in a self-supervised manner for knee abnormality classification. We established a new benchmark in SSL for MRI data, where pretraining on a large supervised data was not required. The state-of-the-art performance, with an accuracy of 89.17% in ACL tear classification, shows that our proposed method can be employed in MR image classification even when the data are limited and ground truth labels are not available.

References

1. Anwar, S.M., et al.: Semi-supervised deep learning for multi-tissue segmentation from multi-contrast MRI. J. Signal Process. Syst. 1–14 (2020)
2. Anwar, S.M., et al.: Medical image analysis using convolutional neural networks: a review. J. Med. Syst. **42**(11), 1–13 (2018)
3. Atito, S., Awais, M., Farooq, A., Feng, Z., Kittler, J.: MC-SSL0.0: towards multi-concept self-supervised learning. arXiv preprint arXiv:2111.15340 (2021)
4. Atito, S., Awais, M., Kittler, J.: SiT: Self-supervised vision transformer. arXiv preprint arXiv:2104.03602 (2021)
5. Atito, S., Awais, M., Kittler, J.: GMML is all you need. arXiv preprint arXiv:2205.14986 (2022)
6. Bien, N., et al.: Deep-learning-assisted diagnosis for knee magnetic resonance imaging: development and retrospective validation of mrnet. PLoS Med. **15**(11), e1002699 (2018)
7. Brown, T.B., et al.: Language models are few-shot learners. arXiv preprint arXiv:2005.14165 (2020)
8. Chen, Z., et al.: Masked image modeling advances 3d medical image analysis. arXiv preprint arXiv:2204.11716 (2022)
9. Devlin, J., Chang, M.W., Lee, K., Toutanova, K.: BERT: pre-training of deep bidirectional transformers for language understanding. arXiv preprint arXiv:1810.04805 (2018)
10. Dosovitskiy, A., et al.: An image is worth 16x16 words: Transformers for image recognition at scale. arXiv preprint arXiv:2010.11929 (2020)
11. Dunnhofer, M., Martinel, N., Micheloni, C.: Improving MRI-based knee disorder diagnosis with pyramidal feature details. In: Medical Imaging with Deep Learning, pp. 131–147. PMLR (2021)
12. Hendrycks, D., Gimpel, K.: Gaussian error linear units (GELUS). arXiv preprint arXiv:1606.08415 (2016)
13. Hung, T.N.K., et al.: Automatic detection of meniscus tears using backbone convolutional neural networks on knee MRI. J. Magn. Reson. Imaging (2022)

14. Irmakci, I., Anwar, S.M., Torigian, D.A., Bagci, U.: Deep learning for musculoskeletal image analysis. In: 2019 53rd Asilomar Conference on Signals, Systems, and Computers, pp. 1481–1485. IEEE (2019)

15. Kittler, J., Hatef, M., Duin, R.P., Matas, J.: On combining classifiers. IEEE Trans. Pattern Anal. Mach. Intell. **20**(3), 226–239 (1998)

16. Krizhevsky, A., Sutskever, I., Hinton, G.E.: Imagenet classification with deep convolutional neural networks. Adv. Neural Inf. Process. Syst. **25**, 1–9 (2012)

17. Liu, Y., et al.: A survey of visual transformers. arXiv preprint arXiv:2111.06091 (2021)

18. Loshchilov, I., Hutter, F.: SGDR: stochastic gradient descent with warm restarts. arXiv preprint arXiv:1608.03983 (2016)

19. Loshchilov, I., Hutter, F.: Fixing weight decay regularization in Adam. arXiv:abs/1711.05101 (2017)

20. Manna, S., Bhattacharya, S., Pal, U.: Self-supervised representation learning for detection of ACL tear injury in knee MR videos. Pattern Recogn. Lett. **154**, 37–43 (2022)

21. Nacey, N.C., Geeslin, M.G., Miller, G.W., Pierce, J.L.: Magnetic resonance imaging of the knee: an overview and update of conventional and state of the art imaging. J. Magn. Reson. Imaging **45**(5), 1257–1275 (2017)

22. Radford, A., Wu, J., Child, R., Luan, D., Amodei, D., Sutskever, I.: Language models are unsupervised multitask learners. OpenAI Blog **1**(8), 9 (2019)

23. Touvron, H., Cord, M., Douze, M., Massa, F., Sablayrolles, A., Jégou, H.: Training data-efficient image transformers & distillation through attention. arXiv preprint arXiv:2012.12877 (2020)

24. Tsai, C.H., Kiryati, N., Konen, E., Eshed, I., Mayer, A.: Knee injury detection using MRI with efficiently-layered network (ELNET). In: Medical Imaging with Deep Learning, pp. 784–794. PMLR (2020)

25. Vaswani, A., et al.: Attention is all you need. arXiv preprint arXiv:1706.03762 (2017)

26. Zhao, H., Gallo, O., Frosio, I., Kautz, J.: Loss functions for image restoration with neural networks. IEEE Trans. Comput. Imaging **3**(1), 47–57 (2016)

27. Zhou, L., Liu, H., Bae, J., He, J., Samaras, D., Prasanna, P.: Self pre-training with masked autoencoders for medical image analysis. arXiv preprint arXiv:2203.05573 (2022)

Optimizing Transformations for Contrastive Learning in a Differentiable Framework

Camille Ruppli[1,3](✉), Pietro Gori[1], Roberto Ardon[3], and Isabelle Bloch[2,3]

[1] LTCI, Télécom Paris, Institut Polytechnique de Paris, Paris, France
[2] Sorbonne Université, CNRS, LIP6, Paris, France
[3] Incepto Medical, Paris, France
`camille.ruppli@incepto-medical.com`

Abstract. Current contrastive learning methods use random transformations sampled from a large list of transformations, with fixed hyper-parameters, to learn invariance from an unannotated database. Following previous works that introduce a small amount of supervision, we propose a framework to find optimal transformations for contrastive learning using a *differentiable* transformation network. Our method increases performances at low annotated data regime both in supervision accuracy and in convergence speed. In contrast to previous work, no generative model is needed for transformation optimization. Transformed images keep relevant information to solve the supervised task, here classification. Experiments were performed on 34000 2D slices of brain Magnetic Resonance Images and 11200 chest X-ray images. On both datasets, with 10% of labeled data, our model achieves better performances than a fully supervised model with 100% labels.

Keywords: Contrastive learning · Semi-supervised learning · Transformations optimization

1 Introduction

When working with medical images, data are increasingly available but annotations are fewer and costly to obtain. Self-supervised methods have been developed to take full advantage of the non-annotated data and increase performances in supervised tasks at low annotated data regime. As part of self-supervised methods, contrastive learning methods [1,2,11,12] train an encoder on non-annotated data to learn invariance between transformed versions of images. Contrastive learning methods are also used with medical images. For instance, the authors of [1] learn local and global features invariance while those of [5] introduce a kernel to take metadata into account in contrastive pretraining.

In most works, the transformations used to learn invariance are randomly sampled from a given list. While many works study the impact of removing some transformations on supervised task performance [2,12], not much investigation has been done on optimizing the transformations and their hyper-parameters. Some authors

G. Zamzmi et al. (Eds.): MILLanD 2022, LNCS 13559, pp. 96–105, 2022.
https://doi.org/10.1007/978-3-031-16760-7_10

[11,15] focus on the role of transformations but without explicit transformations optimization. The work of [11] proposes a formal analysis of transformations composition to select admissible transformations while [15] explores the latent spaces of specific transformations. The authors of [16] introduce a generative network to learn transformations distribution present in the data to use complementary transformations in self-supervised tasks. Unlike our work (see Sect. 2) they need a pretraining step before the contrastive one to learn transformations distribution.

Within supervised training (not self-supervision), some works have proposed to optimize data augmentation. In [4], a pre-training step using reinforcement learning is required. The work of [17] shows that data augmentation should be applied on both discriminator and generator optimization steps but no optimization is performed on augmentation choice. The authors of [8,9] learn a vector containing augmentations probability. They also present a transformations optimization strategy. Unlike our approach (see Sect. 2), transformation parameters are discretized. Optimization is performed on the probability of choosing a family of transformations and a set of parameters.

While supervision is also introduced in contrastive learning in [6,18], few authors used it in order to influence the choice of transformations. Among them, the authors of [14] introduce a transformation generator (a flow-based model based on [7]) to generate transformed images in new color spaces minimizing mutual information while keeping enough information for the supervised task. As transformations only impact color spaces, their application to gray scale images, in particular medical images, is very limited. Furthermore, consistently synthesizing anatomically relevant images with generative models can be difficult [3]. To the best of our knowledge, the approach in [14] is the only existing method optimizing a transformation generator for contrastive learning.

As in [14], the present work uses a small amount of supervision (10%) for transformation optimization. We introduce a differentiable framework on transformations that needs no pre-training, and, unlike [14], is applicable to both color and gray scale images. Our contributions are the following:

- We propose a semi-supervised differentiable framework to optimize the transformations of contrastive learning.
- We demonstrate that our method finds relevant transformations for the downstream task, which are easy to interpret.
- We show that our framework has better performances than fully supervised training at low data regime and contrastive learning [2] without supervision.

2   Transformation Network

Contrastive learning methods train an encoder to bring close together latent representations of positive pairs of images while pushing away representations of negative pairs of images. As in simCLR [2], positive pairs are two transformations of the same image while negative pairs are transformed versions of different images.

Transformations used in most methods are chosen at random from a fixed given list. However, as shown in [14], using positive (transformed) images, that are very similar to each other (i.e., high mutual information), might entail a suboptimal solution since it would not bring additional information to the encoder. By using a small amount of supervision, transformations can be optimized in order to contain relevant information for the targeted supervised task.

In this work, we focus on classification tasks. We introduce a transformation network (M) that minimizes the mutual information between images of a positive pair without compromising the supervised task performance. For each image of the training set, M, implemented as a neural network, outputs a set of parameters (Λ) defining the transformations to apply (T_{Λ_M}). As in [2,15], the latent space of the encoder (f) is optimized using a projection head (g) into a lower dimension space where a contrastive loss function (I_{NCE}) is minimized. Supervision is added on the latent space using a linear classifier (p) that minimizes a classification loss function ($\mathcal{L}$). Figure 1 shows a schematic view of the architecture used (X denotes an image from the training set and X_M its transformed version).

Fig. 1. Proposed architecture (red color indicates a trainable element, blue color indicates a non-trainable element). (Color figure online)

2.1 Optimizing Transformations

We consider a finite set of intensity and geometric transformations acting on images. Each transformation is parameterized by a vector of parameters (for example, the parameter vector of a rotation around a fixed point only contains its angle). The transformation function (T_{Λ_M}) is the composition of transformations applied in a fixed order. The transformation network (M) outputs the transformation function parameters. We propose to train M to find the optimal transformations for the semi-supervised contrastive problem. The network M maps an image to the space of parameter vectors, normalized to $[0,1]$. The order of the transformations in the composition is not optimized, but the impact of this order has been studied and results are shown in Sect. 3.

Let λ_k be the vector of parameters for a given transformation, then the transformation function, noted as T_{Λ_M}, is parameterized by $\Lambda = [\lambda_1, \cdots, \lambda_K]$ (where K is the number of transformations considered).

The optimal transformations for the semi-supervised contrastive problem is then obtained via M, which is thus responsible for finding the optimal Λ_M^*. In contrast with [2], we only transform one version of the image batch. Our experiments show better results in this setting. The optimization goes as follows.

Transformation Network Optimization Steps: (i) M generates a batch of Λ_M vectors defining a transformation T_{Λ_M}. For every image X in a batch, a transformed version is generated: $X_M = T_{\Lambda_M}(X)$. (ii) The transformed and untransformed data batches are passed through the encoder f, the projection head g and the linear classifier p. (iii) The contrastive loss $-I_{NCE}$ (see below, Eq. 2) gradient is computed to update the weights of the network M aiming to minimize mutual information and classification loss function.

Encoder Optimization Steps: (i) From the previous optimization steps of M, one transformed version of the data is generated. Latent projections of the transformed and untransformed data are generated using encoder f and projection head g. (ii) The contrastive loss gradient is computed and parameters of f, g and p are updated. This brings closer positive pairs and further away negative ones, and ensures that transformed images are properly classified.

Formally, these steps aim to solve the following coupled optimization problem where contrastive and classification loss functions are taken into account:

$$
\begin{cases}
\min_M \ \alpha_0 I_{NCE}\Big(g \circ f(X_M), g \circ f(X)\Big) + \alpha_1 \mathcal{L}\Big(p \circ f(X_M), y\Big) \\
\min_{f,p,g} -\alpha_2 I_{NCE}\Big(g \circ f(X_M), g \circ f(X)\Big) + \alpha_3 \mathcal{L}\Big(p \circ f(X_M), y\Big) \\
\quad + \alpha_4 \mathcal{L}\Big(p \circ f(X), y\Big)
\end{cases}
\tag{1}
$$

where α_i are weights balancing each loss term and y are the classification labels when available. The term I_{NCE} is the contrastive loss function as in [2]:

$$
I_{NCE}(X_{Mi}, X_i) = -\sum_i \log \left(\frac{e^{sim(g(f(X_{Mi})), g(f(X_i)))}}{\sum_{j,j \neq i} e^{sim(g(f(X_{Mi})), g(f(X_j)))}} \right)
\tag{2}
$$

where the index i defines positive pairs, j negative ones, and sim is a similarity measure defined as $sim(x, x') = \frac{x^T x'}{\tau}$ where τ is a fixed scalar, here equal to 1. Finally, $\mathcal{L}$ is the binary cross entropy loss function for the supervised constraint.

2.2   Differentiable Formulation of the Transformations

A fundamental difference of the proposed transformation optimization, compared to [8,9,14], is the use of explicit transformations differentiation. During training, gradient computations of Eq. 1 involve the derivative of T_{Λ_M} with respect to the weights (w) of M: $d_w(T_{\Lambda_M}) = dT_{\Lambda_M} \circ d_w M$. This requires the explicit computation of the derivatives of T with respect to its parameters Λ and the differential calculus for each transformation composing T. Thus, we introduce specific formulations and normalized parameterization for the transformations used in our experiments.

We use the following transformations: crop $(Crop)$, Gaussian blur (G), additive Gaussian noise (N), rotation (R) around the center of the image, horizontal

($Flip_0$) and vertical ($Flip_1$) flips. Table 1 lists the expressions of these transformations. The final transformation function is defined as:

$$T_\Lambda = (R \circ Flip_1 \circ Flip_0 \circ Crop \circ N \circ G)(X, \Lambda) \tag{3}$$

and T_Λ thus depends on 7 parameters (the crop has 2 parameters) which are generated by M.

Table 1. Differentiable expressions of the transformations used, parameterized by $\lambda \in [0, 1]$, where S is the sigmoid function, s the size of our images, erfinv the inverse of the error function $2\pi^{-\frac{1}{2}} \int_x^\infty e^{-u^2} du$, $\mathcal{U}$ the uniform distribution and x is a point of the image grid. We fix the maximum Gaussian blur standard deviation to $\sigma_{max} = 2.0$ and the maximum additive noise standard deviation to $\tilde{\sigma}_{max} = 0.1$.

Flip around axis e	$Flip(X, \lambda, e)(x) = (1 - \lambda)X(x) + \lambda X(x - 2\langle x, e \rangle e)$
Crop centered at $c_\lambda = [\lambda_1 s, \lambda_2 s]$	$Crop(X, \lambda)(x) = X(x) \times S(\frac{s}{8} - \|x - c_\lambda\|_\infty)$
Gaussian blur with kernel $g_{\lambda \sigma_{max}}$	$G(X, \lambda) = g_{\lambda \sigma_{max}} * X$
Rotation	$R(X, \lambda)(x) = X\left(\begin{pmatrix} \cos(\lambda 2\pi) & -\sin(\lambda 2\pi) \\ \sin(\lambda 2\pi) & \cos(\lambda 2\pi) \end{pmatrix} x \right)$
Additive Gaussian noise	$N(X, \lambda) = X + \lambda \tilde{\sigma}_{max} \times \sqrt{2} \operatorname{erfinv}(\mathcal{U}[-1, 1])$

2.3   Experimental Settings

Dataset. Experiments were performed on BraTs MRI [10] and Chest X-ray [13] datasets. The Chest X-ray dataset is composed of 10000 images. BraTs volumes were split along the axial axis to get 2D slices. Only slices with less than 80% of black pixels were kept. This resulted in 34000 slices. For both datasets, we studied the supervised task of pathology presence classification (binary classification, present/not present). In medical imaging problems, it is common to have labels only for a small part of the dataset. We thus choose 10% of supervision in all of our experiments. We randomly selected three hold-out test sets of 1000 slices for BraTs experiments. With the Chest dataset, we used the provided test set of 1300 images, from [13], evenly split in three to evaluate variability.

Implementation Details. For every experiment with the BraTs dataset, the encoder f is a fully convolutional network composed of four convolution blocks with two convolutional layers in each block. Following the architecture proposed in [13], the encoder f for experiments on the Chest dataset is a Densenet121. The network M is a fully convolutional network composed of two convolutional blocks with one convolutional layer. The projection head g is a two-layer perceptron as in [2]. On BraTs dataset (resp. Chest dataset), we train with a batch size of 32 (resp. 16) for 100 epochs. In each experiment, the learning rate of f is set to 10^{-4}. When optimizing M with (resp. without) supervision, M learning rate is set to 10^{-3} (resp. 10^{-4}). When using 10% of labeled data for the supervision task, on relatively small databases (10^5 images), there is a risk of overfitting on the classification layer (p in Eq. 1). Contrastive and supervision loss terms need to be carefully balanced while optimizing both the encoder and the transformation generator. To evaluate the impact of hyper-parameters, we carried out experiments with $(\alpha_0, \alpha_2) \in \{1, 0.1\}$ and $(\alpha_1, \alpha_3, \alpha_4) \in \{1, 10\}$. Linear evaluation results (see Sect. 2.4) on BraTs dataset after convergence are summarized in Table 2. Results in Sect. 3 are shown with the best values found for each method.

Table 2. 3-fold cross validation mean linear evaluation AUC after convergence with different α_i values (standard deviation in parentheses).

	α_i values	AUC
Optimizing M	$\alpha_{0,2} = 1, \alpha_{3,4} = 1, \alpha_1 = 10$	**0.884** (0.042)
	$\alpha_0 = 0.1, \alpha_{1,3,4} = 10, \alpha_2 = 0.1$	0.868 (0.030)
	$\alpha_0 = 0.1, \alpha_1 = 10, \alpha_2 = 1, \alpha_{3,4} = 1$	**0.887** (0.013)
Random M	$\alpha_2 = 1, \alpha_{3,4} = 1$	0.874 (0.000)
	$\alpha_2 = 0.1, \alpha_{3,4} = 10$	0.820 (0.037)
	$\alpha_2 = 1, \alpha_{3,4} = 10$	**0.883** (0.003)
Base simCLR [2]		0.730 (0.020)

The fully supervised experiments described in Sect. 3 are optimized with the same encoder architecture and one dense layer followed by a sigmoid activation function for the classification task. For the fully supervised experiments we used a learning rate of 10^{-4}.

Computing Infrastructure. Optimizations were run on Tesla NVIDIA V100 cards.

2.4 Linear Evaluation

To evaluate the representation quality learned by the encoder, we follow the linear evaluation protocol used in the literature [2,12,14]. The encoder is frozen with the weights learned with our framework. One linear layer is added, after removing the projection head (g), and trained with a test set of labeled data, not used in the previous training phase. This means that we first project the test samples in the latent space of the frozen model and then estimate the most discriminative linear model. The rationale here is that a good representation should make the classes of the test data linearly separable.

3 Results and Discussion

To assess the impact of each term in Eq. 1 we performed optimization using the following strategies:

Random (without M, without supervision): each image is transformed with parameters generated by a uniform distribution: $\Lambda = \mathcal{U}\left([0,1]^7\right)$, and $\alpha_{1,3,4} = 0$.

Random with supervision (without M, with supervision): we add the supervision constraint to the random strategy. We set $\alpha_2 = 1$ and $\alpha_{3,4} = 10$.

Self-supervised (with M, without supervision): while setting α_1, α_3 and α_4 to 0, we optimize Eq. 1.

Self-supervised with supervision constraint (with M and supervision): setting $\alpha_1 = 10$ and $\alpha_{0,2,3,4} = 1$, we optimize Eq. 1.

We split the data into pre-training and test sets. Data from the pre-training set are further split into training and validation sets for the perturbator/encoder optimization. For optimizations with supervision constraint (self-supervised and random), all pre-training data are used for self-supervision and a small set of labeled data is used for the supervision constraint. For variability analysis, three optimizations were performed by changing the supervision set. With the BraTs dataset, as slices come from 3D volumes, we split the data ensuring that all slices of the same patient were in the same set.

Linear evaluation was performed on the four optimization strategies with the hold-out test set. Performances were evaluated with the weights obtained at different epochs. We aim to evaluate if our method outputs better representations during training. In Fig. 2, we show performances (mean and standard deviation) on three different test sets for both datasets. We also trained the encoder on the classification task in a fully supervised setting with 10% and 100% labeled data. For the fully supervised training, we used data augmentation composing the tested transformations randomly. Each transformation had a 0.5 probability of being sampled. We performed linear evaluation on the frozen encoder with the hold-out test set and report the obtained AUC as horizontal lines in Fig. 2. Figure 2 also reports linear evaluation results of the base simCLR optimization as in [2] where only one image is transformed by a random composition of the tested transformations. As with the fully supervised experiments, each transformation had a 0.5 probability of being sampled.

Figure 2 shows that optimizing M with supervision helps to have better representations for both datasets. It also shows that optimizing with only 10% of labeled data allows us to reach the same quality of representation as the fully supervised training with 100% of labels.

To investigate the impact of the supervised loss function, we launched an experiment with the supervised contrastive loss introduced in [6] using only 10% of labeled data. After convergence, we obtained a mean AUC of 0.52 ± 0.12 compared to 0.93 ± 0.01 with our method.

On the Chest X-ray database, strong results were obtained in [13] using a network pretrained on ImageNet. Optimizing M with 10% supervision on this ImageNet pretrained network has a smaller impact compared to random transformations (0.96 ± 0.001 for both approaches). However, ImageNet pretrained networks can only be used with 2D slices whereas our strategy could be easily extended to 3D volumes.

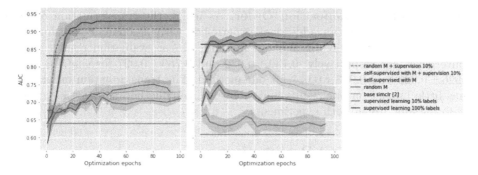

Fig. 2. Linear evaluation results comparing with other methods (left BraTs dataset with batch size 32, right Chest dataset with batch size 16).

Relevance. When optimizing without supervision, the network M needs to minimize the mutual information and it can therefore generate transformations that create images that are very different from the untransformed images but that do not contain relevant information for the downstream task, in particular for medical images. Without the supervision constraint, the optimal crop can be found, for instance, in a corner, leading to an image with a majority of zero values (i.e., entirely black), thus useless for the supervised task. The supervision constraint helps M to generate relevant images that keep pathological pixels (see some examples in Fig. 3).

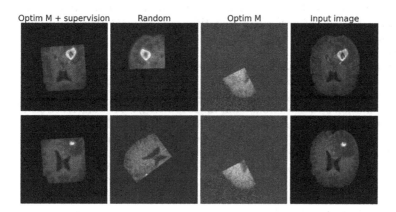

Fig. 3. Two examples (row 1 and 2) of generated transformations in the BraTs dataset with different optimization strategies (red contour highlights the tumor). (Color figure online)

Runtime. The addition of the network M increases the training computational time of around 20–25% which is balanced by a performance gain.

Transformation Composition Order. As in [2], the transformation order is fixed. We launched an additional experiment with a different transformation order for both simCLR and our method. Linear evaluation results after convergence are respectively: 0.730 ± 0.020 and 0.760 ± 0.027 for simCLR and 0.926 ± 0.020 and 0.923 ± 0.021 for our method. The transformation order has thus little impact on our results and, above all, our method substantially outperforms simCLR in both experiments.

4 Conclusions and Perspectives

We proposed a method to optimize usual transformations employed in contrastive learning with very little supervision. Extensive experiments on two datasets showed that our method finds more relevant transformations and obtains better latent representations, in terms of linear evaluation. Future works will try to optimize the transformations composition order. Furthermore, in a weakly-supervised setting, we could also investigate constraining latent space representations of non labeled data with pseudo-labels and nearest neighbor clustering.

References

1. Chaitanya, K., Erdil, E., Karani, N., Konukoglu, E.: Contrastive learning of global and local features for medical image segmentation with limited annotations. In: NeurIPS, vol. 33, pp. 12546–12558 (2020)
2. Chen, T., Kornblith, S., Norouzi, M., Hinton, G.: A simple framework for contrastive learning of visual representations. In: 37th International Conference on Machine Learning. Proceedings of Machine Learning Research, vol. 119, pp. 1597–1607. PMLR (2020)
3. Cohen, J.P., Luck, M., Honari, S.: Distribution matching losses can hallucinate features in medical image translation. In: MICCAI (2018)
4. Cubuk, E.D., Zoph, B., Mane, D., Vasudevan, V., Le, Q.V.: AutoAugment: learning augmentation strategies from data. In: 2019 IEEE/CVF Conference on Computer Vision and Pattern Recognition (CVPR), pp. 113–123 (2019)
5. Dufumier, B., et al.: Contrastive learning with continuous proxy meta-data for 3D MRI classification. In: MICCAI (2021)
6. Khosla, P., et al.: Supervised contrastive learning. In: Advances in Neural Information Processing Systems, vol. 33, pp. 18661–18673 (2020)
7. Kingma, D.P., Dhariwal, P.: Glow: generative flow with invertible 1x1 convolutions. In: NeurIPS, vol. 31 (2018)
8. Li, Y., Hu, G., Wang, Y., Hospedales, T., Robertson, N.M., Yang, Y.: Differentiable automatic data augmentation. In: Vedaldi, A., Bischof, H., Brox, T., Frahm, J.-M. (eds.) ECCV 2020. LNCS, vol. 12367, pp. 580–595. Springer, Cham (2020). https://doi.org/10.1007/978-3-030-58542-6_35
9. Liu, A., Huang, Z., Huang, Z., Wang, N.: Direct differentiable augmentation search. In: 2021 IEEE/CVF International Conference on Computer Vision (ICCV) (2021)
10. Menze, B.H., et al.: The multimodal brain tumor image segmentation benchmark (BRATS). IEEE Trans. Med. Imaging **34**(10), 1993–2024 (2015)

11. Patrick, M., et al.: On compositions of transformations in contrastive self-supervised learning. In: IEEE/CVF International Conference on Computer Vision (ICCV), pp. 9577–9587 (2021)
12. Perakis, A., Gorji, A., Jain, S., Chaitanya, K., Rizza, S., Konukoglu, E.: Contrastive learning of single-cell phenotypic representations for treatment classification. In: MLMI - MICCAI, pp. 565–575 (2021)
13. Tang, Y., et al.: Automated abnormality classification of chest radiographs using deep convolutional neural networks. NPJ Digit. Med. **3**, 1–8 (2020)
14. Tian, Y., Sun, C., Poole, B., Krishnan, D., Schmid, C., Isola, P.: What makes for good views for contrastive learning? In: NeurIPS (2020)
15. Xiao, T., Wang, X., Efros, A.A., Darrell, T.: What should not be contrastive in contrastive learning. In: International Conference on Learning Representations (2021)
16. Yang, S., Das, D., Chang, S., Yun, S., Porikli, F.M.: Distribution estimation to automate transformation policies for self-supervision. In: Advances in Neural Information Processing Systems (2021)
17. Zhao, S., Liu, Z., Lin, J., Zhu, J.Y., Han, S.: Differentiable augmentation for data-efficient GAN training. In: Advances in Neural Information Processing Systems, vol. 33, pp. 7559–7570 (2020)
18. Zhao, X., et al.: Contrastive learning for label efficient semantic segmentation. In: IEEE/CVF International Conference on Computer Vision (ICCV), pp. 10623–10633 (2021)

Stain Based Contrastive Co-training for Histopathological Image Analysis

Bodong Zhang[1,2(✉)] ⓘ, Beatrice Knudsen[3] ⓘ, Deepika Sirohi[3] ⓘ,
Alessandro Ferrero[2] ⓘ, and Tolga Tasdizen[1,2] ⓘ

[1] Electrical and Computer Engineering, University of Utah, Salt Lake City, UT, USA
[2] Scientific Computing and Imaging Institute, University of Utah, Salt Lake City,
UT, USA
{bodong.zhang,alessandro.ferrero}@utah.edu, tolga@sci.utah.edu
[3] Huntsman Cancer Institute, University of Utah, Salt Lake City, UT, USA
beatrice.knudsen@path.utah.edu, deepika.sirohi@hsc.utah.edu

Abstract. We propose a novel semi-supervised learning approach for classification of histopathology images. We employ strong supervision with patch-level annotations combined with a novel co-training loss to create a semi-supervised learning framework. Co-training relies on multiple conditionally independent and sufficient views of the data. We separate the hematoxylin and eosin channels in pathology images using color deconvolution to create two views of each slide that can partially fulfill these requirements. Two separate CNNs are used to embed the two views into a joint feature space. We use a contrastive loss between the views in this feature space to implement co-training. We evaluate our approach in clear cell renal cell and prostate carcinomas, and demonstrate improvement over state-of-the-art semi-supervised learning methods.

Keywords: Histopathology · Semi-supervised learning · Co-training

1 Introduction

Convolutional neural networks (CNNs) are commonly used in histopathology. Because digital whole slide images (WSIs) in pathology are much larger than typical input sizes for CNNs, workflows typically first tile the WSI into many smaller patches. There are two main approaches for training classification models with WSIs: strong and weak supervision. Strong supervision uses labels for the individual tiles, which requires expert annotation at a high cost [7]. Weak supervision applies multiple instance learning with slide level labels [6,10,12,20]. Weakly supervised methods have become popular due to the ease of obtaining labels for learning directly from pathology reports [5]. However, successful model training with weak learning requires thousands of WSIs, and strong supervision is still essential when a smaller number of WSIs are available for learning.

Expert annotation at the tile level is infeasible to obtain beyond a small number of WSIs. Semi-supervised learning (SSL) seeks to leverage unlabeled

© The Author(s), under exclusive license to Springer Nature Switzerland AG 2022
G. Zamzmi et al. (Eds.): MILLanD 2022, LNCS 13559, pp. 106–116, 2022.
https://doi.org/10.1007/978-3-031-16760-7_11

data to improve the accuracy of models when only a limited amount of labeled data is available. One of the recent trends in SSL, consistency regularization [9, 16], has also found application in the classification of histopathology images. Teacher-student consistency [19] has been used to supplement tile-level labels for quantifying prognostic features in colorectal cancer [17] and in combination with weak supervision for Gleason grade classification in prostate cancer [11]. The MixMatch model [3] has been tested on histology datasets with open-set noise [13]. Weak/strong data transformation consistency (FixMatch) [18] has been applied to detection of dysplasia of the esophagus [13]. State-of-the-art SSL methods rely on enforcing prediction/representation consistency between various transformations of the data. Whereas consistency under model perturbations has been proposed [16], it is a less explored area. On the other hand, the co-training [4] approach to SSL can provide excellent results when multiple views of each sample are available that meet the criteria of sufficiency (each view should be able to support accurate classification on its own) and conditional independence given the label of a sample.

Hematoxylin (H) and Eosin (E) are chemical stains that are used to highlight features of tissue architecture in formalin-fixed and paraffin-embedded tissue sections. H and E provide complementary information for pathologists. H is a basic chemical compound that binds negatively charged nucleotides in DNA and RNA to provide a blue color. In contrast, E is acidic and reacts with basic side chains of amino acids resulting in pink coloration. Whereas proteins bind to DNA and RNA lead to overlapping H and E staining in the cell nucleus and cytoplasm, the extracellular matrix and vascular structures supporting cancer cells interact primarily with E since they are devoid of DNA and RNA. In contrast to RGB channels that cannot easily be linked to a biological interpretation, H and E allow separation of nuclei versus cytoplasm and extracellular matrix. Therefore, we hypothesize that H and E stains, when separated into their own channels, can provide two views that can, to a large extent, satisfy the co-training assumptions. We also formulate a novel contrastive co-training with H and E views. We validate our approach on a dataset of 53 WSIs from clear cell renal cell carcinoma (ccRCC) patients for histologic growth pattern (HGP) classification and of 45 WSIs from prostate cancer patients for cancer vs. benign gland classification. We demonstrate that our approach outperforms state-of-the-art SSL methods. We perform further experiments to explain the suitability of H and E channels for co-training as opposed to RGB channels.

2   Stain Based Contrastive Co-training

2.1   Stain Separation

We adopt an approach that separates an H&E image in the RGB space into individual H and E stain channels using non-linear pixel-wise functions derived from dominant color profiles of each stain [15]. Concretely, we use the following approximate transformation between the two spaces:

$$\begin{bmatrix} H \\ E \end{bmatrix} = \begin{bmatrix} 1.838 & 0.034 & -0.760 \\ -1.373 & 0.772 & 1.215 \end{bmatrix} \begin{bmatrix} \log_{10} 255/R \\ \log_{10} 255/G \\ \log_{10} 255/B \end{bmatrix}. \qquad (1)$$

The H and E channels are normalized to the range $[0,1]$ after the transformation.

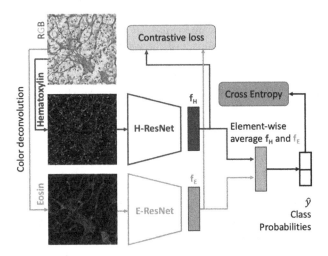

Fig. 1. H&E RGB image is separated into H and E channels and processed separately to generate two feature sets f_H and f_E trained with the proposed contrastive loss.

2.2   Contrastive Co-training

We propose two ResNet models [8] (same architecture, separate parameters) for H and E channels, respectively (Fig. 1). Existing co-training methods enforce consistency of prediction between classifier outputs operating on different views of the data. The disadvantage of this approach is that the individual classifiers only make use of their respective views and are sub-optimal. Instead, we propose a contrastive loss in the feature space to implement co-training and define a single classifier which uses a combined view by averaging the features from the two channels (Fig. 1). Our approach is inspired by recent works that use contrastive learning to create a shared feature space between multimodal data [21,22]. We use a contrastive loss to create a shared feature space between features extracted by the H and E networks. Let $f_H(x)$ and $f_E(x)$ denote the H and E features for input tile x, respectively. We use a triplet loss

$$\mathcal{L}_{c.t.}(x_i) = \max\left(\| f_H(x_i) - f_E(x_i) \|_2 - \| f_H(x_i) - f_E(x_k) \|_2 + m, 0 \right), \qquad (2)$$

where random $k \neq i$, $\| a \|_2$ denotes the L2 norm of vector a, and m is the margin hyperparameter. The triplet loss encourages (f_H, f_E) pairs from the same H&E tile x_i to be mapped closer together than (f_H, f_E) pairs from mismatched input tiles x_i and x_k. Note that the output of the model is a linear+softmax layer applied to $0.5(f_H + f_E)$. Therefore, pushing the features f_H and f_E closer for the same tile also implicitly minimizes the difference between individual predictions, similar to co-training, if the final layer were applied to f_H and f_E alone.

Let $L = \{x_j, y_j\}$ denote the labeled training set where y_i is the label corresponding to input tile x_i. Let $U = \{x_i\}$ denote the unlabeled training set. The overall learning strategy combines supervised learning with cross-entropy on the labeled dataset with the triplet loss (2) on the entire dataset:

$$\mathcal{L} = \sum_{x_j \in L} y_j \log \hat{y}_j + \lambda \sum_{x_i \in L \cup U} \mathcal{L}_{c.t.}(x_i), \tag{3}$$

where $\hat{y}_j$ denotes the output of the model for input x_j and λ is a hyperparameter controlling the relative contributions from the labeled and unlabeled losses.

3   Experiments

3.1   Datasets

ccRCC. H&E slides from ccRCC patients at our institution were retrieved from the pathology archive and scanned at 40× magnification. HGPs in 53 WSIs were annotated by drawing polygons around them in QuIP [2] by a GU-subspecialty trained pathologist. HGPs were divided into nested vs. diffuse (non-nested) histologic classes [1]. Diffuse HGPs are associated with a higher risk of cancer recurrence and metastatic progression. Each WSI contains multiple polygons. Images were downsampled by a factor of 2× and a tile size of 400 × 400 pixels was chosen to capture the visual characteristics of the HGPs after discussion with pathologists (Fig. 2). We sampled overlapping tiles by choosing a stride of 200 pixels. We extracted 3014 tiles with nested HGPs and 2566 tiles with diffuse HGPs from the annotated polygons. We separated the WSIs into training, validation and testing sets to ensure a realistic experimental setting. This separation resulted in 2116/1990 nested/diffuse tiles for training, 386/246 nested/diffuse tiles for validation and 512/330 nested/diffuse tiles for testing. The validation set was used for choosing hyperparameters as discussed below. The test set was for final model evaluation. Tiles from same patient were in the same set. For the SSL experiments, we divided the annotated polygons from the training set into 10 groups and randomly picked one group to draw labeled tiles from in each run of our experiments. This is a more realistic and challenging scenario than randomly choosing 10% of the training tiles as labeled data because tiles from the same polygon usually represent a smaller range of variations for learning.

Prostate Cancer. We collected 6992 benign gland images and 6992 prostate cancer images from our institution as training set using the same process as with the ccRCC dataset. The tile size was chosen as 256 × 256, which is sufficient to characterize gland features. The validation and test sets are from the The Cancer Genome Atlas Program (TCGA). We collected 477 benign and 472 cancer tiles from 18 cases. In each experiment, we randomly selected 8 cases for validation

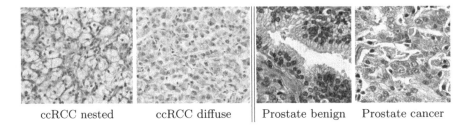

| ccRCC nested | ccRCC diffuse | Prostate benign | Prostate cancer |

Fig. 2. Examples of ccRCC and prostate gland tiles.

and 10 cases for testing. Examples of prostate gland images are shown in Fig. 2. For SSL, we randomly divided training images into 20 groups and used one group as labeled data. The image sets from our institution are available through a material transfer agreement and the TCGA set is publicly available.

3.2 Model Selection, Training and Hyperparameters

Considering the small number of training samples, we chose ImageNet pretrained ResNet18 [8] for all experiments. ResNet is a state-of-the-art model which has better performance with less parameters. For models that use single channel inputs, i.e., the H and E CNN pathways in Fig. 1, we summed the convolutional weights of the R, G and B channels in the first layer of ResNet18. The final layer of the ResNet18 was also changed for binary classification.

We used color jittering, random rotation, crop to 256×256 (ccRCC) or 224×224 (prostate) pixels, random horizontal/vertical flip and color normalization as data augmentation. For validation and test tiles, we performed center crop and color normalization to follow the same data format as in training. For the co-training model, H and E channels have independent color jitters but the rest of the augmentations are common, e.g., the same random rotation angle is applied to the H and E channels from the same tile. The rationale for independent color jitters is that color variations due to the amount of H or E chemical tissue stains used are common in practice, which leads to independent brightness variations in these channels.

We used the Adam optimizer with an initial learning rate of 10^{-3}(100% label only) or 10^{-4} and used a decaying learning rate. A batch size of 64 was used in ccRCC dataset and 128 in prostate cancer dataset. Hyperparameters in (3) were chosen as $\lambda = 0.2 \times p$ and $m = 40$, where p is the percentage of training data used as labeled data. All hyperparameters were chosen to optimize accuracy over the validation set, including experiments on other state-of-the-art models. Batch normalization was applied to the features before computing the contrastive loss.

For comparison with other state-of-the-art SSL methods, we used consistency regularization [9,16], MixMatch [3] and FixMatch [18]. The same augmentations discussed above were used for the SSL experiments. We ran all experiments for 250 epochs in ccRCC experiments and 100 epochs in prostate cancer dataset and chose the epoch with the best validation accuracy. Each experimental setting was run 5 times to calculate mean accuracy and standard deviation.

We used Python 3.7.11 + Pytorch 1.9.0 + torchvision 0.10.0 + CUDA 10.2 on virtual environment and ran on NVIDIA TITAN X and NVIDIA TITAN RTX. We also used Python 3.9.0 + Pytorch 1.7.1 + torchvision 0.8.2 + CUDA 11.0 and ran on NVIDIA RTX A6000. With batchsize fixed to 64, co-training experiment on ccRCC occupied around 5300 MB memory on GPU and needed 1.5–2.0 min for each epoch. The code is available at https://github.com/BzhangURU/Paper_2022_Co-training.

3.3   Results

We compared proposed co-training with H and E views to a baseline ResNet18 model that uses RGB H&E images as input, as well as other state-of-the-art SSL methods, such as MixMatch and FixMatch, considering they are already widely used in histopathology image analysis [13]. The approaches were compared under two settings: using 100% of the available labeled tiles in training set for supervised learning and using only a subset (10% in ccRCC, 5% in prostate) of the available tiles for supervised learning. The proposed model also employed the unsupervised co-training loss with 100% of the training data (unlabeled) to set up an SSL method. Mean accuracy and standard deviation over 5 runs reported for all methods are shown in Table 1 for both datasets.

Table 1. Mean accuracy and standard deviations of different models for the test sets in ccRCC and prostate experiments. Best performing model results for the 100% and 10%/5% labeled data setting are shown in bold.

ccRCC model	Test accuracy	Prostate model	Test accuracy
100% label RGB ResNet	$84.8 \pm 2.4\%$	100% label RGB ResNet	$77.5 \pm 2.5\%$
100% label H/E co-train	$\mathbf{92.0 \pm 2.6\%}$	100% label H/E co-train	$\mathbf{79.1 \pm 2.0\%}$
10% label RGB ResNet	$76.9 \pm 5.9\%$	5% label RGB ResNet	$73.4 \pm 1.0\%$
10% label RGB consis	$86.8 \pm 3.3\%$	5% label RGB consis	$74.7 \pm 1.3\%$
10% label RGB MixMatch	$85.9 \pm 5.7\%$	5% label RGB MixMatch	$73.7 \pm 5.0\%$
10% label RGB FixMatch	$88.3 \pm 3.8\%$	5% label RGB FixMatch	$78.2 \pm 3.8\%$
10% label H/E co-train	$\mathbf{92.3 \pm 2.1\%}$	5% label H/E co-train	$\mathbf{78.7 \pm 1.9\%}$

We note that the contrastive co-training strategy improved test accuracy, by a large margin in the case of ccRCC, when 100% of the labeled data were used for supervised training (row 2 vs. 1, Table 1), which suggests it provides a strong regularization effect against overfitting. Note that training accuracy for the fully supervised RGB ResNet and H/E co-train models were $99.97 \pm 0.02\%$ and $99.78 \pm 0.15\%$, respectively, in the ccRCC dataset. The same models achieve $98.34 \pm 0.64\%$ and $98.32 \pm 0.55\%$ training accuracy in prostate cancer. The fact that test accuracies on prostate cancer are lower than on ccRCC for all models is likely due to domain shift. In ccRCC dataset, all training, validation and test sets come from our institution. While in prostate cancer dataset, only training set comes our institution, the validation and test set come from TCGA dataset. Another possible reason is the fact that sometimes the gland size in prostate cancer is much smaller than the size of tiles, which could carry much less distinguishable features.

As expected, the proposed co-training strategy significantly outperforms the baseline approach (row 7 vs. 3, Table 1) under the limited labeled data setting. Consistency regularization based SSL methods significantly improve the accuracy of RGB ResNet baseline when a limited amount of training data is available (rows 4–6 vs. 3, Table 1). In line with results from computer vision, FixMatch even surpasses the baseline model trained with the entire labeled dataset. However, our proposed method outperformed all other SSL methods we compared against including FixMatch for both datasets. We note that hyperparameters for all SSL methods were independently fine-tuned to obtain the best validation accuracy. Finally, contrastive co-training was able to reach the same accuracy levels independent of the amount of labeled data that was used for supervised training (rows 2 and 7, Table 1).

3.4   Co-training View Analysis

In this section, we further study the suitability of the H and E channels for co-training in the context of the ccRCC dataset. First, we explore whether the H and E channels are sufficient on their own to provide a basis for accurate classification in a supervised setting. We train models that only use the H or only use the E channel as input. The 100% labeled results in Table 2 show that both channels carry sufficient information for the classification problem at hand. This is especially true for the E-channel, which is particularly informative for the nested vs diffuse classification task. However, as expected, the accuracy for both channels drops significantly when the labeled data is limited.

Table 2. H-only and E-only models test accuracy for the ccRCC dataset.

Model	Accuracy	Model	Accuracy
100% label H ResNet	$79.4 \pm 3.7\%$	10% label H ResNet	$73.5 \pm 4.0\%$
100% label E ResNet	$94.0 \pm 1.4\%$	10% label E ResNet	$82.3 \pm 7.0\%$

We next explore if the H and E channels are better suited for co-training than R, G and B channels due to a higher degree of independence. We trained an image-to-image regression model using the U-Net architecture [14] between various channels, e.g., predicting the E-channel from the H-channel of the same tile. The final layer of the U-Net architecture was chosen to be linear, and we used the mean square error function for training. Table 3 reports the coefficient of determination (R^2) achieved for various input/output channel combinations. We observe that the H and E channels are harder to predict from each other (lower R^2) compared to the R, G and B channels, hence demonstrating a higher degree of independence and suitability for co-training.

Table 3. Coefficient of determination (R^2) of image mapping between various channels on ccRCC validation set at epoch with the lowest MSE.

Experiments	R^2 value	Experiments	R^2 value
H $\Rightarrow$ E	0.5223	E $\Rightarrow$ H	0.4613
R $\Rightarrow$ G	0.8464	G $\Rightarrow$ R	0.7833
R $\Rightarrow$ B	0.8207	B $\Rightarrow$ R	0.7713
G $\Rightarrow$ B	0.8522	B $\Rightarrow$ G	0.8824

3.5 Ablation Studies

We also conducted ablation studies to separately analyze the role of the contrastive loss and the H and E channel selection in terms of classification accuracy on ccRCC. Omitting the contrastive loss from training while using the H and E channel inputs lowered the accuracy from $92.0 \pm 2.6\%$ to $84.7 \pm 5.2\%$ for 100% labeled data and from $92.3 \pm 2.1\%$ to $78.7 \pm 8.0\%$ for 10% labeled data. In the next ablation experiment, we used various pairs from the RGB channels as the basis for our co-training method, and compared with ResNet using the same pair as input, e.g., using only the R and B channels to form 2-channel images as input for ResNet. Results are reported in Table 4. Unlike the H and E models, we observe that the results are approximately the same, which is expected considering the higher level of dependence among RGB channels shown in Sect. 3.4. These observations suggest that the benefit of the proposed model is due to the contrastive co-training loss applied to the H and E view inputs rather than simply due to the change in the input space or the contrastive loss individually.

Table 4. Ablation study on ccRCC. Test set accuracy of ResNet and co-training models taking only 2 channels from RGB as input with 10% labeled data in training.

Model	Accuracy	Model	Accuracy	Model	Accuracy
RB ResNet	$77.5 \pm 6.6\%$	RG ResNet	$80.2 \pm 6.4\%$	GB ResNet	$78.4 \pm 9.7\%$
R/B co-train	$78.2 \pm 4.5\%$	R/G co-train	$79.8 \pm 5.6\%$	G/B co-train	$76.6 \pm 7.3\%$

4   Conclusion

We proposed a novel co-training approach for pathology image classification that leverages deconvolution of an H&E image into individual H and E stains. We demonstrated the advantages of the proposed approach over fully supervised learning and other state-of-the-art SSL methods in the context of ccRCC and prostate cancer. The proposed method could be used after segmentation of cancer regions from a WSI to drive prognostic markers. In future work, we will investigate finer-grained classification for further improved prognostic value.

Since our proposed approach uses a complementary learning strategy to consistency regularization approaches that use data transformations, a potential avenue for future research is to combine them for further improvements. Another potential direction for further research is to investigate whether a more sophisticated separation into H and E stain channels can provide improved results with co-training. Methods based on Cycle-GAN have been used for stain-to-stain translation such as H&E to immunohistochemistry and they could also be used for separation of H and E stains. However, this would require the acquisition of additional datasets with H only and E only stains for the discriminators.

Acknowledgements. We are grateful for the support of the Computational Oncology Research Initiative (CORI) at the Huntsman Cancer Institute, University of Utah. We also acknowledge support of ARUP Laboratories and the Department of Pathology at University of Utah.

References

1. Sirohi, D., et al.: Histologic growth patterns in clear cell renal cell carcinoma stratify patients into survival risk groups. Clin. Genitourin. Cancer **22**, 17–9 (2022). https://doi.org/10.1016/j.clgc.2022.01.005. epub ahead of print. PMID: 35125301
2. Saltz, J., et al.: A containerized software system for generation, management, and exploration of features from whole slide tissue images. Cancer Res. **77**, e79–e82 (2017)
3. Berthelot, D., Carlini, N., Goodfellow, I., Papernot, N., Oliver, A., Raffel, C.A.: Mixmatch: a holistic approach to semi-supervised learning. In: Advances in Neural Information Processing Systems, vol. 32. Curran Associates, Inc. (2019). https://proceedings.neurips.cc/paper/2019/file/1cd138d0499a68f4bb72bee04bbec2d7-Paper.pdf
4. Blum, A., Mitchell, T.: Combining labeled and unlabeled data with co-training. In: COLT: Proceedings of the Workshop on Computational Learning Theory, pp. 92–100 (1998)
5. Bulten, W., et al.: Artificial intelligence for diagnosis and Gleason grading of prostate cancer: the panda challenge. Nat. Med. **28**(1), 154–163 (2022). https://doi.org/10.1038/s41591-021-01620-2
6. Campanella, G., et al.: Clinical-grade computational pathology using weakly supervised deep learning on whole slide images. Nat. Med. **25**(8), 1301–1309 (2019). https://doi.org/10.1038/s41591-019-0508-1

7. Dimitriou, N., Arandjelović, O., Caie, P.D.: Deep learning for whole slide image analysis: an overview. Front. Med. **6** (2019). https://doi.org/10.3389/fmed.2019.00264. https://www.frontiersin.org/article/10.3389/fmed.2019.00264
8. He, K., Zhang, X., Ren, S., Sun, J.: Deep residual learning for image recognition. In: 2016 IEEE Conference on Computer Vision and Pattern Recognition (CVPR), pp. 770–778 (2016)
9. Laine, S., Aila, T.: Temporal ensembling for semi-supervised learning. In: 5th International Conference on Learning Representations, ICLR 2017, Toulon, France, 24–26 April 2017, Conference Track Proceedings. OpenReview.net (2017). https://openreview.net/forum?id=BJ6oOfqge
10. Lerousseau, M., et al.: Weakly supervised multiple instance learning histopathological tumor segmentation. In: MICCAI 2020 - Medical Image Computing and Computer Assisted Intervention, Lima, Peru, pp. 470–479, October 2020. https://doi.org/10.1007/978-3-030-59722-1_45. https://hal.archives-ouvertes.fr/hal-03133239
11. Otálora, S., Marini, N., Müller, H., Atzori, M.: Semi-weakly supervised learning for prostate cancer image classification with teacher-student deep convolutional networks. In: Cardoso, J., et al. (eds.) IMIMIC/MIL3ID/LABELS -2020. LNCS, vol. 12446, pp. 193–203. Springer, Cham (2020). https://doi.org/10.1007/978-3-030-61166-8_21
12. Chikontwe, P., Kim, M., Nam, S.J., Go, H., Park, S.H.: Multiple instance learning with center embeddings for histopathology classification. In: Martel, A.L., et al. (eds.) MICCAI 2020. LNCS, vol. 12265, pp. 519–528. Springer, Cham (2020). https://doi.org/10.1007/978-3-030-59722-1_50
13. Pulido, J.V., et al.: Semi-supervised classification of noisy, gigapixel histology images. In: 2020 IEEE 20th International Conference on Bioinformatics and Bioengineering (BIBE), pp. 563–568 (2020). https://doi.org/10.1109/BIBE50027.2020.00097
14. Ronneberger, O., Fischer, P., Brox, T.: U-Net: convolutional networks for biomedical image segmentation. In: Navab, N., Hornegger, J., Wells, W.M., Frangi, A.F. (eds.) MICCAI 2015. LNCS, vol. 9351, pp. 234–241. Springer, Cham (2015). https://doi.org/10.1007/978-3-319-24574-4_28
15. Ruifrok, A.C., Johnston, D.A.: Quantification of histochemical staining by color deconvolution. Anal. Quant. Cytol. Histol. **23**(4), 291–9 (2001)
16. Sajjadi, M., Javanmardi, M., Tasdizen, T.: Regularization with stochastic transformations and perturbations for deep semi-supervised learning. In: Lee, D., Sugiyama, M., Luxburg, U., Guyon, I., Garnett, R. (eds.) Advances in Neural Information Processing Systems, vol. 29. Curran Associates, Inc. (2016). https://proceedings.neurips.cc/paper/2016/file/30ef30b64204a3088a26bc2e6ecf7602-Paper.pdf
17. Shaw, S., Pajak, M., Lisowska, A., Tsaftaris, S.A., O'Neil, A.Q.: Teacher-student chain for efficient semi-supervised histology image classification. arXiv abs/2003.08797 (2020)
18. Sohn, K., et al.: Fixmatch: simplifying semi-supervised learning with consistency and confidence. In: Larochelle, H., Ranzato, M., Hadsell, R., Balcan, M.F., Lin, H. (eds.) Advances in Neural Information Processing Systems, vol. 33, pp. 596–608. Curran Associates, Inc. (2020)
19. Tarvainen, A., Valpola, H.: Mean teachers are better role models: weight-averaged consistency targets improve semi-supervised deep learning results. In: Guyon, I., et al. (eds.) Advances in Neural Information Processing Systems, vol. 30. Curran Associates, Inc. (2017). https://proceedings.neurips.cc/paper/2017/file/68053af2923e00204c3ca7c6a3150cf7-Paper.pdf

20. Huang, Y., Chung, A.C.S.: Evidence localization for pathology images using weakly supervised learning. In: Shen, D., et al. (eds.) MICCAI 2019. LNCS, vol. 11764, pp. 613–621. Springer, Cham (2019). https://doi.org/10.1007/978-3-030-32239-7_68
21. Yuan, X., et al.: Multimodal contrastive training for visual representation learning. In: 2021 IEEE/CVF Conference on Computer Vision and Pattern Recognition (CVPR), pp. 6991–7000 (2021)
22. Zhang, Y., Jiang, H., Miura, Y., Manning, C., Langlotz, C.: Contrastive learning of medical visual representations from paired images and text (2020)

Active and Continual Learning

CLINICAL: Targeted Active Learning for Imbalanced Medical Image Classification

Suraj Kothawade[1](✉), Atharv Savarkar[2], Venkat Iyer[2],
Ganesh Ramakrishnan[2], and Rishabh Iyer[1]

[1] University of Texas at Dallas, Richardson, USA
`suraj.kothawade@utdallas.edu`
[2] Indian Institute of Technology, Bombay, Mumbai, India

Abstract. Training deep learning models on medical datasets that perform well for all classes is a challenging task. It is often the case that a suboptimal performance is obtained on some classes due to the natural class imbalance issue that comes with medical data. An effective way to tackle this problem is by using *targeted active learning*, where we iteratively add data points that belong to the rare classes, to the training data. However, existing active learning methods are ineffective in targeting rare classes in medical datasets. In this work, we propose CLINICAL (targeted aCtive Learning for ImbalaNced medICal imAge cLassification) a framework that uses submodular mutual information functions as acquisition functions to mine critical data points from rare classes. We apply our framework to a wide-array of medical imaging datasets on a variety of real-world class imbalance scenarios - namely, *binary* imbalance and *long-tail* imbalance. We show that CLINICAL outperforms the state-of-the-art active learning methods by acquiring a diverse set of data points that belong to the rare classes.

1 Introduction

Owing to the advancement of deep learning, medical image classification has made tremendous advances in the past decade. However, medical datasets are naturally imbalanced at the class level, *i.e.*, some classes are comparatively rarer than the others. For instance, cancerous classes are naturally rarer than non-cancerous ones. In such scenarios, the over-represented classes *overpower* the training process and the model ends up learning a biased representation. Deploying such biased models results in incorrect predictions, which can be catastrophic and even lead to loss of life. Active learning (AL) is a promising solution to mitigate this imbalance in the training dataset. The goal of AL is to select data points from an unlabeled set for addition to the training dataset at an additional

---

Supplementary Information The online version contains supplementary material available at https://doi.org/10.1007/978-3-031-16760-7_12.

labeling cost. The model is then retrained with the new training set and the process is repeated. Reducing the labeling cost using the AL paradigm is crucial in domains like medical imaging, where labeling data requires expert supervision (*e.g.*, doctors), which makes the process extremely expensive. However, current AL methods are inefficient in selecting data points from the rare classes in medical image datasets. Broadly, they use acquisition functions that are either: i) based on the uncertainty scores of the model, which are used to select the top uncertain data points [26], or ii) based on diversity scores, where data points having diverse gradients are selected [3,25]. They mainly focus on improving the overall performance of the model, and thereby fail to target these rare yet critical classes. Unfortunately, this leads to a wastage of expensive labeling resources when the goal is to improve performance on these rare classes.

In this work, we consider two types of class imbalance that recur in a wide array of medical imaging datasets. The first scenario is *binary* imbalance, where a subset of classes is rare/infrequent and the remaining subset is relatively frequent. The second scenario is that of *long-tail* imbalance, where the frequency of data points from each class keeps *steeply* reducing as we go from the most frequent class to the rarest class (see Fig. 1). Such class imbalance scenarios are particularly challenging in the medical imaging domain since there exist subtle differences which are barely visually evident (see Fig. 1). In Sect. 3, we discuss CLINICAL, a

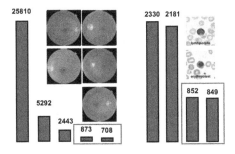

Fig. 1. Motivating examples of two main class imbalance scenarios occurring in medical imaging. **Left:** Long-tail imbalance (Diabetic retinopathy grading from retinal images in APTOS-2019 [10]). **Right:** Binary imbalance (Microscopic peripheral blood cell image classification in Blood-MNIST [1]). Red boxes in both scenario denote targeted rare classes. (Color figure online)

targeted active learning algorithm that acquires a subset by maximizing the submodular mutual information with a set of *misclassified* data points from the rare classes. This enables us to focus on data points from the unlabeled set that are critical and belong to the rare classes.

1.1 Related Work

Uncertainty Based Active Learning. Uncertainty based methods aim to select the most uncertain data points according to a model for labeling. The most common techniques are - 1) ENTROPY [26] selects data points with maximum entropy, 2) LEAST CONFIDENCE [28] selects data points with the lowest confidence, and 3) MARGIN [24] selects data points such that the difference between the top two predictions is minimum.

Diversity Based Active Learning. The main drawback of uncertainty based methods is that they lack diversity within the acquired subset. To mitigate this, a number of approaches have proposed to incorporate diversity. The CORESET method [25] minimizes a coreset loss to form coresets that represent the geometric structure of the original dataset. They do so using a greedy k-center clustering. A recent approach called BADGE [3] uses the last linear layer gradients to represent data points and runs K-MEANS++ [2] to obtain centers that have a high gradient magnitude. The centers being representative and having high gradient magnitude ensures uncertainty and diversity at the same time. However, for batch AL, BADGE models diversity and uncertainty only within the batch and *not* across all batches. Another method, BATCHBALD [15] requires a large number of Monte Carlo dropout samples to obtain significant mutual information which limits its application to medical domains where data is scarce.

Class Imbalanced and Personalized Active Learning. Closely related to our method CLINICAL, are methods which optimize an objective that involves a held-out set. GRADMATCH [13] uses an orthogonal matching pursuit algorithm to select a subset whose gradient closely matches the gradient of a validation set. Another method, GLISTER-ACTIVE [14] formulates an acquisition function that maximizes the log-likelihood on a held-out validation set. We adopt GRAD-MATCH and GLISTER-ACTIVE as baselines that *targets* rare classes in our class imbalance setting and refer to it T-GRADMATCH and T-GLISTER in Sect. 4. Recently, [16] proposed the use of submodular information measures for active learning in realistic scenarios, while [17] used them to find rare objects in an autonomous driving object detection dataset. Finally, [19] use the submodular mutual information functions (used here) for personalized speech recognition. Our proposed method uses the submodular mutual information to target selecting data points from the rare classes via using a small set of *misclassified* data points as exemplars, which makes our method applicable to binary as well as long-tail imbalance scenarios.

1.2 Our Contributions

We summarize our contributions as follows: **1**) We emphasize on the issue of binary and long-tail class imbalance in medical datasets that leads to poor performance on rare yet critical classes. **2**) Given the limitations of current AL methods on medical datasets, we propose CLINICAL, a novel AL framework that can be applied to any class imbalance scenario. **3**) We demonstrate the effectiveness of our framework for a diverse set of image classification tasks and modalities on Pneumonia-MNIST [12], Path-MNIST [11], Blood-MNIST [1], APTOS-2019 [10], and ISIC-2018 [4] datasets. Furthermore, we show that CLINICAL outperforms the state-of-the-art AL methods by up to $\approx 6\%-10\%$ on an average in terms of the average rare classes accuracy for binary imbalance scenarios and long-tail imbalance scenarios. **4**) We provide valuable insights about the *choice* of submodular functions to be used for subset selection based on the *modality* of medical data.

2 Preliminaries

Submodular Functions: We let $\mathcal{V}$ denote the *ground-set* of n data points $\mathcal{V} = \{1, 2, 3, ..., n\}$ and a set function $f : 2^{\mathcal{V}} \to \mathbb{R}$. The function f is submodular [5] if it satisfies diminishing returns, namely $f(j|\mathcal{X}) \geq f(j|\mathcal{Y})$ for all $\mathcal{X} \subseteq \mathcal{Y} \subseteq \mathcal{V}, j \notin \mathcal{Y}$. Facility location, graph cut, log determinants, *etc.* are some examples [9].

Submodular Mutual Information (SMI): Given a set of items $\mathcal{A}, \mathcal{Q} \subseteq \mathcal{V}$, the submodular mutual information (MI) [6,8] is defined as $I_f(\mathcal{A}; \mathcal{Q}) = f(\mathcal{A}) + f(\mathcal{Q}) - f(\mathcal{A} \cup \mathcal{Q})$. Intuitively, this measures the similarity between $\mathcal{Q}$ and $\mathcal{A}$ and we refer to $\mathcal{Q}$ as the query set. [18] extend SMI to handle the case when the *target* can come from a different set $\mathcal{V}'$ apart from the ground set $\mathcal{V}$. In the context of imbalanced medical image classification, $\mathcal{V}$ is the source set of images and the query set $\mathcal{Q}$ is the target set containing the rare class images. To find an optimal subset given a query set $\mathcal{Q} \subseteq \mathcal{V}'$, we can define $g_{\mathcal{Q}}(\mathcal{A}) = I_f(\mathcal{A}; \mathcal{Q})$, $\mathcal{A} \subseteq \mathcal{V}$ and maximize the same.

2.1 Examples of SMI Functions

For targeted active learning, we use the recently introduced SMI functions in [6,8] and their extensions introduced in [18] as acquisition functions. For any two data points $i \in \mathcal{V}$ and $j \in \mathcal{Q}$, let s_{ij} denote the similarity between them.

Graph Cut MI (GCMI): The SMI instantiation of graph-cut (GCMI) is defined as: $I_{GC}(\mathcal{A}; \mathcal{Q}) = 2 \sum_{i \in \mathcal{A}} \sum_{j \in \mathcal{Q}} s_{ij}$. Since maximizing GCMI maximizes the joint pairwise sum with the query set, it will lead to a summary similar to the query set Q. In fact, specific instantiations of GCMI have been intuitively used for query-focused summarization for videos [27] and documents [20,21].

Facility Location MI (FLMI): We consider two variants of FLMI. The first variant is defined over $\mathcal{V}$(FLVMI), the SMI instantiation can be defined as: $I_{FLV}(\mathcal{A}; \mathcal{Q}) = \sum_{i \in \mathcal{V}} \min(\max_{j \in \mathcal{A}} s_{ij}, \max_{j \in \mathcal{Q}} s_{ij})$. The first term in the $\min(.)$ of FLVMI models diversity, and the second term models query relevance.

For the second variant, which is defined over $\mathcal{Q}$ (FLQMI), the SMI instantiation can be defined as: $I_{FLQ}(\mathcal{A}; \mathcal{Q}) = \sum_{i \in \mathcal{Q}} \max_{j \in \mathcal{A}} s_{ij} + \sum_{i \in \mathcal{A}} \max_{j \in \mathcal{Q}} s_{ij}$. FLQMI is very intuitive for query relevance as well. It measures the representation of data points that are the most relevant to the query set and vice versa.

Log Determinant MI (LOGDETMI): The SMI instantiation of LOGDETMI can be defined as: $I_{LogDet}(\mathcal{A}; \mathcal{Q}) = \log \det(S_{\mathcal{A}}) - \log \det(S_{\mathcal{A}} - S_{\mathcal{A}, \mathcal{Q}} S_{\mathcal{Q}}^{-1} S_{\mathcal{A}, \mathcal{Q}}^{T})$. $S_{\mathcal{A}, \mathcal{Q}}$ denotes the cross-similarity matrix between the items in sets $\mathcal{A}$ and $\mathcal{Q}$.

3   CLINICAL: Our Targeted Active Learning Framework for Binary and Long-Tail Imbalance

In this section, we propose our targeted active learning framework, CLINICAL (see Fig. 2), and show how it can be applied to datasets with class imbalance. Concretely, we apply the SMI functions as acquisition functions for improving a model's accuracy on rare classes at a given additional labeling cost (B instances) without compromising on the overall accuracy. The main idea in CLINICAL, is to use *only the misclassified* data points from a held-out target set $\mathcal{T}$ containing data points from the rare classes. Let $\hat{\mathcal{T}} \subseteq \mathcal{T}$ be the subset of misclassified data points. Then, we optimize the SMI function $I_f(\mathcal{A}; \hat{\mathcal{T}})$ using a greedy strategy [23].

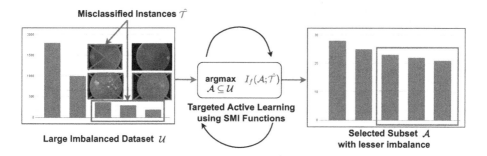

Fig. 2. The CLINICAL framework. We use a set of misclassified instances $\hat{\mathcal{T}}$ as the query set $\mathcal{Q}$ in the SMI function. We then maximize $I_f(\mathcal{A}; \hat{\mathcal{T}})$ in an AL loop to target the imbalance and gradually mine data points from the rare classes.

Note that since $\hat{\mathcal{T}}$ contains only the misclassified data points, it would contain more data points from classes that are comparatively *rarer* or the worst performing. Moreover, $\hat{\mathcal{T}}$ is updated in every AL round, this mechanism helps the SMI functions to focus on classes that require the most attention. For instance, in the long-tail imbalance scenario (see Fig. 1), CLINICAL would focus more on the tail classes in the initial rounds of AL. Next, we discuss the CLINICAL algorithm in detail:

Algorithm: Let $\mathcal{L}$ be an initial training set of labeled instances and $\mathcal{T}$ be the target set containing examples from the rare classes. Let $\mathcal{U}$ be a large unlabeled dataset and $\mathcal{M}$ be the trained model using $\mathcal{L}$. Next, we compute $\hat{\mathcal{T}}$ as the subset of data points from $\mathcal{T}$ that were misclassified by $\mathcal{M}$. Using last layer gradients as a representation for each data point which are extracted from $\mathcal{M}$, we compute similarity kernels of elements within $\mathcal{U}$, within $\hat{\mathcal{T}}$ and between $\mathcal{U}$ and $\hat{\mathcal{T}}$ to instantiate an SMI function $I_f(\mathcal{A}; \hat{\mathcal{T}})$ and maximize it to compute an optimal subset $\mathcal{A} \subseteq \mathcal{U}$ of size B given $\hat{\mathcal{T}}$ as target (query) set. We then augment $\mathcal{L}$ with labeled $\mathcal{A}$ (i.e. $L(\mathcal{A})$) and re-train the model to improve the model on the rare classes.

Algorithm 1. CLINICAL: Targeted AL for binary and long-tail imbalance
___
Require: Initial Labeled set of data points: $\mathcal{L}$, unlabeled dataset: $\mathcal{U}$, target set: $\mathcal{T}$, Loss
    function $\mathcal{H}$ for learning model $\mathcal{M}$, batch size: B, number of selection rounds: N
1: **for** selection round $i = 1 : N$ **do**
2:     Train $\mathcal{M}$ with loss $\mathcal{H}$ on the current labeled set $\mathcal{L}$ and obtain parameters θ_i
3:     Compute $\hat{\mathcal{T}} \subseteq \mathcal{T}$ that were misclassified by the trained model $\mathcal{M}$
4:     Use $\mathcal{M}_{\theta_i}$ to compute gradients using hypothesized labels $\{\nabla_\theta \mathcal{H}(x_j, \hat{y_j}, \theta), \forall j \in \mathcal{U}\}$
    and obtain a pairwise similarity matrix X. {where $X_{ij} = \langle \nabla_\theta \mathcal{H}_i(\theta), \nabla_\theta \mathcal{H}_j(\theta) \rangle$}
5:     Instantiate a submodular function f based on X.
6:     $\mathcal{A}_i \leftarrow \text{argmax}_{\mathcal{A} \subseteq \mathcal{U}, |\mathcal{A}| \leq B} I_f(\mathcal{A}; \hat{\mathcal{T}})$
7:     Get labels $L(\mathcal{A}_i)$ for batch $\mathcal{A}_i$, and $\mathcal{L} \leftarrow \mathcal{L} \cup L(\mathcal{A}_i), \mathcal{U} \leftarrow \mathcal{U} - \mathcal{A}_i$
8:     $\mathcal{T} \leftarrow \mathcal{T} \cup \mathcal{A}_i^\mathcal{T}$, augment $\mathcal{T}$ with new data points that belong to target classes.
9: **end for**
10: Return trained model $\mathcal{M}$ and parameters θ_N.
___

4   Experiments

In this section, we evaluate the effectiveness of CLINICAL on binary imbalance (Sect. 4.1) and long-tail imbalance (Sect. 4.2) scenarios. We do so by comparing the accuracy and class selections of various SMI functions with the existing state-of-the-art AL approaches. In our experiments, we observe that different SMI functions outperform existing approaches depending on the modality of the medical data. We show that the choice of the SMI based acquisition function is imperative and varies based on the imbalance scenario and the modality of medical data.

Baselines in all Scenarios. We compare the performance on CLINICAL against a variety of state-of-the-art uncertainty, diversity and targeted selection methods. The uncertainty based methods include ENTROPY, LEAST CONFIDENCE (LEAST-CONF), and MARGIN. The diversity based methods include CORESET and BADGE. The targeted selection methods include T-GLISTER and T-GRADMATCH. We discuss the details of all baselines in Sect. 1.1. For a fair comparison with CLINICAL, we use the same target set of misclassified data points $\hat{\mathcal{T}}$ as the held out validation set used in T-GLISTER and T-GRADMATCH. Lastly, we compare with random sampling (RANDOM).

Experimental Setup: We use the same training procedure and hyperparameters for all AL methods to ensure a fair comparison. For all experiments, we train a ResNet-18 [7] model using an SGD optimizer with an initial learning rate of 0.001, the momentum of 0.9, and a weight decay of 5e−4. For each AL round, the weights are reinitialized using Xavier initialization and the model is trained till 99% training accuracy. The learning rate is decayed using cosine annealing [22] in every epoch. We run each experiment 5× on a V100 GPU and provide the error bars (std deviation). We discuss dataset splits for each our experiments below and provide more details in Appendix. B.

4.1   Binary Imbalance

Datasets: We apply our framework to **1)** Pneumonia-MNIST (pediatric chest X-ray) [12,29], **2)** Path-MNIST (colorectal cancer histology) [11,29], and **3)**Blood-MNIST (blood cell microscope) [1,29] medical image classification datasets. To create a more realistic medical scenario, we create a custom dataset that simulates binary class imbalance for each of these datasets for our experiments. Let $\mathcal{C}$ be the set of data points from the rare classes and $\mathcal{D}$ be the set of data points from the over-represented classes. We create the initial labeled set $\mathcal{L}$ (seed set) in AL, $|\mathcal{D_L}| = \rho|\mathcal{C_L}|$ and an unlabeled set $\mathcal{U}$ such that $|\mathcal{D_U}| = \rho|\mathcal{C_U}|$, where ρ is the imbalance factor. We use a small held out target set $\mathcal{T}$ which contains data points from the rare classes. For Path-MNIST and PneumoniaMNIST, we use $\rho = 20$, and for Blood-MNIST, we use $\rho = 7$ due to the small size of the dataset. For Pneumonia-MNIST, $|\mathcal{C_L}| + |\mathcal{D_L}| = 105$, $|\mathcal{C_U}| + |\mathcal{D_U}| = 1100$, $B = 10$ (AL batch size) and, $|\mathcal{T}| = 5$. Following the natural class imbalance, we use the 'pneumonia' class as the rare class. For Path-MNIST, $|\mathcal{C_L}| + |\mathcal{D_L}| = 3550$, $|\mathcal{C_U}| + |\mathcal{D_U}| = 56.8K$, $B = 500$ and, $|\mathcal{T}| = 20$. Following the natural class imbalance, we use two classes from the dataset ('mucus', 'normal colon mucosa') as rare classes. For Blood-MNIST, $|\mathcal{C_L}| + |\mathcal{D_L}| = 228$, $|\mathcal{C_U}| + |\mathcal{D_U}| = 1824$, $B = 20$

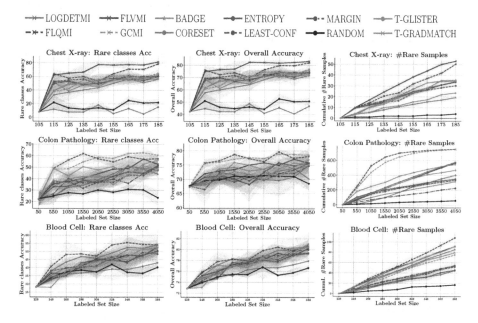

Fig. 3. AL for binary imbalanced medical image classification on Pneumonia-MNIST [12] (**first** row), Path-MNIST [11] (**second** row), and Blood-MNIST [1] (**third** row). CLINICAL outperforms the existing AL methods by $\approx 2\%-12\%$ on the rare classes acc. (**left** col.) and $\approx 2\%-6\%$ on overall acc. (**center** col.). SMI functions select the most number of rare class samples (**right** col.)

and, $|\mathcal{T}| = 20$. Following the natural class imbalance, we use four classes from the dataset ('basophil', 'eosinophil', 'lymphocyte', 'neutrophil') as rare classes.

Results: The results for the binary imbalance scenario are shown in Fig. 3. We observe that the CLINICAL consistently outperform other methods by $\approx$ 2%−12% on the rare classes accuracy (Fig. 3(left column)) and $\approx$ 2%−6% on overall accuracy (Fig. 3(center column)). This is due to the fact that the SMI functions are able to select significantly more data points that belong to the rare classes (Fig. 3(right column)). Particularly, we observe that when the data modality is *X-ray* (Pneumonia-MNIST), the facility location based SMI variants, FLVMI and FLQMI perform significantly better than other acquisition functions due to their ability to model *representation*. For the *colon pathology* modality (Path-MNIST), GCMI and FLQMI functions that model *query-relevance* significantly outperform other methods. Lastly, for the blood cell microscope modality (Blood-MNIST), we observe some improvement using FLQMI, although it selects many points from the rare classes.

4.2   Long-Tail Imbalance

Datasets: We apply CLINICAL to two datasets that naturally show a long-tail distribution: **1)** The ISIC-2018 skin lesion diagnosis dataset [4] and **2)** APTOS-2019 [10] for diabetic retinopathy (DR) grading from retinal fundus images. We evaluate all AL methods on a balanced test set to obtain a fair estimate of accuracy across all classes. We split the remaining data randomly with 20% into the initial labeled set $\mathcal{L}$ and 80% into the unlabeled set $\mathcal{U}$. We use a small held-out

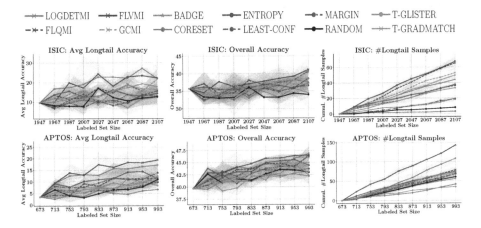

Fig. 4. Active learning for long-tail imbalanced medical image classification on ISIC-2018 [4] (**first** row) and APTOS-2019 [10] (**second** row). CLINICAL outperforms the state-of-the-art AL methods by $\approx$ 10%−12% on the average long-tail accuracy (**left** col.) and $\approx$ 2%−5% on overall accuracy (**center** col.). SMI functions select the most number of long-tail class samples (**right** col.)

target set $\mathcal{T}$ with data points from the classes at the tail of the distribution (long-tail classes, see Fig. 1). For ISIC-2018, we use the bottom three infrequent skin lesions from the tail of the distribution as long-tail classes ('bowen's disease', 'vascular lesions', and 'dermatofibroma'). We set $B = 40$ and $|\mathcal{T}| = 15$. For APTOS-2019 we use the bottom two infrequent DR gradations as long-tail classes ('severe DR' and 'proliferative DR') (see Fig. 1). We set $B = 20$ and $|\mathcal{T}| = 10$.

Results: We present the results for the long-tail imbalance scenario in Fig. 4. We observe that CLINICAL consistently outperform other methods by $\approx 10\%-12\%$ on the average long-tail classes accuracy (Fig. 4(left column)) and $\approx 2\%-5\%$ on the overall accuracy (Fig. 4(center column)). This is because the SMI functions select significantly more data points from the long-tail classes (Fig. 4(right column)). On both datasets, we observe that the functions modeling query-relevance *and* diversity (FLVMI and LOGDETMI) outperform the functions modeling *only* query-relevance (FLQMI and GCMI).

5 Conclusion

We demonstrate the effectiveness of CLINICAL for a wide range of medical data modalities for binary and long-tail imbalance. We empirically observe that the current methods in active learning cannot be directly applied to medical datasets with rare classes, and show that a targeting mechanism like SMI can greatly improve the performance on rare classes.

References

1. Acevedo, A., Merino, A., Alférez, S., Molina, Á., Boldú, L., Rodellar, J.: A dataset of microscopic peripheral blood cell images for development of automatic recognition systems. Data Brief **30** (2020). ISSN 2352-3409
2. Arthur, D., Vassilvitskii, S.: k-means++: the advantages of careful seeding. In: SODA 2007: Proceedings of the Eighteenth Annual ACM-SIAM Symposium on Discrete Algorithms, pp. 1027–1035. Society for Industrial and Applied Mathematics, Philadelphia (2007)
3. Ash, J.T., Zhang, C., Krishnamurthy, A., Langford, J., Agarwal, A.: Deep batch active learning by diverse, uncertain gradient lower bounds. In: ICLR (2020)
4. Codella, N., et al.: Skin lesion analysis toward melanoma detection 2018: a challenge hosted by the international skin imaging collaboration (ISIC). arXiv preprint arXiv:1902.03368 (2019)
5. Fujishige, S.: Submodular Functions and Optimization. Elsevier, Amsterdam (2005)
6. Gupta, A., Levin, R.: The online submodular cover problem. In: ACM-SIAM Symposium on Discrete Algorithms (2020)
7. He, K., Zhang, X., Ren, S., Sun, J.: Deep residual learning for image recognition. In: Proceedings of the IEEE Conference on Computer Vision and Pattern Recognition, pp. 770–778 (2016)

8. Iyer, R., Khargoankar, N., Bilmes, J., Asnani, H.: Submodular combinatorial information measures with applications in machine learning. arXiv preprint arXiv:2006.15412 (2020)

9. Iyer, R.K.: Submodular optimization and machine learning: theoretical results, unifying and scalable algorithms, and applications. Ph.D. thesis (2015)

10. Kaggle: Aptos 2019 blindness detection (2019). https://www.kaggle.com/c/aptos2019-blindness-detection/data

11. Kather, J.N., et al.: Predicting survival from colorectal cancer histology slides using deep learning: a retrospective multicenter study. PLoS Med. **16**(1), e1002730 (2019)

12. Kermany, D.S., et al.: Identifying medical diagnoses and treatable diseases by image-based deep learning. Cell **172**(5), 1122–1131 (2018)

13. Killamsetty, K., Durga, S., Ramakrishnan, G., De, A., Iyer, R.: Grad-match: gradient matching based data subset selection for efficient deep model training. In: International Conference on Machine Learning, pp. 5464–5474. PMLR (2021)

14. Killamsetty, K., Sivasubramanian, D., Ramakrishnan, G., Iyer, R.: Glister: generalization based data subset selection for efficient and robust learning. In: AAAI (2021)

15. Kirsch, A., Van Amersfoort, J., Gal, Y.: Batchbald: efficient and diverse batch acquisition for deep Bayesian active learning. arXiv preprint arXiv:1906.08158 (2019)

16. Kothawade, S., Beck, N., Killamsetty, K., Iyer, R.: Similar: submodular information measures based active learning in realistic scenarios. In: Advances in Neural Information Processing Systems, vol. 34 (2021)

17. Kothawade, S., Ghosh, S., Shekhar, S., Xiang, Y., Iyer, R.: Talisman: targeted active learning for object detection with rare classes and slices using submodular mutual information. arXiv preprint arXiv:2112.00166 (2021)

18. Kothawade, S., Kaushal, V., Ramakrishnan, G., Bilmes, J., Iyer, R.: Prism: a rich class of parameterized submodular information measures for guided subset selection. arXiv preprint arXiv:2103.00128 (2021)

19. Kothyari, M., Mekala, A.R., Iyer, R., Ramakrishnan, G., Jyothi, P.: Personalizing ASR with limited data using targeted subset selection. arXiv preprint arXiv:2110.04908 (2021)

20. Li, J., Li, L., Li, T.: Multi-document summarization via submodularity. Appl. Intell. **37**(3), 420–430 (2012)

21. Lin, H.: Submodularity in natural language processing: algorithms and applications. Ph.D. thesis (2012)

22. Loshchilov, I., Hutter, F.: SGDR: stochastic gradient descent with warm restarts. arXiv preprint arXiv:1608.03983 (2016)

23. Mirzasoleiman, B., Badanidiyuru, A., Karbasi, A., Vondrák, J., Krause, A.: Lazier than lazy greedy. In: Proceedings of the AAAI Conference on Artificial Intelligence, vol. 29 (2015)

24. Roth, D., Small, K.: Margin-based active learning for structured output spaces. In: Fürnkranz, J., Scheffer, T., Spiliopoulou, M. (eds.) ECML 2006. LNCS (LNAI), vol. 4212, pp. 413–424. Springer, Heidelberg (2006). https://doi.org/10.1007/11871842_40

25. Sener, O., Savarese, S.: Active learning for convolutional neural networks: a core-set approach. In: International Conference on Learning Representations (2018)

26. Settles, B.: Active learning literature survey. Technical report, University of Wisconsin-Madison, Department of Computer Sciences (2009)

27. Vasudevan, A.B., Gygli, M., Volokitin, A., Van Gool, L.: Query-adaptive video summarization via quality-aware relevance estimation. In: Proceedings of the 25th ACM International Conference on Multimedia, pp. 582–590 (2017)
28. Wang, D., Shang, Y.: A new active labeling method for deep learning. In: 2014 International Joint Conference on Neural Networks (IJCNN), pp. 112–119. IEEE (2014)
29. Yang, J., et al.: MedMNIST v2: A large-scale lightweight benchmark for 2D and 3D biomedical image classification. arXiv preprint arXiv:2008 (2021)

Real Time Data Augmentation Using Fractional Linear Transformations in Continual Learning

Arijit Patra[(✉)]

Data and Translational Sciences, UCB Biopharma UK, Slough SL1 3WE, UK
`Arijit.Patra@ucb.com`

Abstract. Over recent years, deep learning algorithms have gained prominence in medical image analysis research. Like other connectionist systems, such networks have been found to be prone to catastrophic forgetting effects. This makes generalization a challenge as new additions to prediction requirements at runtime would invariably require retraining on not only the new dataset, but also substantial portions of older task data. This is a difficult task in clinical imaging where retention of datasets over extended time is challenged by legal and infrastructure constraints. Thus, there is a requirement of algorithmic designs that address forgetting as a part of base and incremental task learning. This has been cast as an incremental learning problem recently. We propose a novel approach to the incremental class addition problem, where a retention of limited numbers of exemplars of old classes helps reduce forgetting instead of large scale data storage, using a strategy of incremental time augmentation with Mobius transformations and weighted distillation objectives to correct evolving class imbalance effects.

Keywords: Knowledge distillation · Incremental learning · Mobius augmentation

1 Introduction

Deep learning based methods have become common in medical imaging research [31, 35]. In realistic situations, clinical imaging systems often do not have access to all the required data initially but data arrives in incremental chunks over time, acquired with multiple devices and across different centers. This problem is pronounced in healthcare systems in low and middle countries (LMIC) where data acquisition and quality assurance infrastructure may not be as developed. Such cases of variable data accessibility require machine learning algorithms to be robust to adaptations on new data distributions over time and be generalizable to novel classes of data, in order to remain clinically significant and reliably aid diagnostic efforts throughout their shelf lives under evolving requirements. This requirement for continual adaptation in deep networks for clinical imaging implies a need to ensure that model parameters remain relevant to both old and new tasks in incremental data regimes. This needs to occur without storing large numbers of exemplars from past classes over subsequent learning schedules [33] owing to constraints on long-term storage of clinical data in terms of fairness [36], legal and

© The Author(s), under exclusive license to Springer Nature Switzerland AG 2022
G. Zamzmi et al. (Eds.): MILLanD 2022, LNCS 13559, pp. 130–140, 2022.
https://doi.org/10.1007/978-3-031-16760-7_13

privacy issues [37]. Thus the ideal joint training condition of optimizing models with all datasets ever used at each incremental retraining is challenging in clinical imaging.

Prior Work. Adaptation of existing models to learn new classes was attempted by transfer learning [2]. Transfer learning, despite helping prior learning to enhance future task learning, was found to inefficiently balance old and new task knowledge. Studies show a decline in past performances or catastrophic forgetting [1], as information pre-viously learnt is lost causing high validation losses on past data. Recent work has pursued mitigation of forgetting in deep networks with parameter expansion [3], exemplar replay [4], generative rehearsal [5, 6] and weight regularization [7]. Knowledge distillation, where representations learnt by a model are transferred to another, are often used in model compression [8]. It has been used for incremental learning as the representation from one learning session can help regularize a future session, with the old tasks' logits regularizing the learning on new data. Such methods include Learning without Forgetting (LwF) [4] with distillation and cross-entropy objectives, iCaRL [10] which incrementally learns representations, learning using human insights [11] where distillation and gaze-based salience enable model compression, progressive retrospection (PDR) [12] using distillation from both old and new models. In clinical imaging, data availability is often not immediate and models learning incrementally over time without affecting past performance have been researched [32], such as pixel regularization for MRI segmentation [13], modelling Alzheimers progression [14], weight consolidation and distillation [15, 34], hierarchical continual learning [16] etc. While data augmentation has been extensively used in machine learning [9, 17], there has been relatively little research on runtime augmentation on examples retained in incremental learning. We study Mobius transformations for incremental time augmentation in histology imaging. Mobius transformations have been studied in projective geometry [18], design of com-plex valued networks [19], optimizing deep compositional spatial models [20], extending sample-level diversity [21], hyperbolic networks [22] and approximating Choquet integrals [23]. We extend Mobius functions to data augmentation regimes in histology for incremental learning and study their interaction with distillation methods.

Contributions. We propose a novel approach for incremental learning without storing a large number of samples in the analysis of histology images, using a dataset of colorectal carcinoma images [24] to show a proof-of-concept. This is achieved by propagating sample diversity through a novel online augmentation over a limited number of past tasks' samples, while performing a weighted cross-distillation over the logits of the past classes while training on new class data for the available model. Our key contributions are: a) a concept of incremental time data augmentation strategy using Mobius transformations b) weighted cross-distillation for continual learning of new classes c) an online adaptation of Mobius augmentation in incremental learning tasks.

We first describe Mobius transformations and its interpretation as a composition of elementary operations like translation, rotation and so on, which individually form the basis of many sample-level data augmentation methods. Next, we describe our distillation approach where class specific accuracy is used to apportion importance to the over-all past logits vector. The combination of the two steps involves a few samples from old classes being subjected to an online augmentation using Mobius transformation to improve representation of previously seen classes as the model is optimized for new classes. During the optimization over new classes, the old class logits after being weighted without images being stored, and summed up to reflect an overall representation of old tasks allow the model to have a snapshot of the past learning and prevent a catastrophic perturbation to the parameter space along with cross-entropy optimization that enables the new task learning to account for both old class knowledge and the new class sample information.

2 Methodology

Datasets. Anonymized colorectal cancer HE stained tissue slides were obtained using an Aperio ScanScope scanner at 20× magnification. These are digitized and anonymized images of formalin-fixed paraffin embedded human colorectal adenocarcinomas and made publicly available through the pathology archives at the University Medical Center Mannheim [24]. These slides contain contiguous tissue areas that are manually annotated and tessellated. These are converted to $150 \times 150 \times 3$ RGB patches. Overall, 5000 images were obtained for different tissue classes. In this study, 8 classes with 625 samples each were considered: *1. Tumor epithelium; 2. Simple stroma (homogeneous with tumor stroma, extra-tumoral stroma and smooth muscle); 3. Complex stroma (single tumor cells and immune cells); 4. Debris (necrosis, hemorrhage and mucus); 5. Immune cells (immune cell conglomerates and sub-mucosal lymphoid follicles); 6. Normal mucosal glands; 7. Adipose tissue; 8. Background.*

Problem Definition. Consider a problem where the model needs to be trained in an *M*-stage fashion, with each stage being a classification task with classes as $Xt = \{Xt,i\}^{Kt}_{i=1}$, $t \in [1, M]$, with each X being a class and includes samples $xt \in Xt$ and Kt being the number of classes in each stage t. The classifier learning in stage $t-1$, after incrementally being optimized over the classes at the tth stage, shouldn't show marked de-clines in inference capacity over validation set instances from $(t-1)^{th}$ stage or prior stages. Here, we design an incremental learning experiment with four classes in the initial training stage and four in the incremental stage ($M = 2, K1 = K2 = 4$).

This study is modelled as a sequential class learning task as above, with a proportion of classes being learnt as '**base classes**' during an initial training stage. Next, the remaining classes are learnt as '**incremental classes**' in a subsequent learning stage, leading to a multistage learning system over a temporal interval. The base classes are the *tumour epithelium (TE), simple stroma (SS), Immune cells (IC)* and *Adipose tissue (AT)*. The incrementally learnt classes include *complex stroma (CS), debris (De), normal mucosal glands (NMG)* and *background (BG)*. The former are used to optimize for the initial task (Task 1) and the latter help train the model trained over base classes for the incremental task (Task 2), thus simulating a continual learning scenario (Figs. 1 and 2).

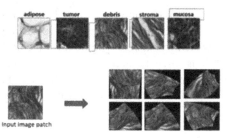

Fig. 1. Sample images from the colorectal histology dataset used (*top*); Mobius transformed augmented examples during incremental learning (*bottom*)

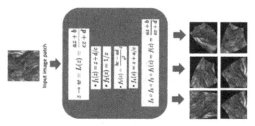

Fig. 2. Interpretation of Mobius transformations as a composition of basic transformations enables an algorithmic implementation to plug into the incremental learning step at real-time.

Mobius Augmentation. Many sample-level data augmentation methods at training time belong to a set of affine transformations, which includes a group of mappings like rotation, scaling, translation and flipping. Such operations can be modelled as a bijective mapping in a complex plane as $z \rightarrow az + b$, where the variable z, parameters $a, b \in C$, the set of complex numbers. A generalization of this mapping considers the presence of non-zero imaginary parts of the complex numbers in the transformation and the affine mapping being performed in the Argand plane [19]. This expands the superset of possible image transformations with valid label preservation. The denominator of a linear transformation $z \rightarrow az + b$ can be assumed as unity. This can also be obtained by treating the denominator as a complex number $cz + d$, such that the real part of this complex quantity is unity and the imaginary part is zero. This hints at the next stage of abstraction by introducing a denominator with non-zero real and imaginary components $(c, z \neq 0)$. This creates a group of transformations in the set of complex numbers:

$$f(z) = (az + b)/(cz + d) \tag{1}$$

where $a, b, c, d \in C$ and $ad - bc \neq 0$ is the invertibility condition. This encapsulates a superset of basic mappings including inversion, translation, rotation and flipping and is termed a Mobius transformation if $z \in C$, $f(z)$ is not constant and $cz + d \neq 0$ [19]. A point z is mapped from one complex plane to another using parameters a, b, c, d. This can pro-ceed without an explicit imaginary part defined for the complex entity z, as every real number can have a form $x + iy$, where $x \in R$, and $y = 0$. This enables us to define points on the image to estimate a, b, c and d. We choose 3 points at random on the image space with different combinations allowing for a different output at the conclusion of the mapping operation with label information preserved. This allows expansion in sample diversity per input in available datasets, with a much larger set of possible modifications for a particular class compared to existing sample-level methods. With a transformed appearance in 2D, the Mobius augmentation improves model generalization and robustness to noise and dataset shifts. Assuming 3 points in the initial plane as $z1, z2, z3$ and in a target plane as $w1, w2, w3$, then considering the preservation of anharmonic ratios [19]:

$$\frac{(w - w_1)(w_2 - w_3)}{(w - w_3)(w_2 - w_1)} = \frac{(z - z_1)(z_2 - z_3)}{(z - z_3)(z_2 - z_1)} \tag{2}$$

$$\frac{(w - w_1)}{(w - w_3)} = \frac{(z - z_1)(z_2 - z_3)(w_2 - w_1)}{(z - z_3)(z_2 - z_1)(w_2 - w_3)} \tag{3}$$

where,

$$w = \frac{(Aw_3 - w_1)}{A - 1}$$

$$A = \frac{(z - z_1)(z_2 - z_3)(w_2 - w_1)}{(z - z_3)(z_2 - z_1)(w_2 - w_3)}$$

This implies that we can express the transformation function in a reduced form as:

$$f(z) = w = \frac{(Aw_3 - w_1)}{A - 1} = \frac{az + b}{cz + d} \tag{4}$$

Then, we obtain the values of coefficients a, b, c, d in terms of the chosen points $(z1, z2, z3)$ and $(w1, w2, w3)$ through substitution in equations (1), (3) and (4):

$$a = w_1 w_2 z_1 - w_1 w_3 z_1 - w_1 w_2 z_2 + w_2 w_3 z_2 + w_1 w_3 z_3 - w_2 w_3 z_3 \tag{5a}$$

$$b = w_1 w_3 z_1 z_2 - w_2 w_3 z_1 z_2 - w_1 w_2 z_1 z_3 + w_2 w_3 z_1 z_3 + w_1 w_2 z_2 z_3 - w_1 w_3 z_2 z_3 \tag{5b}$$

$$c = w_2 z_1 - w_3 z_1 - w_1 z_2 + w_3 z_2 + w_1 z_3 - w_2 z_3 \tag{5c}$$

$$d = w_1 z_1 z_2 - w_2 z_1 z_2 - w_1 z_1 z_3 + w_3 z_1 z_3 + w_2 z_2 z_3 - w_3 z_2 z_3 \tag{5d}$$

Based on Liouville's theorem [25], a Mobius transformation can be expressed as a composition of translations, orthogonal transformations and inversions, encompassing a superset of a number of common augmentation operations in deep learning. This helps us design an algorithmic framework for real-time generation of Mobius transformations using values of a, b, c, d from (5a, 5b, 5c, 5d) to form subspaces of compositions on basic transformations from a superset of the generalized Mobius transformation. While an infinite number of Mobius samples can be obtained, the number of samples is bounded by randomly assigned cutoffs at runtime within $[1, R]$, where R is the maximum number of samples allowed by memory constraints. We set R at 250 based on our RAM settings.

Weighted Distillation. Representations learnt by models can also be thought of as representing a 'dark knowledge' [8] about the model-data dynamics in a compact vec-torized form. This process was termed as knowledge distillation since the heavier models' learning is 'distilled' into an essential, compact representation that can be used in the other tasks. We use this vector as a 'memory' of past class learning to regularize incremental training. Based on the initial learning, we retain class averaged logits per class by saving to memory the validation logits at the conclusion of the training sched-ule of the initial (Task 1) training. Next, we compute the weighted logits by applying weighting factors to logits of individual classes, the weights being numerical inverses of class-specific validation accuracies. This allows our distillation logits to reflect class-wise biases in proportion to their difficulty for the model to learn. The initial classes' training employs a cross-entropy loss. The probability vector of the initial task, is $p = softmax\ (z) \in 1$, where z is the set of logits. The objective in the initial training stage:

$$L_{crossent}(y, p) = -\sum_{i=1}^{K_1} y_i \cdot \log(p_i) \tag{6}$$

Here p_i is the predicted probability score vector for each class in the new task, y_i is the associated ground truth in a one-hot encoding form. In next sessions, a distillation term is added to the objective, to enable representation of past knowledge in the learn-ing process ($y'y$ are final layer class scores for new task classes before softmax steps):

$$L_{distillation}(z_{old}, y') = -\sum_{i=1}^{N} soft\max(\frac{z_{old}}{T}) . \log(soft\max\left(\frac{y'_i}{T}\right)) \tag{7}$$

Logits and predictions are scaled with a temperature term T in a softening process. Softening with a temperature hyperparameter helps reduce the disparity between the class label with the highest confidence score in the probability vector with respect to the other class labels and helps better reflect inter-class relationships at the representation learning stage. Considering the overall logit vector for old classes, after weighting as z_{old}, class-specific logits are weighted to obtain a sum of class-weighted logits as:

$$z_{old} = \sum_{i=1}^{k_1} u_i \cdot z_i \tag{8}$$

The logits from individual classes $z_i, i \in [1, K1]$ are calculated by averaging pre-soft-max probability values (after sigmoid activation) for examples from each of $K1$ classes. The weights $(u1, u2, ..., uk1)$ are computed as inverse of class-specific accuracy on valida-tion sets of the initial classes. The idea is to boost logits from classes which are inherently difficult to learn for the model (lower the class-specific accuracy, higher the class weight). This reduces the disparity among classes in their contribution towards the overall sessional representation vector to be saved as an imprint of Stage 1 learning. Overall, the net incremental objective for learning beyond initial sessions is (= 0.5):

$$L = \gamma L_{crossent} + (1 - \gamma)L_{distillation} \tag{9}$$

3   Experiments, Results and Discussion

The experiment is split into two sequential tasks, labeled Task 1 and Task 2. The initial task proceeds with a standard cross-entropy objective and Task 2, the incremental task utilizes a joint loss with a cross-entropy term and a distillation loss. We utilize a ResNet-50 feature extractor, removing layers subsequent to the last residual block and adding to the last residual block a fully-connected (FC) layer of 512 units, followed by a FC layer with 4 units (number of classes) and loss heads. The pre-softmax layer generates probability scores by a sigmoid operation. An 80:20 split is used for the *train:test* split on the dataset. Input images are resized to *224 × 224* and a batch size of 50 is used with a learning rate of 0.001 and adaptive moment optimization (Adam) [26]. Task 1 models are trained for 150 epochs on a (*N,label*) set for all *N* frames. In Task 2, models are trained for 150 epochs on (*N', label, logit*) tuples- *N'* having Mobius transformed versions of selectively retained old samples besides new class data. Note that we don't perform training time data augmentation except for the retained samples in incremental training. This is a departure from most machine learning efforts in clinical imaging but our aim is to analyze specific effects of Mobius transformations on incremental learning performance with distillation and otherwise. Thus, boosting base model accuracy is not aimed in the study. We set $T = 4.0$ after grid search in $T \in [1, 5]$. Two 32 GB Nvidia V100 GPUs, 512 MB RAM used with ResNet 50 based models with ~24.8 million parameters, average training time of 102s per epoch in both tasks. Mobius augmentation modules and deep models are coded in Python 3.7.1 and Tensorflow 2.0 respectively.

Table 1. Accuracy (%) for task 1/Stage 1 classes, after Task 1 is trained for, and after task 2 is incrementally added in Stage 2. The difference in accuracies on the validation set of Task 1 classes represents forgetting on them due to Task 2 addition

Stage	Stage 1					Stage 2					ΔAcc
	TE	SS	IC	AT	Avg(T1)	TE	SS	IC	AT	Avg(T2)	T2-T1
Our(MT+wKD)	91.66	90.40	87.35	88.72	89.53	90.33	87.50	85.46	87.15	87.61	1.92
Our(MT+KD)	91.66	90.40	87.35	88.72	89.53	84.67	83.15	81.25	80.67	82.44	7.09
Our (KD)	91.66	90.40	87.35	88.72	89.53	77.20	72.33	70.54	73.25	73.33	16.20
Our (MT+FT)	91.66	90.40	87.35	88.72	89.53	75.24	68.10	67.11	70.77	70.31	19.22
Ours (FT)	91.66	90.40	87.35	88.72	89.53	55.45	48.67	47.05	51.10	50.57	38.96
LwF.ewc [15]	91.66	90.40	87.35	88.72	89.53	72.50	68.95	64.71	67.90	68.51	21.02
LwM [11]	91.66	90.40	87.35	88.72	89.53	76.95	73.85	69.20	73.35	73.34	16.19
PDR [12]	91.66	90.40	87.35	88.72	89.53	73.09	70.21	67.33	70.55	70.30	19.23

For the incremental task (Task 2), we use data from the 4 classes that are incrementally added. Mobius transformations for augmentation are exclusively applied to retained exemplars from Task 1 classes. Guided by memory constraints, we choose the top 20 examples for retention sorting by the magnitude of the class confidence scores after the validation set if passed through the trained models after Task 1. Trivially, including a greater number of samples can improve performance as theoretically shown in [2], with full joint training being an upper bound on incremental performance. Local storage conditions constrain our memory buffer available and we need to economise on memory similar to several clinical imaging workflows worldwide. Thus, we stop at 20 instances for retention sets. The reduction in forgetting (Table 1) is pronounced for weighted distillation methods with a ΔAcc (difference in overall accuracy on Task 1 validation set before and after Task 2 training) of *1.92*. In Table 1, methods using both weighted distillation and Mobius augmentation are labeled as '*Our(MT+wKD)*', and as '*Our(MT+KD)*' if using unweighted distillation. '*Our(MT+FT)*' is the method where finetuning is combined with Mobius augmentation. For incremental tasks and in the overall accuracies for all classes after Task 2 training concludes, significant gains are seen with methods using Mobius operations to retained exemplars for initial task classes before interspersing with incremental class batches both for distillation and finetuning approaches. Overall, a clear advantage is seen when using distillation compared to finetuning alone. The best results are seen for combined distillation and Mobius aug-mentation before incremental optimization. This underscores the value of augmentation of old retained samples. This is different from most distillation-based methods that retain some old samples without incremental augmentation for retained samples while data augmentation is used only in initial sessions and the new incremental data.

Baselines from literature are used with ResNet-50 backbones and original incremental training configurations molded to suit the two-task incremental aspect of our study. Table 2 shows the performance of final model on Task 2. While one may conventionally expect to have near equal accuracies across methods, we see slight differences in prediction accuracies within same Task 2 classes. The forward transfer effects of Task 1 training coupled with distillation based regularization is more optimal when using an intermediate Mobius augmentation step on old examples creating a diverse sample set for incremental training. Distilled models perform better on the new task overall due to distillation induced regularizations on parameter shifts unlike the unregularized optimization in finetuning (FT). We also compare (Table 2; *right*) Mobius transformation based incremental augmentation (MT) with other augmentation ideas like cutout [27], Adatransform [28], AutoAugment [17], Population Based Augmentation (PBA) [29], RandAugment [30], rotation with $20°$ steps and translation with a 10px window. This comparison of Δacc values shows Mobius augmentation outperforming several sample-level methods in reducing forgetting by augmenting old task samples prior to incremental training. Future work can focus on studying the efficacy of Mobius transforms on other tasks like segmentation, comparing to generative augmentation methods and exploring Mobius augmentation in combination with concurrent methods in literature.

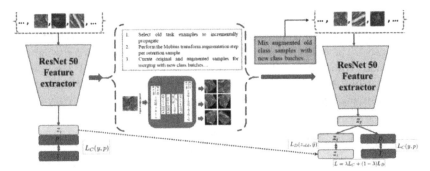

Fig. 3. Illustration of our overall pipeline. The initial training is performed (*left*) followed by a curation of old task exemplars, a Mobius augmentation step and interspersing with new class batches, followed by incremental task training under joint cross-entropy and distillation (*right*).

Table 2. Accuracy (%) for Task 2/Stage 2 classes. Benefits of forward transfer on new class data is evident (*left*); ΔAcc comparison of Mobius transforms and existing methods for augmentation on select old task exemplars over distillation and finetuning.

Stage 2	CS	De	NMG	BG	Avg.(T2)
Our(MT+wKD)	87.42	88.14	85.30	81.54	85.60
Our (MT+KD)	87.05	86.91	84.77	81.28	85.02
Our (KD)	85.21	83.80	82.63	77.25	82.22
Our (MT+FT)	86.30	84.37	85.02	78.33	83.51
Our (FT)	80.12	80.45	82.11	78.62	80.33
LwF.ewc [15]	82.33	84.21	83.70	80.16	82.60
LwM [11]	85.16	85.27	84.09	81.67	84.05
PDR [12]	83.67	82.19	80.56	79.94	81.59

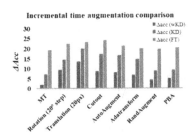

4 Conclusion

We presented a novel method of data augmentation using Mobius transformations. Subsequently, we explore the value of the generalized Mobius transformations for performing augmentation of an exemplar set in a distillation-based incremental learning setting, introducing a new concept of incremental augmentation for retained exemplars. All of this was validated on a real-world dataset of colorectal carcinoma histology images.

References

1. Goodfellow, I.J., Mirza, M., Xiao, D., Courville, A., Bengio, Y. An empirical investigation of catastrophic forgetting in gradient-based neural networks. arXiv:1312.6211 (2013)
2. Ravishankar, H., et al.: Understanding the mechanisms of deep transfer learning for medical images. In: Carneiro, G., et al. (eds.) LABELS/DLMIA -2016. LNCS, vol. 10008, pp. 188–196. Springer, Cham (2016). https://doi.org/10.1007/978-3-319-46976-8_20
3. Patra, A., Chakraborti, T.: Learn more, forget less: cues from human brain. In: Proceedings of the Asian Conference on Computer Vision (2020)

4. Li, Z., Hoiem, D.: Learning without forgetting. IEEE Trans. Pattern Anal. Mach. Intell. **40**(12), 2935–2947 (2017)
5. Kemker, R., Kanan, C.: Fearnet: brain-inspired model for incremental learning. arXiv:1711. 10563 (2017)
6. Patra, A., Cai, Y., Chatelain, P., Sharma, H., Drukker, L., Papageorghiou, A.T., Noble, J.A.: Multimodal continual learning with sonographer eye-tracking in fetal ultrasound. In: International Workshop on Advances in Simplifying Medical Ultrasound, pp. 14–24 (2020)
7. Kirkpatrick, J., et al.: Overcoming catastrophic forgetting in neural networks. In: Proceedings of the National Academy of Sciences, pp. 3521–3526 (2017)
8. Hinton, G., Vinyals, O., Dean, J.: Distilling the knowledge in a neural network. In: NIPS 2014 Deep Learning Workshop (2014)
9. Patra, A., Noble, J.A.: Multi-anatomy localization in fetal echocardiography videos. In: 2019 IEEE 16th International Symposium on Biomedical Imaging (ISBI 2019), pp. 1761–1764 (2019)
10. Rebuffi, S.A., Kolesnikov, A., Sperl, G., Lampert, C.H.: iCaRl: incremental classifier and representation learning. In: Proceedings of the IEEE CVPR, pp. 2001–2010 (2017)
11. Patra, A., et al.: Efficient ultrasound image analysis models with sonographer gaze assisted distillation. In: Shen, D., et al. (eds.) MICCAI 2019. LNCS, vol. 11767, pp. 394–402. Springer, Cham (2019). https://doi.org/10.1007/978-3-030-32251-9_43
12. Hou, S., Pan, X., Loy, C.C., Wang, Z., Lin, D.: Lifelong learning via progressive distillation and retrospection. In: Ferrari, V., Hebert, M., Sminchisescu, C., Weiss, Yair (eds.) ECCV 2018. LNCS, vol. 11207, pp. 452–467. Springer, Cham (2018). https://doi.org/10.1007/978-3-030-01219-9_27
13. Ozdemir, F., Fuernstahl, P., Goksel, O.: Learn the new, keep the old: Extending pretrained models with new anatomy and images. In: Frangi, A., Schnabel, J., Davatzikos, C., Alberola-López, C., Fichtinger, G. (eds.) International Conference on Medical Image Computing and Computer-Assisted Intervention. MICCAI 2018, LNIP, vol. 11073. Springer, Cham (2018). https://doi.org/10.1007/978-3-030-00937-3_42
14. Zhang, J., Wang, Y.: Continually modeling Alzheimer's disease progression via deep multi-order preserving weight consolidation. In: International Conference on Medical Image Computing and Computer-Assisted Intervention. LNIP, vol. 11765, pp. 850–859. Springer, Cham (2019). https://doi.org/10.1007/978-3-030-32245-8_94
15. Kim, H.E., Kim, S., Lee, J.: Keep and learn: continual learning by constraining the latent space for knowledge preservation in neural networks. In: International Conference on Medical Image Computing and Computer-Assisted Intervention, LNCS. Springer, Cham (2018). https://doi.org/10.1007/978-3-030-00928-1_59
16. Patra, A., Noble, J.A.: Hierarchical class incremental learning of anatomical structures in fetal echocardiography videos. IEEE J. Biomed. Health Inf. **24** (2020)
17. Cubuk, E. D., Zoph, B., Mane, D., Vasudevan, V. and Le, Q. V., Autoaugment: Learning augmentation strategies from data. In: Proceedings of the IEEE Conference on Computer ViSion and Pattern Recognition, pp. 113–123 (2019)
18. Ahlfors, L., Möbius Transformations in Several Dimensions. University of Minnesota, 1989
19. Özdemir, N., Iskender, B.B., Özgür, N.Y.: Complex valued neural network with Mö-bius activation function. Commun. Nonlinear Sci. Numer. Simul. **16**(12), 4698–4703 (2011)
20. Zammit-Mangion, A., Ng, T.L.J., Vu, Q., Filippone, M.: Deep compositional spatial models. arXiv preprint arXiv:1906.02840 (2019)
21. Zhou, S., Zhang, J., Jiang, H., Lundh, T., Ng, A.Y.: Data augmentation with Mobius transformations. arXiv preprint arXiv:2002.02917 (2020)
22. Ganea, O., Bécigneul, G., Hofmann, T.: Hyperbolic neural networks. In: Advances in Neural Information Processing Systems, pp. 5345–5355 (2018)

23. Islam, M.A., Anderson, D.T., Pinar, A., Havens, T.C., Scott, G., Keller, J.M.: Enabling explainable fusion in deep learning with fuzzy integral neural networks. IEEE Trans. Fuzzy Syst **28** (2019)

24. Kather, J., Weis, C., Bianconi, F., Melchers, S.M., Schad, L.R., Gaiser, T., Marx, A., Zöllner, F.G.: Multi-class texture analysis in colorectal cancer histology.' In Scientific re-ports (2016)

25. Liouville, J.: Extension au cas des trois dimensions de la question du tracé géographique. Note VI, pp. 609–617 (1850)

26. Kingma, D.P., Adam, J.B.: A method for stochastic optimization. arXiv:1412.6980

27. DeVries, T., Taylor, G.W.: Improved regularization of convolutional neural networks with cutout. arXiv preprint arXiv:1708.04552 (2017)

28. Tang, Z., Peng, X., Li, T., Zhu, Y., Metaxas, D.N.: Adatransform: adaptive data transformation. In: Proceedings of the IEEE International Conference on Computer Vision, pp. 2998–3006 (2019)

29. Ho, D., Liang, E., Stoica, I., Abbeel, P., Chen, X.: Population based augmentation: efficient learning of augmentation policy schedules. arXiv preprint arXiv:1905.05393 (2019)

30. Cubuk, E.D., Zoph, B., Shlens, J., Le, Q.V.: Randaugment: practical data augmentation with no separate search. arXiv preprint arXiv:1909.13719 (2019)

31. Omar, H.A., Patra, A., Domingos, J.S., Leeson, P., Noblel, A.J.: Automated myocardial wall motion classification using handcrafted features vs a deep cnn-based mapping. In: 2018 40th Annual International Conference of the IEEE Engineering in Medicine and Biology Society (EMBC), pp. 3140–3143. IEEE (2018)

32. Lee, C.S., Lee, A.Y.: Clinical applications of continual learning in machine learning. In: The Lancet Digital Health 2.6, pp. 279–e281 (2020)

33. Patra, A., Noble, J.A.: Sequential anatomy localization in fetal echocardiography videos. arXiv preprint arXiv:1810.11868 (2019)

34. Patra, A., Noble, J.A.: Incremental learning of fetal heart anatomies using interpretable saliency maps. In: Zheng, Y., Williams, B., Chen, K. (eds.) Medical Image Understanding and Analysis. MIUA 2019. Communications in Computer and Information Science, CCIS. vol. 1065, pp. 129–141. Springer, Cham (2019). https://doi.org/10.1007/978-3-030-39343-4_11

35. Patra, A., Huang, W., Noble, J.A.: Learning spatio-temporal aggregation for fetal heart analysis in ultrasound video. In: Cardoso, M.J., et al. (eds.) DLMIA/ML-CDS -2017. LNCS, vol. 10553, pp. 276–284. Springer, Cham (2017). https://doi.org/10.1007/978-3-319-67558-9_32

36. Chakraborti, T., Patra, A., Noble, J.A.: Contrastive fairness in machine learning. IEEE Lett. Comput. Soc. **3**(2), 38–41 (2020)

37. Omar, H.A., Domingos, J.S., Patra, A., Leeson, P., Noble, J.A.: Improving visual detection of wall motion abnormality with echocardiographic image enhancing methods. In: 2018 40th Annual International Conference of the IEEE Engineering in Medicine and Biology Society (EMBC), pp. 1128–1131. IEEE (2018)

38. Food, Drug Administration, et al.: Proposed regulatory framework for modifications to artificial intelligence/machine learning (AI/ML)-based software as a medical device (SaMD) - discussion paper (2019)

DIAGNOSE: Avoiding Out-of-Distribution Data Using Submodular Information Measures

Suraj Kothawade[1]($\boxtimes$), Akshit Shrivastava[2], Venkat Iyer[2],
Ganesh Ramakrishnan[2], and Rishabh Iyer[1]

[1] University of Texas at Dallas, Dallas, USA
suraj.kothawade@utdallas.edu
[2] Indian Institute of Technology, Bombay, Mumbai, India

Abstract. Avoiding out-of-distribution (OOD) data is critical for training supervised machine learning models in the medical imaging domain. Furthermore, obtaining labeled medical data is difficult and expensive since it requires expert annotators like doctors, radiologists, *etc.* Active learning (AL) is a well-known method to mitigate labeling costs by selecting the most diverse or uncertain samples. However, current AL methods do not work well in the medical imaging domain with OOD data. We propose DIAGNOSE (avoiDing out-of-dIstribution dAta usinG submodular iNfOrmation meaSurEs), an active learning framework that can jointly model similarity and dissimilarity, which is crucial in mining in-distribution data and avoiding OOD data at the same time. Particularly, we use a small number of data points as exemplars that represent a query set of in-distribution data points and another set of exemplars that represent a private set of OOD data points. We illustrate the generalizability of our framework by evaluating it on a wide variety of real-world OOD scenarios. Our experiments verify the superiority of DIAGNOSE over the state-of-the-art AL methods across multiple domains of medical imaging.

1 Introduction

Deep learning based models are widely used for medical image computing. However, it is critical to mitigate incorrect predictions for avoiding a catastrophe when these models are deployed at a health-care facility. It is known that deep models are data hungry, which leads us to two problems before we can train a high quality model. **Firstly,** procuring medical data is difficult due to limited availability and privacy constraints. **Secondly,** acquiring the *right* labeled data to train a supervised model which has minimum dissimilarity with the test (deployment) distribution can be challenging [19]. This difficulty is particularly because the unlabeled dataset consists of out-of-distribution (OOD) data caused due to changes in data collection procedures, treatment protocols, demographics

Supplementary Information The online version contains supplementary material available at https://doi.org/10.1007/978-3-031-16760-7_14.

of the target population, *etc.* [4]. In this paper, we study active learning (AL) strategies in order to mitigate *both* these problems.

Current AL techniques are designed to acquire data points that are either the most uncertain, or the most diverse, or a mix of both. Unfortunately, this makes the current techniques susceptible to picking data points that are OOD which gives rise to two more problems: **1)** Wastage of expensive labeling resources, since expert annotators need to filter out OOD data points rather than focusing on annotating the in-distribution data points. **2)** Drop in model performance, since OOD data points may sink into the labeled set due to human errors. To tackle the above problems, we propose DIAGNOSE, an active learning framework that uses the submodular information measures [7] as acquisition functions to model similarity with the in-distribution data points and dissimilarity with the OOD data points.

1.1   Problem Statement: OOD Scenarios in Medical Data

We consider a diverse set of *four* OOD scenarios with increasing levels of difficulty. We present three scenarios in Fig. 1. We present the details for each scenario in the context of image classification below:

Scenario A - Unrelated Images: Avoid images that are completely unassociated for the task. For instance, real-world images mixed with skin lesion images (first column in Fig. 1).

Scenario B - Incorrectly Acquired: Avoid images that are either captured incorrectly or post-processed incorrectly. For instance, incorrectly cropped/positioned images, blurred images, or images captured using a different procedure *etc.* (second column in Fig. 1). OOD images of this type are harder to filter than scenario A since there may be some overlap with the semantics of the in-distribution images.

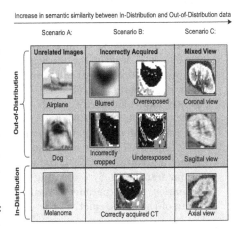

Fig. 1. The out-of-distribution (OOD) images in three scenarios are contrasted with the in-distribution (ID) images. A: Inputs that are unrelated to the task. B: Inputs which are incorrectly acquired. C: Inputs that belong to a different view of anatomy. Note that these scenarios become *increasingly* difficult as we go from A → C since the semantic similarity between OOD and ID increases.

Scenario C - Mixed View: Avoid images captured with a different view of the anatomy than the deployment scenario. For example, images from a coronal or sagittal view are OOD when the deployment is on axial view images (third column in Fig. 1). Note that this scenario is further challenging than scenario B since *only* the viewpoint of the *same* organ makes it ID or OOD.

1.2   Related Work

Uncertainty Based Active Learning. Uncertainty based methods aim to select the most uncertain data points according to a model for labeling. The most common techniques are - 1) ENTROPY [21] selects data points with maximum entropy, and 2) MARGIN [18] selects data points such that the difference between the top two predictions is minimum.

Diversity Based Active Learning. The main drawback of uncertainty based methods is that they lack diversity within the acquired subset. To mitigate this, a number of approaches have proposed to incorporate diversity. The CORESET method [20] minimizes a coreset loss to form coresets that represent the geometric structure of the original dataset. They do so using a greedy k-center clustering. A recent approach called BADGE [2] uses the last linear layer gradients to represent data points and runs K-MEANS++ [1] to obtain centers each having high gradient magnitude. Having representative centers with high gradient magnitude ensures uncertainty and diversity at the same time. However, for batch AL, BADGE models diversity and uncertainty only within the batch and *not* across all batches. Another method, BATCHBALD [11] requires a large number of Monte Carlo dropout samples to obtain reliable mutual information which limits its application to medical domains where data is scarce.

Active Learning for OOD Data. To the best of our knowledge, only a small minority of AL methods tackle OOD data. Our work is closest to and inspired from SIMILAR [12], which uses the SCMI functions (see Sect. 2) for *simulated* OOD scenarios on *toy* datasets with thumbnail images (CIFAR-10 [14]) and black and white digit images (MNIST [15]). In contrast, DIAGNOSE tackles a wide range of real-world OOD scenarios in the medical imaging domain. Another related AL baseline is GLISTER-ACTIVE [10] with an acquisition formulation that maximizes the log-likelihood on a held-out validation set.

1.3   Our Contributions

We summarize our contributions as follows: **1)** We emphasize on *four* diverse OOD data scenarios in the context of medical image classification (see Fig. 1). **2)** Given the limitations of current AL methods on medical datasets, we propose DIAGNOSE, a novel AL framework that can jointly model similarity with the in-distribution (ID) data points and dissimilarity with the OOD data points. We observe that the submodular conditional mutual information functions that jointly model similarity and dissimilarity acquire the most number of ID data points (see Fig. 3, 3, 4). **3)** We demonstrate the effectiveness of our framework for multiple modalities, namely, dermatoscopy, Abdominal CT, and histopathology. Furthermore, we show that DIAGNOSE consistently outperforms the state-of-the-art AL methods on all OOD scenarios. **4)** Through rigorous ablation studies, we compare the effects of maximizing mutual information and conditional gain functions.

2 Preliminaries

Submodular Functions: We let $\mathcal{V}$ denote the *ground-set* of n data points $\mathcal{V} = \{1, 2, 3, ..., n\}$ and a set function $f : 2^{\mathcal{V}} \to \mathbb{R}$. The function f is submodular [5] if it satisfies the diminishing marginal returns, namely $f(j|\mathcal{A}) \geq f(j|\mathcal{B})$ for all $\mathcal{A} \subseteq \mathcal{B} \subseteq \mathcal{V}, j \notin \mathcal{B}$. Different submodular functions model different properties. For *e.g.*, facility location, $f(\mathcal{A}) = \sum_{i \in \mathcal{V}} \max_{j \in \mathcal{A}} S_{ij}$, selects a representative subset and log determinant, $f(\mathcal{A}) = \log \det(S)$ selects a diverse subset [8], where S is a matrix containing pariwise similarity values S_{ij}.

Table 1. Instantiations of Submodular Information Measures (SIM).

(a) SMI and SCG functions.

SMI	$I_f(\mathcal{A}; \mathcal{Q})$
FLMI	$\sum_{i \in \mathcal{U}} \min(\max_{j \in \mathcal{A}} S_{ij}, \max_{j \in \mathcal{Q}} S_{ij})$
LogDetMI	$\log \det(S_{\mathcal{A}}) - \log \det(S_{\mathcal{A}} - S_{\mathcal{A},\mathcal{Q}} S_{\mathcal{Q}}^{-1} S_{\mathcal{A},\mathcal{Q}}^T)$

SCG	$f(\mathcal{A}|\mathcal{P})$
FLCG	$\sum_{i \in \mathcal{U}} \max(\max_{j \in \mathcal{A}} S_{ij} - \max_{j \in \mathcal{P}} S_{ij}, 0)$
LogDetCG	$\log \det(S_{\mathcal{A}} - S_{\mathcal{A},\mathcal{P}} S_{\mathcal{P}}^{-1} S_{\mathcal{A},\mathcal{P}}^T)$

(b) SCMI functions.

SCMI	$I_f(\mathcal{A}; \mathcal{Q}|\mathcal{P})$
FLCMI	$\sum_{i \in \mathcal{U}} \max(\min(\max_{j \in \mathcal{A}} S_{ij}, \max_{j \in \mathcal{Q}} S_{ij})$ $- \max_{j \in \mathcal{P}} S_{ij}, 0)$
LogDetCMI	$\log \dfrac{\det(I - S_{\mathcal{P}}^{-1} S_{\mathcal{P},\mathcal{Q}} S_{\mathcal{Q}}^{-1} S_{\mathcal{P},\mathcal{Q}}^T)}{\det(I - S_{\mathcal{A}\cup\mathcal{P}}^{-1} S_{\mathcal{A}\cup\mathcal{P},\mathcal{Q}} S_{\mathcal{Q}}^{-1} S_{\mathcal{A}\cup\mathcal{P},\mathcal{Q}}^T)}$

Submodular Information Measures (SIM): Given a set of items $\mathcal{A}, \mathcal{Q}, \mathcal{P} \subseteq \mathcal{V}$, the submodular conditional mutual information (SCMI) [7] is defined as $I_f(\mathcal{A}; \mathcal{Q}|\mathcal{P}) = f(\mathcal{A} \cup \mathcal{P}) + f(\mathcal{Q} \cup \mathcal{P}) - f(\mathcal{A} \cup \mathcal{Q} \cup \mathcal{P}) - f(\mathcal{P})$. Intuitively, this jointly measures the similarity between $\mathcal{Q}$ and $\mathcal{A}$ and the dissimilarity between $\mathcal{P}$ and $\mathcal{A}$. We refer to $\mathcal{Q}$ as the query set and $\mathcal{P}$ as the private or conditioning set. Kothawade *et al.* [13] extend the SIM to handle the case when $\mathcal{Q}$ and $\mathcal{P}$ can come from a different set $\mathcal{V}'$ which is disjoint from the ground set $\mathcal{V}$. In the context of medical image classification in scenarios with OOD data, $\mathcal{V}$ is the source set of images, whereas $\mathcal{Q}$ contains data points from the in-distribution classes that we are interested in selecting, and $\mathcal{P}$ contains OOD data points that we want to avoid. As discussed in [12], we can use the SCMI formulation to obtain the submodular mutual information (SMI) by setting $\mathcal{Q} \leftarrow \mathcal{Q}$ and $\mathcal{P} \leftarrow \emptyset$. The SMI is defined as: $I_f(\mathcal{A}; \mathcal{Q}) = f(\mathcal{A}) + f(\mathcal{Q}) - f(\mathcal{A} \cup \mathcal{Q})$. Similarly, the submodular conditional gain (SCG) formulation can be obtained by setting $\mathcal{Q} \leftarrow \emptyset$ and $\mathcal{P} \leftarrow \mathcal{P}$. The SCG is defined as: $f(\mathcal{A}|\mathcal{P}) = f(\mathcal{A} \cup \mathcal{P}) - f(\mathcal{P})$. To find an optimal subset given $\mathcal{Q}, \mathcal{P} \subseteq \mathcal{V}'$, we can define $g_{\mathcal{Q},\mathcal{P}}(\mathcal{A}) = I_f(\mathcal{A}; \mathcal{Q}|\mathcal{P})$, $\mathcal{A} \subseteq \mathcal{V}$ and maximize the same. In Table 1, we present the instantiations of various SCMI, SCG and, SCMI functions with the naming convention abbreviated as the 'function name' + 'CMI/MI/CG'. The submodular functions that we use include 'Facility Location' (FL) and 'Log Determinant' (LogDet) [7,13].

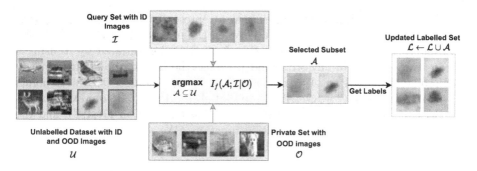

Fig. 2. One round of active learning using DIAGNOSE. We optimize the SCMI function to jointly model similarity with the query set $\mathcal{I}$ with ID images and dissimilarity with the private set $\mathcal{O}$ with OOD images.

3   Leveraging Submodular Information Measures for Multiple Out-of-Distribution Scenarios

In this section, we present DIAGNOSE (see Fig. 2), a one-stop framework that uses the SCMI functions as AL acquisition functions to tackle OOD scenarios (Fig. 1). The main idea in our approach is to exploit the joint modeling of similarity and

---

Algorithm 1. DIAGNOSE: Avoiding OOD using SIM

Require: Initial labeled set: $\mathcal{L}$, Initial set of ID points: $\mathcal{I} \leftarrow \mathcal{L}$, Initial set of OOD points: $\mathcal{O} \leftarrow \emptyset$ large unlabeled dataset: $\mathcal{U}$ with ID and OOD points, Loss function $\mathcal{H}$ for learning model $\mathcal{M}$, batch size: B, number of selection rounds: N

1: **for** selection round $i = 1 : N$ **do**
2:    Train $\mathcal{M}_{\theta_i}$ with loss $\mathcal{H}$ on the current labeled set $\mathcal{L}$.
3:    $\mathcal{G}_{\mathcal{U}} \leftarrow \{\nabla_{\theta_i}\mathcal{H}(x_j, \hat{y_j}, \theta_i), \forall j \in \mathcal{U}\}$ {Compute gradients using hypothesized labels}

4:    $\mathcal{G}_{\mathcal{I}}, \mathcal{G}_{\mathcal{O}} \leftarrow \{\nabla_{\theta_i}\mathcal{H}(x_j, y_j, \theta_i), \forall j \in \mathcal{I}, \mathcal{O}\}$ {Compute gradients using true labels}
5:    $\mathcal{X} \leftarrow$ COSINE_SIMILARITY $(\{\mathcal{G}_{\mathcal{I}} \cup \mathcal{G}_{\mathcal{O}}\}, \mathcal{G}_{\mathcal{U}})$ $\{X \in \mathbb{R}^{|\mathcal{I} \cup \mathcal{O}| \times |\mathcal{U}|}\}$
6:    Instantiate a SCMI function I_f based on $\mathcal{X}$.
7:    $\mathcal{A}_i \leftarrow \text{argmax}_{\mathcal{A} \subseteq \mathcal{U}, |\mathcal{A}| \leq B} I_f(\mathcal{A}; \mathcal{I}|\mathcal{O})$
8:    Get labels $L(\mathcal{A}_i)$ for batch $\mathcal{A}_i$ and $\mathcal{L} \leftarrow \mathcal{L} \cup L(\mathcal{A}_i), \mathcal{U} \leftarrow \mathcal{U} - \mathcal{A}_i$
9:    $\mathcal{I} \leftarrow \mathcal{I} \cup \mathcal{A}_i^{\mathcal{I}}, \mathcal{O} \leftarrow \mathcal{O} \cup \mathcal{A}_i^{\mathcal{O}}$ {Add new ID points to $\mathcal{I}$ and new OOD points to $\mathcal{O}$}
10: **end for**
11: Return trained model $\mathcal{M}$ and parameters θ.

---

dissimilarity in SCMI functions to acquire the desired in-distribution (ID) data and avoid the out-of-distribution (OOD) data. We do so by maintaining two sets, *viz.*: $\mathcal{I}$ containing the ID data points, and $\mathcal{O}$ containing the OOD data points that we have encountered so far in the batch active learning loop. Next, we assign the query set $\mathcal{Q} \leftarrow \mathcal{I}$ and the private set $\mathcal{P} \leftarrow \mathcal{O}$ in the SCMI formulation (see Sect. 2). Using last layer gradients as a representation for each data point, we compute the similarity matrix $\mathcal{X}$ between the unlabeled set $\mathcal{U}$ and $\{\mathcal{I} \cup \mathcal{O}\}$. We then optimize the resulting function $I_f(\mathcal{A}; \mathcal{I}|\mathcal{O})$ instantiated by $\mathcal{X}$ using a greedy strategy [17]. In any AL round i, we use the ID data points from newly acquired labeled set $A_i^{\mathcal{I}} \subseteq A_i$ to augment $\mathcal{I} \leftarrow \mathcal{I} \cup A_i^{\mathcal{I}}$, and new OOD data points $A_i^{\mathcal{O}} \subseteq A_i$ to augment $\mathcal{O} \leftarrow \mathcal{O} \cup A_i^{\mathcal{O}}$. Note that $\mathcal{A}_i \leftarrow \mathcal{A}_i^{\mathcal{I}} \cup \mathcal{A}_i^{\mathcal{O}}$. In our experiments (see Sect. 4), we also use the corresponding SMI formulation $I_f(\mathcal{A}; \mathcal{I})$, and the SCG formulation $f(\mathcal{A}|\mathcal{O})$ as acquisition functions. We summarize DIAGNOSE in Algorithm 1 and discuss its scalability aspects in Appendix C.

4   Experimental Results

In this section, we evaluate the effectiveness of DIAGNOSE on three diverse medical imaging OOD data scenarios (A - C) with increasing levels of difficulty. We discuss these scenarios in detail in Sect. 1.1. For evaluation, we compare the test accuracy and the number of in-distribution data points selected by the SCMI functions and existing state-of-the-art baselines in each round of active learning (see Fig. 3). We conduct ablation studies for each OOD data scenario to study the individual effect of only using a query set via the SMI functions and only using the private set via the SCG functions. We present the ablation study for one of the scenarios in (see Fig. 4). In a nutshell, our experiments show that jointly modeling of similarity and dissimilarity using the SCMI functions not only outperforms the existing AL baselines but also the SMI and SCG functions across multiple OOD scenarios in medical data.

Baselines in All Scenarios: We compare the performance on DIAGNOSE against a variety of state-of-the-art uncertainty, diversity and targeted selection methods. The uncertainty based methods include ENTROPY and MARGIN. The diversity based methods include CORESET and BADGE. For GLISTER, we maximize the log-likelihood with the set of ID points $\mathcal{I}$, for a fair comparison with the SCMI based acquisition functions. We discuss the details of all baselines in Sect. 1.2. Lastly, we compare against random sampling (RANDOM).

Experimental Setup: We use the same training procedure and hyperparameters for all AL methods to ensure a fair comparison. For all experiments, we use a ResNet-18 [6] model instantiated using $(n + 1)$ classes, where n is the number of ID classes and all other classes are grouped as a single OOD class. We train this model using an SGD optimizer with an initial learning rate of 0.001, the momentum of 0.9, and a weight decay of 5e-4. For each AL round, the weights are reinitialized using Xavier initialization and the model is trained till 99% training accuracy. The learning rate is decayed using cosine annealing [16] in every epoch. We run each experiment 5× on a V100 GPU and provide the error bars (std deviation). We discuss dataset splits for each of our experiments below and provide more details in Appendix B.3.

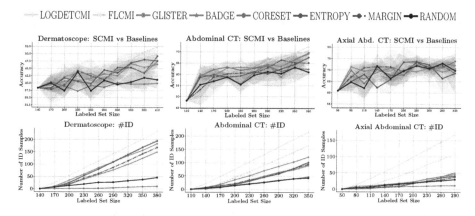

Fig. 3. Active learning with medical OOD scenarios. **Top row:** SCMI vs Baselines. **Bottom row:** Number of ID points selected by each method. **First column - Scenario A:** We observe that facility location functions that balance representation and query-relevance are ideal for scenario A. Particularly, FLCMI consistently outperforms baselines by ≈5%–7%. **Second column - Scenario B:** The SCMI functions (LOGDETCMI, FLCMI) outperform baselines by ≈4%–5%. **Third column - Scenario C:** We observe that LOGDETCMI outperforms the baselines by ≈2%–4%. LOGDETCMI selects the most number of ID points in all scenarios.

4.1   Scenario A - Unrelated Images

Dataset: In this scenario, we apply DIAGNOSE to avoid data points that are unrelated to the medical imaging domain. We use the Derma-MNIST (dermatoscopy of pigmented skin lesions) [9,22] skin lesion image classification dataset as in-distribution (ID) data and CIFAR-10 [14] as OOD data. We create an initial labeled set $|\mathcal{L}| = 140$ using only ID data and an unlabeled set $\mathcal{U}$ containing both ID data ($|\mathcal{I}_\mathcal{U}| = 1061$) and OOD data ($|\mathcal{O}_\mathcal{U}| = 5000$) with AL batch size $B = 30$.

Results: We present results for the unrelated images OOD scenario in Fig. 3 (first column) and observe that the FLCMI consistently outperforms both uncertainty (ENTROPY, MARGIN) and diversity based (BADGE, CORESET) methods by ≈5%–7% on overall accuracy. Moreover, we observe that FLCMI outperforms LOGDETCMI which suggests that using a submodular function like facility location that models *representation* is useful for scenarios where the OOD data is obviously unrelated to the ID data. This also entails that a representative subset is imperative for obtaining a high accuracy on dermatoscopy modality datasets.

4.2   Scenario B - Incorrectly Acquired Images

Dataset: We apply DIAGNOSE to avoid CT scan images that are incorrectly prepared. Examples include images that are blurry, overexposed, underexposed or incorrectly cropped. We use OrganA-MNIST (Abdominal CT scans in an

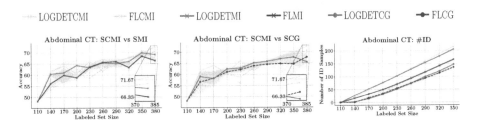

Fig. 4. Ablation studies comparing the performance of SCMI functions with SMI functions (**left** plot) and SCG functions (**right** plot) for scenario B. We see that SCMI functions outperform their SMI and SCG counterparts, particularly in later rounds of AL.

Axial plane) [9,22] organ image classification dataset as ID data. Following [3], we obtain OOD data by simulating different pre- and post-processing errors on CT scans such as inappropriate brightness, incorrect padding, cropping, and blurry images. We create the initial labeled set $|\mathcal{L}| = 110$ using only ID data and an unlabeled set $\mathcal{U}$ containing both ID data ($|\mathcal{I_U}| = 1650$) and OOD data ($|\mathcal{O_U}| = 8000$) with AL batch size $B = 30$.

Results: We present results for the incorrectly prepared medical images OOD scenario in Fig. 3 (second column). We observe that the SCMI functions (LOGDETCMI, FLCMI) outperform baselines by ≈4%–5%. The log determinant based functions that balance between *diversity* and *query-relevance* (LOGDETCMI, LOGDETMI) select the most number of ID data points and perform well in this scenario.

Ablation Study: Interestingly, the conditional gain functions (FLCG, LOGDETCG) do not select as many ID points but still perform at par with the SMI functions (see Fig. 4). This suggests the need for conditioning in difficult OOD scenarios where the ID and OOD points have a high semantic similarity. Hence, jointly maximizing the conditional gain and mutual information is imperative, as done in the SCMI functions.

4.3   Scenario C - Mixed View Images

Dataset: We apply DIAGNOSE to avoid Abdominal CT scan images that are captured from a different view of the anatomy. We use OrganA-MNIST (axial plane) [9,22] organ image classification dataset as ID data, and a combination of OrganC-MNIST (coronal plane) [9,22] and OrganS-MNIST (sagittal plane) [9, 22] as OOD data. We create the initial labeled set $|\mathcal{L}| = 50$ using only ID data an unlabeled set $\mathcal{U}$ containing both ID data ($|\mathcal{I_U}| = 750$) and OOD data ($|\mathcal{O_U}| = 8000$) with AL batch size $B = 30$.

Results: We present results for the mixed view medical images OOD scenario in Fig. 3 (third column). We observe that LOGDETCMI outperforms the baselines by ≈2%–4%. We observe from scenarios B and C that the log determinant functions select significantly more ID data points from the unlabeled set and outperform other methods when the modality is CT. This entails that selecting a diverse subset is one of the key factors for CT modality data.

5 Conclusion

We demonstrate the effectiveness of DIAGNOSE across a diverse set of out-of-distribution (OOD) scenarios in medical data. We observe that SCMI functions outperform other baselines along with SMI and SCG functions. Which submodular function works best depends on the modality of medical data and the type of OOD scenario. Importantly, we note that jointly maximizing both components, mutual information and conditional gain, works the best for scenarios with OOD data. Lastly, as expected, we observe a drop in accuracy gain as the difficulty of OOD scenarios increases.

References

1. Arthur, D., Vassilvitskii, S.: k-means++: the advantages of careful seeding. In: SODA 2007: Proceedings of the Eighteenth Annual ACM-SIAM Symposium on Discrete Algorithms, pp. 1027–1035. Society for Industrial and Applied Mathematics, Philadelphia (2007)
2. Ash, J.T., Zhang, C., Krishnamurthy, A., Langford, J., Agarwal, A.: Deep batch active learning by diverse, uncertain gradient lower bounds. In: ICLR (2020)
3. Cao, T., Huang, C.W., Hui, D.Y.T., Cohen, J.P.: A benchmark of medical out of distribution detection. arXiv preprint arXiv:2007.04250 (2020)
4. Finlayson, S.G., et al.: The clinician and dataset shift in artificial intelligence. N. Engl. J. Med. **385**(3), 283 (2021)
5. Fujishige, S.: Submodular Functions and Optimization. Elsevier, Amsterdam (2005)
6. He, K., Zhang, X., Ren, S., Sun, J.: Deep residual learning for image recognition. In: Proceedings of the IEEE Conference on Computer Vision and Pattern Recognition, pp. 770–778 (2016)
7. Iyer, R., Khargoankar, N., Bilmes, J., Asnani, H.: Submodular combinatorial information measures with applications in machine learning. arXiv preprint arXiv:2006.15412 (2020)
8. Iyer, R.K.: Submodular optimization and machine learning: theoretical results, unifying and scalable algorithms, and applications. Ph.D. thesis (2015)
9. Kermany, D.S., et al.: Identifying medical diagnoses and treatable diseases by image-based deep learning. Cell **172**(5), 1122–1131 (2018)
10. Killamsetty, K., Sivasubramanian, D., Ramakrishnan, G., Iyer, R.: Glister: generalization based data subset selection for efficient and robust learning. In: AAAI (2021)
11. Kirsch, A., Van Amersfoort, J., Gal, Y.: Batchbald: efficient and diverse batch acquisition for deep bayesian active learning. arXiv preprint arXiv:1906.08158 (2019)
12. Kothawade, S., Beck, N., Killamsetty, K., Iyer, R.: Similar: submodular information measures based active learning in realistic scenarios. In: Advances in Neural Information Processing Systems, vol. 34 (2021)

13. Kothawade, S., Kaushal, V., Ramakrishnan, G., Bilmes, J., Iyer, R.: Prism: a rich class of parameterized submodular information measures for guided subset selection. arXiv preprint arXiv:2103.00128 (2021)
14. Krizhevsky, A., Hinton, G., et al.: Learning multiple layers of features from tiny images (2009)
15. LeCun, Y., Cortes, C., Burges, C.: MNIST handwritten digit database. AT&T Labs (2010)
16. Loshchilov, I., Hutter, F.: SGDR: stochastic gradient descent with warm restarts. arXiv preprint arXiv:1608.03983 (2016)
17. Mirzasoleiman, B., Badanidiyuru, A., Karbasi, A., Vondrák, J., Krause, A.: Lazier than lazy greedy. In: Proceedings of the AAAI Conference on Artificial Intelligence, vol. 29 (2015)
18. Roth, D., Small, K.: Margin-based active learning for structured output spaces. In: Fürnkranz, J., Scheffer, T., Spiliopoulou, M. (eds.) ECML 2006. LNCS (LNAI), vol. 4212, pp. 413–424. Springer, Heidelberg (2006). https://doi.org/10.1007/11871842_40
19. Saria, S., Subbaswamy, A.: Tutorial: safe and reliable machine learning. arXiv preprint arXiv:1904.07204 (2019)
20. Sener, O., Savarese, S.: Active learning for convolutional neural networks: a core-set approach. In: International Conference on Learning Representations (2018)
21. Settles, B.: Active learning literature survey. Technical report, University of Wisconsin-Madison Department of Computer Sciences (2009)
22. Yang, J., et al.: MedMNIST v2: a large-scale lightweight benchmark for 2D and 3D biomedical image classification. arXiv preprint arXiv:2008 (2021)

Transfer Representation Learning

Auto-segmentation of Hip Joints Using MultiPlanar UNet with Transfer Learning

Peidi Xu[1](✉), Faezeh Moshfeghifar[1], Torkan Gholamalizadeh[1,3],
Michael Bachmann Nielsen[2], Kenny Erleben[1], and Sune Darkner[1]

[1] Department of Computer Science, University of Copenhagen,
Copenhagen, Denmark
peidi@di.ku.dk
[2] Department of Diagnostic Radiology, Copenhagen University Hospital,
Copenhagen, Denmark
[3] 3Shape A/S, Copenhagen, Denmark

Abstract. Accurate geometry representation is essential in developing finite element models. Although generally good, deep-learning segmentation approaches with only few data have difficulties in accurately segmenting fine features, e.g., gaps and thin structures. Subsequently, segmented geometries need labor-intensive manual modifications to reach a quality where they can be used for simulation purposes. We propose a strategy that uses transfer learning to reuse datasets with poor segmentation combined with an interactive learning step where fine-tuning of the data results in anatomically accurate segmentations suitable for simulations. We use a modified MultiPlanar UNet that is pre-trained using inferior hip joint segmentation combined with a dedicated loss function to learn the gap regions and post-processing to correct tiny inaccuracies on symmetric classes due to rotational invariance. We demonstrate this robust yet conceptually simple approach applied with clinically validated results on publicly available computed tomography scans of hip joints. Code and resulting 3D models are available at: https://github.com/MICCAI2022-155/AuToSeg.

Keywords: Segmentation · Finite element modeling · Transfer learning

1 Introduction

Precise segmentation of medical images such as computed tomography (CT) scans, is widely used for generating finite element (FE) models of humans for patient-specific implants [2]. A requirement in generating FE models is a proper geometrical representation of the anatomical structures [9]. In our case, an *accurate* segmentation of the hip joint (HJ) should essentially detail the shape and boundaries of the femur and hip bones and identify the inter-bone cavities. The segmented geometries should be closed, non-intersecting, and without spikes. As manual segmentation is labor-intensive and time-consuming [9], automated segmentation tools are usually necessary to generate accurate FE models.

G. Zamzmi et al. (Eds.): MILLanD 2022, LNCS 13559, pp. 153–162, 2022.
https://doi.org/10.1007/978-3-031-16760-7_15

Convolutional Neural Networks with encoder-decoder structures are widely used for auto semantic segmentation, among which the most successful one is the UNet structure [10]. The architecture uses skip connection on high-resolution feature maps in the encoding path to include more fine-grained information. Although more recent models are proposed on segmenting natural images, e.g., DeepLabV3+, UNet still provides some of the best segmentation results in medical images [1]. Therefore, the variation of UNet, e.g., 3D UNet, is a straightforward way to segment 3D medical data like CT scans and has shown its state-of-the-art performance [3]. Applying 3D convolutions directly to large 3D images may overflow memory. Therefore, 3D models are usually trained on small patches, which results in a limited field of view and subsequent loss of global information. As an alternative with far less memory usage, the MultiPlanar UNet (MPUNet) model was proposed by Perslev et al. [8] which uses a 2D UNet to learn representative semantic information.

Most studies on auto-segmentation of the HJs focus on designing more powerful neural networks that separate anatomical structures with little manual intervention [12,13]. These studies focus primarily on the bone morphology and not on the inter-bone gaps. The consequence is that although they reach fairly high Dice scores, the segmentation results are anatomically inaccurate and are unsuitable for generating HJ 3D models. This limits the usability of the existing deep learning models for FE simulations [7].

We require the deep learning models to provide anatomically correct segmentation of the bones and the existing gap in the HJ as shown in Fig. 1 [12,13]. Due to the limited number of accurate training data, we propose a deep learning-based strategy for enhancing publicly available poorly annotated scans using only a few accurately segmented data to learn an accurate model and in our case the gap regions in HJ. Besides using the idea of MultiPlanar, our backbone model is a standard UNet with batch normalization. Therefore, the proposed pipeline is both parameter and memory efficient.

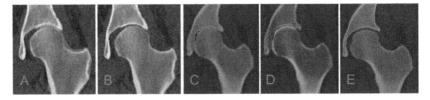

Fig. 1. Illustration of gap generation: inferior ground truth of a training image from public dataset (A) and results by fine-tuned model (B). Results on a test image with model trained only on public dataset (C) with erroneous prediction detection (D) and fine-tuned (E)

To enforce the cartilage gap with few annotated data, we apply MPUNet with a dedicated loss function penetrated more on the gap regions combined with transfer learning and a post-processing step. Our framework uses an interactive learning pipeline involving pre-training MPUNet on a public dataset with inferior HJ segmentation to learn general semantic features of the bones [5]. The model is then fine-tuned using a few highly accurate segmentation to learn the correct labeling of the gaps. We show that our proposed approach allows the model to learn the gap and generate anatomically accurate segmentation, using the pre-trained model and only four accurate segmentations for fine-tuning. Our work is validated on a set of HJs from which we construct FE models and report the Dice with the manually corrected segments used for biomechanical models.

2   Method

Our strategy for accurate HJ segmentation with very few accurate training images relies on the following: (i) we use the idea of MPUNet that segments 3D medical images using 2D models while preserving as much spatial information as possible by segmenting different views of the data. (ii) we use a relatively simple yet powerful backbone model for performing the segmentation to avoid overfitting and memory issues. (iii) we pre-train the model using publicly available datasets with poor labels, which are then fine-tuned with a very small set of accurately annotated data. (iv) we use a dedicated weighted distance loss to enforce the gap between the bones. (v) we introduce a post-processing step that solves the internal problem of MPUNet on images with symmetric features.

Model: As a baseline model, we use the MPUNet proposed by Perslev et al. [8] to segment the 3D HJs using 2D UNet while preserving as much 3D information as possible by generating views from different perspectives. During training, the model $f(x; \theta)$ takes a set 2D image slices of size $w \times h$, from different views, and outputs a probabilistic segmentation map $P \in R^{w \times h \times K}$ for K classes for each slice. Standard pixel-wise loss function is then applied for back-propagation. Our experiment uses a standard categorical cross-entropy loss augmented by the weighted distance map. We found no improvement using a class-wise weighted cross-entropy loss or the dice loss. In the inference phase, we run 3D reconstruction in each view separately over the segmentation results on all the parallel slices to get the volume back. This results in a volume probability map of size $m \times w \times h \times K$ for each view. Unlike original MPUNet [8] which suggests training another fusion model using validation data, we simply sum over the results (P) from different views followed by an argmax over last dimension to get the final label map. This strategy achieves good results on the validation data.

Transfer Learning: The accurate segmentation and fast convergence rely partially on pre-training the model using publicly available datasets with poor labeling, which is subsequently fine-tuned with a small set of accurate data. We detail two modifications that differ from standard transfer learning settings. First, we also transfer the weight in the last softmax layer for a much faster convergence because we work on exactly the same classes as before. Then, instead of freezing encoder and only fine-tuning decoder, it is necessary to explicitly learn encoder to detect the gap, as the gap must be encoded correctly first.

Weighted Distance Map: For the model to be fined-tuned to learn the gap between the bones, we enforce a voxel-wise weight-map $w(x)$ to the loss function based on the distances to the border of the foreground classes. This strategy was initially suggested in the original UNet paper, which we employ in a modified version for 3D data [8,10]. We define $w(x)$ as follows,

$$w(x) = w_c(x) + w_0 \cdot e^{-\frac{(d_1(x)+d_2(x))^2}{2\sigma^2}} \tag{1}$$

where d_1 and d_2 denotes the distance to the border of the nearest foreground class and the second nearest foreground class respectively. We follow original UNet paper and set $w_0 = 10$ and $\sigma = 5$. $w_c : \Omega \to R$ is used to balance the class frequencies, which we do not enforce, thus we set $w_c = 1$ for every c.

During fine-tuning, the corresponding slice of the 3D weight map is sampled together with the images and labels. We apply an element-wise multiplication of the weight map with the cross-entropy loss of predictions and labels on each pixel before reduction. Figure 2 (left & middle) shows an example training slice. Note that we do not plot the prediction since it consists of multi-class probabilities.

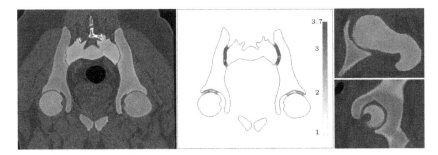

Fig. 2. (left) A sample training slice of true labels overlaid on top of raw image. (middle) Corresponding weight map computed with Eq. (1) overlaid on top of label boundaries. (right) Results of training with weight map calculated over eroded labels(orange contour), which shows a smoother and more complete contour near the boundaries than the results trained without erosion (blue contour). (Color figure online)

We also notice that the model is prone to overfitting to the gap, producing a broader gap than usual if we assign higher weights only to the gap regions in Eq. (1). Instead, we would like to assign more weight to the boundaries around the gap to avoid false negatives. This is accomplished by applying a mathematical erosion to the labels over a ball with a radius of 3 voxels before calculating the weight map, as demonstrated in Fig. 2 (middle). To compensate for the increased value of $d_1 + d_2$ introduced by erosion, we double w_0 to 20.

Sampling Strategies: Sampling and interpolation are necessary to retrieve corresponding 2D slices from a 3D medical image viewed from a random orientation other than the standard RAS axes. We follow the idea in [8] by sampling pixel with dimension $d \in \mathcal{Z}^+$ on isotropic grids within a sphere of diameter $m \in \mathcal{R}^+$ centered at the origin of the scanner coordinate system in the physical scanner space. We differ in that these two numbers are chosen as the 75 percentile across all axes and images during training but as maximum value during inference. This ensures both efficient training and complete predictions near the boundaries.

Post-processing: Although MPUNet is both parameter and memory efficient, the model is trained on 2D slices with a possibly limited field of view near the boundaries. Furthermore, it is trained to segment the input viewed from different perspectives by sampling from planes of various orientations. This introduces some rotational invariance but makes it hard to distinguish between symmetric classes with very similar semantic features. For example, it is hard to be consistent with the left and right femurs when viewing the input from various perspectives. Therefore, some part of the left femur near the boundaries is misclassified as the right femur respectively, and vice versa, as shown in Fig. 3.

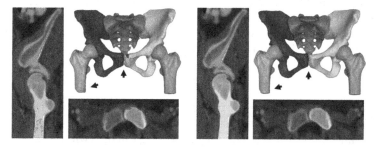

Fig. 3. Segmentation (left) with post-processing (right) where falsely predicted symmetric groups are recovered.

In order to solve this problem automatically, we propose a symmetric connected component decomposition. We only keep the largest connected component for each symmetric class pair while assigning the corresponding symmetric class value to all the other components. By doing this instead of just removing small components, those parts predicted as the left femur on the right femur are mapped correctly to the right femur, and vice versa. We then apply a standard connected component decomposition while keeping only the largest connected component for each foreground class to remove floating points (false positives).

We acknowledge that our post-processing is highly task-specific but could also be generalized to other segmentation tasks with symmetric classes that share similar semantic features and are disconnected from each other.

3   Data and Experiments

We use 35 CT scans from The Cancer Imaging Archive and crop the region of interest on the images to roughly cover the area around the HJs, including the sacrum, both hip bones, and both proximal femurs [4]. Each scan comprises $(415 \pm 47) \times (244 \pm 30) \times (266 \pm 29)$ voxels, with a voxel size of $(0.78 \pm 0.11) \times (0.77 \pm 0.1) \times (0.96 \pm 0.17)$ mm^3. For the pre-training step, we use 10 scans and their associated inferior segmentations from a publicly available dataset of *segmented CT pelvis scans with annotated anatomical landmarks* (CTPEL) [5,12]. We only use two scans with accurate segmentation to fine-tune the model in the first place, In the next step, two other unseen scans are used to get the segmentation results of the model. Then, we manually correct these two results and fine-tune the model again. The second fine-tuning process could be re-iterated, but four images is sufficient to obtain accurate results. We evaluate the segmentation results of our approach with minimal required fine-tuning data. A clinical expert evaluated the segmentation results of the 21 test cases.

Interactive Learning Setup: Using prior anatomical knowledge that each class should be disconnected by at least a certain distance, contradicting cases in the model output indicate false positives (collisions) on at least one of the classes. We thus apply another Euclidean transform over the output segmentation P such that each point in a predicted foreground class is mapped to the nearest distance to other foreground classes. We can then find those collision points set E by applying a threshold ϵ to the distance map, as shown in Fig. 1(D).

$$E = \{x | P(x) \neq 0 \wedge d(x) \leq \epsilon\} \tag{2}$$

Since E only roughly captures the collision points, directly setting them to background will not be accurate and may introduce false negatives. However, the size of it ($|E|$) can be used as a metric for model performance without ground truth to decide when to terminate the interactive learning process. In our experiment where $\epsilon = 2$, the model without fine-tuning gives $|E| \approx 24803$, while fine-tuning with two and another two accurate data reduces $|E|$ to 1000 and 200 respectively.

Pre-processing: We pre-process the data by first filtering out all negative values in the volume because both bones and cartilages should have positive Hounsfield unit values. We then apply a standardization based on the equation $X_{\text{scale}} = (x_i - x_{\text{mean}})/(x_{75} - x_{25})$, where x_{25} and x_{75} are the 1st and 3rd quartiles respectively. This removes the median and scales the intensity based on quartiles and is more robust to outliers. No other pre-processing is applied to avoid any manual errors that can easily propagate in a neural network.

Experimental Setup: The network is trained on NVIDIA GeForce RTX 3090 with a batch size of 10 using the Adam optimizer for 40 epochs with a learning rate of 1e–5 and reduced by 10% for every two consecutive epochs without performance improvements. We apply early stopping if the performance of five consecutive epochs does not improve. Pre-training takes approximately one day, while fine-tuning takes about six hours to reach convergence.

Augmentations: We follow MPUNet by applying Random Elastic Deformations to generate images with deformed strength and smoothness [11] and assign a weight value of 1/3 for the deformed samples during training [8].

4   Results

To have suitable geometries for FE models, the auto-segmentation framework must separate bones and generate accurate results near the boundaries, which is essential for generating cartilage layers for HJ. Therefore, any standard evaluation metric such as the Dice score could be misleading. Hence, our results, including the bone outlines and the existing gap in the joints, are first validated by a senior consultant radiologist as our clinical expert.

The clinical expert initially scrolls through all the segmented slices to verify the bone contours and the gaps between the hip and femoral bones. Then, he verifies the anatomical shape and smoothness of the reconstructed 3D model. This procedure justifies our method in obtaining precise HJ geometries.

Figure 3 illustrates the results of the fined-tuned model on the test set and demonstrates the effect of post-processing, where it shows that the misclassified regions in symmetric classes are successfully recovered by the post-processing step. With the distance weight applied to loss, the model can detail the gap accurately. The final result is accurate and requires little or no human intervention for subsequent simulation experiments, e.g., FE analysis. Results in 3D are available at GitHub Repo. As an example, we have generated the cartilage geometry on the segmented HJ with a method proposed by [6] to analyze the stress distributions as shown in Fig. 4. The results show a smooth stress pattern indicating that our method's output is suitable for use in FE simulations.

Table 1. Test results with various design choices

	Dice ↑	GapDice ↑	HD (#$voxels$) ↓
Ours	**98.63 ± 0.56**	**96.47 ± 1.60**	**3.67 ± 1.13**
NoPretrain	97.82 ± 0.59	95.13 ± 1.42	5.26 ± 2.10
NoWeight	98.12 ± 0.47	94.35 ± 2.19	4.58 ± 1.50
3DUNet	93.36 ± 1.84	87.48 ± 3.01	7.02 ± 1.09
Ours(2)	**97.59 ± 0.74**	**95.19 ± 1.14**	**5.18 ± 2.08**
NoPretrain(2)	90.80 ± 9.29	91.13 ± 8.53	11.20 ± 7.19
NoWeight(2)	96.28 ± 2.91	93.91 ± 1.74	6.30 ± 2.95

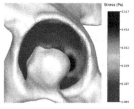

Fig. 4. Smooth von Mises stress pattern

4.1   Numerical Validation and Ablation Study

Although numerical results could be misleading regarding the final FE simulations, we include them as a validation and ablation study of our several design choices. Table 1 shows the numerical validations on the test set, including nine images with manually corrected ground truth segmentations. We test the performance by varying one of the design choices each time while keeping the others fixed. (i) The strategy mentioned in Sect. 2 (ours), (ii) Training without using ten inaccurate public data (NoPretrain), (iii) Training without enforcing distance weight map (NoWeight), (iv) Using 3D UNet as the backbone (3DUNet). We also test and report the performance in the first stage when fine-tuned with only two manually corrected data except for (iv) because of its poor performance.

Besides the standard Dice score, we are especially interested in the surface and gap regions. Therefore, two more evaluation metrics are introduced. We use Hausdorff distance (HD) as surface measurement by computing the largest distance between the result and the nearest point on the ground truth.

$$\text{HD}(P, Y) = \max(\max_{p \in P} \min_{y \in Y} \|p - y\|_2, \ \max_{y \in Y} \min_{p \in P} \|p - y\|_2) \quad (3)$$

We also propose a GapDice in Eq. (4) to measure the average Dice score between the segmentation result and the ground truth only around the gap regions. Given the segmentation results P and ground truth segmentation Y, we compute the Euclidean distance transformation map Y_d of Y, corresponding to the $d_1 + d_2$ term from Eq. (1). The gap region G is defined as the locations where $Y_d < \epsilon$. Dice score between P and Y is calculated in the standard way inside G. Here we choose $\epsilon = 10$ as we found it to be a good indicator of both the gap and boundary regions. Figure 2 (middle) shows the region computed by eroded labels, which is also an indication of G. Please refer to GitHub Repo for generated G.

$$\text{GapDice}(P, Y) = \frac{2 * |P \cap Y \cap G|}{|P \cap G| + |Y \cap G|} \quad (4)$$

The results show that MPUNet (all the first three models) works significantly better than 3D UNet in a data scarcity setting. Our pipeline outperforms in all three metrics. Especially, although the difference of the Dice score is not significant in our fine tuned model with four manually corrected data, pretraining on inaccurate data and enforcing the weight map shows a significantly better GapDice score and HD, which is vital for further simulation. The benefit of pretraining is much clearer in the first round when fine-tuned with only two accurate data, which is crucial to have minimal manual work to be fine tuned again. We acknowledge that the ground truth for test data is manually modified over the results from our pipeline, giving a bias when comparing multiple models, but the general goal is to show that our pipeline suits well for further simulation.

5   Conclusion

We presented an auto-segmentation framework for accurate segmentation from CT scans considering the bone boundaries and inter-bone cavities. Our framework uses a modified MPUNet pre-trained on a public dataset with coarse segmentation and fine-tunes with very few data with accurate segmentation in a transfer and interactive learning setup. We demonstrate that our simple yet robust model can detail crucial features such as the gap where the cartilage resides.

This work is tested out on HJ CT scans and provides anatomically accurate segmentation, which has both been verified by a clinical expert and shown superior numerical results, reaching an overall Dice score above 98% and above 96% around gap regions. Our method can be used to enhance anatomically incorrect and poorly annotated datasets with a few accurately annotated scans. The FE analysis shows that the generated models produce smooth stress patterns without any geometry-related artifacts. Thereby, the segmentation result of this work can be used for generating FE models with little or no manual modifications.

Acknowledgements. This project has received funding from the European Union's Horizon 2020 research and innovation programme under the Marie Sklodowska-Curie grant agreement No. 764644. This paper only contains the author's views, and the Research Executive Agency and the Commission are not responsible for any use that may be made of the information it contains.

References

1. Chen, L.-C., Zhu, Y., Papandreou, G., Schroff, F., Adam, H.: Encoder-decoder with atrous separable convolution for semantic image segmentation. In: Proceedings of the European Conference on Computer vision (ECCV), pp. 801–818 (2018)
2. Xiaojun Chen, L.X., Wang, Y., Hao, Y., Wang, L.: Image-guided installation of 3d-printed patient-specific implant and its application in pelvic tumor resection and reconstruction surgery. Comput. Methods Prog. Biomed. **125**, 66–78 (2016)
3. Çiçek, Ö., Abdulkadir, A., Lienkamp, S.S., Brox, T., Ronneberger, O.: 3D U-Net: learning dense volumetric segmentation from sparse annotation. In: Ourselin, S., Joskowicz, L., Sabuncu, M.R., Unal, G., Wells, W. (eds.) MICCAI 2016. LNCS, vol. 9901, pp. 424–432. Springer, Cham (2016). https://doi.org/10.1007/978-3-319-46723-8_49
4. Clark, K., et al.: The cancer imaging archive (TCIA): maintaining and operating a public information repository. J. Digit. Imag. **26**(6), 1045–1057 (2013)
5. Connolly, B., Wang, C.: Segmented CT pelvis scans with annotated anatomical landmarks (2019)
6. Moshfeghifar, F., Kragballe Nielsen, M., Tascón-Vidarte, J.D., Darkner, S., Erleben, K.: A direct geometry processing cartilage generation method using segmented bone models from datasets with poor cartilage visibility (2022)
7. Nishii, T., Sugano, N., Sato, Y., Tanaka, H., Miki, H., Yoshikawa, H.: Three-dimensional distribution of acetabular cartilage thickness in patients with hip dysplasia: a fully automated computational analysis of MR imaging. Osteoar. Cartil. **12**(8), 650–657 (2004)
8. Perslev, M., Dam, E.B., Pai, A., Igel, C.: One network to segment them all: a general, lightweight system for accurate 3D medical image segmentation. In: Shen, D., et al. (eds.) MICCAI 2019. LNCS, vol. 11765, pp. 30–38. Springer, Cham (2019). https://doi.org/10.1007/978-3-030-32245-8_4
9. Poelert, S., Valstar, E., Weinans, H., Zadpoor, A.M.: Patient-specific finite element modeling of bones. Proc. Inst. Mech. Eng. Part H. J. Eng. Med. **227**(4), 464–478 (2013)
10. Ronneberger, O., Fischer, P., Brox, T.: U-Net: convolutional networks for biomedical image segmentation. In: Navab, N., Hornegger, J., Wells, W.M., Frangi, A.F. (eds.) MICCAI 2015. LNCS, vol. 9351, pp. 234–241. Springer, Cham (2015). https://doi.org/10.1007/978-3-319-24574-4_28
11. Simard, P.Y., Steinkraus, D., Platt, J.C., et al.: Best practices for convolutional neural networks applied to visual document analysis. In: ICDAR, vol. 3 (2003)

12. Wang, C., Connolly, B., de Oliveira Lopes, P.F., Frangi, A.F., Smedby, Ö.: Pelvis segmentation using multi-pass U-Net and iterative shape estimation. In: Vrtovec, T., Yao, J., Zheng, G., Pozo, J.M. (eds.) MSKI 2018. LNCS, vol. 11404, pp. 49–57. Springer, Cham (2019). https://doi.org/10.1007/978-3-030-11166-3_5
13. Weston, A.D., et al.: Complete abdomen and pelvis segmentation using U-Net variant architecture. Med. Phy. **47**(11), 5609–5618 (2020)

Asymmetry and Architectural Distortion Detection with Limited Mammography Data

Zhenjie Cao[1]([✉]), Xiaoyun Zhou[1], Yuxing Tang[1], Mei Han[1], Jing Xiao[2], Jie Ma[3], and Peng Chang[1]

[1] PingAn Tech, US Research Lab, Palo Alto, USA
zhenjiecaoaccnt@gmail.com
[2] Ping An Technology, Shenzhen, China
[3] Shenzhen People's Hospital, Shenzhen, China

Abstract. Detection of the asymmetry (AS) and architectural distortion (AD) on mammograms is important for early breast cancer diagnosis. However, this is a challenging task because there are very limited mammography data containing these two lesions. In this paper, we tackle this problem by presenting a novel transfer learning framework of Supervised mass-Transferred Pre-training (STP) followed by Supervised Constrained Contrastive Fine-tuning (SC^2F). While STP can leverage the commonly available mass data to help with detecting the rarely available AS and AD as pre-training, SC^2F can depart the mass, AS, and AD in the embedding space as far as possible with a carefully designed constrained contrastive loss. In addition, a novel detection network - AsAd-Net, is proposed for the AS and AD detection. The validation results on the largest-so-far AS and AD dataset show state-of-the-art (SOTA) detection performance.

Keywords: Mammogram · Asymmetry · Architectural distortion · Contrastive learning · Transfer learning · Detection

1 Introduction

Breast cancer accounted for 11.7% of the total new cancer cases diagnosed worldwide in 2020, surpassing lung cancer as the most common cancer for the first time [25]. Developing a Computer-Aided Diagnosis (CAD) system that can reliably improve the efficiency of mammogram interpretation is of great importance. As shown in Fig. 1, the mass, calcification, asymmetry (**AS**), and architectural distortion (**AD**) are the four typical lesion findings that radiologists use as indications for potential breast cancer on mammograms. Among them, the mass and calcification are more commonly seen, while the AS and AD are considerably more limited, found in approximately 7% of all mammograms [3]. An AS refers to an area of increased density in one breast compared to the corresponding region in the contralateral breast [11]. An AD is defined as distorted normal

G. Zamzmi et al. (Eds.): MILLanD 2022, LNCS 13559, pp. 163–173, 2022.
https://doi.org/10.1007/978-3-031-16760-7_16

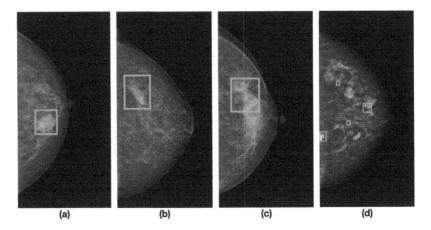

Fig. 1. Examples of different lesion types on mammograms: (a) mass, (b) asymmetry (AS), (c) architectural distortion (AD), (d) calcification.

architecture with no definite mass visible. A key observation is that from both mammography appearance and pathology point of view, the AS and AD are more related to the mass and distinctively different from the calcification, with some actually being caused by the mass.

Compared to the mass and calcification, few studies focus on detecting the AS and AD, mainly attributed to the scarcity of high-quality labeled data. In the public dataset DDSM [4], there are only 155 cases of combined ASs and ADs out of a total of 2,620 cases. Previous research based on such a small dataset only leads to preliminary results [2,31]. Thus, we collaborate with three hospitals to build the largest-so-far AS and AD dataset, which contains 1,004 pixel-level labeled ASs and ADs mammograms out of a total of 29,159 mammograms.

We propose a comprehensive transfer learning framework with Supervised mass-Transferred Pre-training (**STP**) followed by Supervised Constrained Contrastive Fine-tuning (**SC^{2}F**) to tackle this problem. During STP, since the AS and AD are related to the mass both radiographically and pathologically [3], we pre-train a detector with the AS and AD data together with the sufficiently available mass data by detecting the mass, AS, and AD as a joint class first and pushing samples from all classes towards one "root" cluster in the embedding space. Then, in SC^{2}F phase, a carefully designed *constrained* contrastive learning step optimally separates the mass, AS, and AD apart. However, a general distance-based contrastive learning that pulls samples indefinitely far is against their radiographic feature that the AS and AD are related to the mass. Thus, we propose a novel constrained contrastive learning in SC^{2}F that departs the mass, AS, and AD samples in the embedding space as far as possible while still constraining them in the same "root" cluster from STP. In addition, a novel AsAdNet with dual-view inputs is designed for detecting the AS and AD.

The main contributions of this paper include 1) a novel transfer learning framework of **STP** + **SC^{2}F** which uses the sufficiently available mass data to help solve the data scarcity problem of the AS and AD as pre-training, 2) a novel constrained contrastive learning technique in SC^{2}F that separates the mass, AS and AD in the embedding space under certain constraints as fine-tuning, 3) a novel AsAdNet for the AS and AD detection on mammograms, and 4) based on our best knowledge, we achieve state-of-the-art (SOTA) performance on the AS and AD detection on our collected largest-so-far dataset.

2   Related Work

Mass and calcification are the two most common lesions in mammography, and many efficient works have been proposed to detect them [6,29,30]. In comparison, the AS and AD are rare and related works mainly focus on image/patch-level classifications [10,12,18,21,27,33]. Oyelade et al. [23] provides the most up-to-date survey of the AD detection and states that Ari et al. [2] is the existing baseline. To the best of our knowledge, Zeng et al. [31] proposes the best-so-far approach for the AS detection.

Most contrastive learning works have been conducted within the realm of self-supervised learning [1,8,9,15,16,22,28,32], involving different forms of contrastive loss [13]. The recent work of *SimCLR-v2* [9] shows that self-supervised contrastive learning can compete with its supervised counterpart after fine-tuning on downstream tasks. The work of *SupCon* [19] generalizes the contrastive loss to the supervised setting. Contrastive InfoNCE loss [14] proves its effectiveness for representation learning. In medical imaging, Cao et al. [5] applies contrastive pre-training followed by a supervised fine-tuning for mammography screening.

3   Method

Overall Framework. The overall architecture of the STP + SC^{2}F framework is illustrated in Fig. 2. We first pre-train a fully supervised AsAdNet to detect the mass, AS, and AD as one class in STP. Then, we use a novel constrained contrastive learning to depart them in SC^{2}F as fine-tuning. We define mammogram images with pixel-level labels as $I_{pixel} \in \mathbb{R}^{H \times W}$ and their corresponding labels as $L_{pixel} \in \mathbb{R}^{H \times W \times 2}$. H, W are the height and width of images. $L_{pixel}^{(:,:,1)} = 1$ indicates the background pixel while $L_{pixel}^{(:,:,2)} = 1$ indicates the foreground.

STP. AsAdNet detects the mass, AS, and AD as one class without distinguishing between them. The general idea is to transfer the largely available mass knowledge onto the detection of the rarely available AS and AD. We want to push samples from the three classes towards one "root" cluster in the embedding space, with optimizing the model parameters Θ:

$$\min_{\Theta} \sum_{n=1}^{N} E_{pixel}(f(I_{pixel}^n; \Theta), L_{pixel}^n), \tag{1}$$

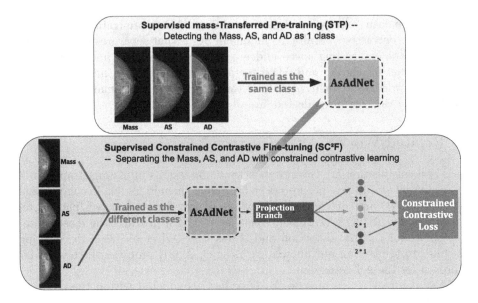

Fig. 2. The architecture of STP + SC^{2}F framework. The pre-trained AsAdNet in STP is transferred into SC^{2}F as the magenta arrow shows.

where N is the batch size, $f(\cdot)$ is the detection model parameterized by Θ and E_{pixel} is the pixel-wise focal loss as in Eq. 3.

$$E_{pixel}^{(w,h,n)} = -\sum_{c=1}^{2} \alpha^{(c)}(1 - P_{prob}^{(c)})^{\gamma} L_{pixel}^{(c)} log(P_{prob}^{(c)}) \qquad (2)$$

$$E_{pixel} = -\frac{1}{H \times W \times N} \sum_{w=0}^{W} \sum_{h=0}^{H} \sum_{n=0}^{N} E_{pixel}^{(w,h,n)} \qquad (3)$$

where $P_{prob} \in \mathbb{R}^{H \times W \times 2}$ is the probability map generated by AsAdNet as illustrated in Fig. 4; $\alpha^{(c)} = \alpha$, if $c = 2$, while $\alpha_c = 1 - \alpha$, if $c = 1$, α is a weight set empirically to balance the loss of the foreground ($c = 2$) and the background ($c = 1$); γ is a customized exponent. After the training converges, we add a projection branch onto the AsAdNet to provide a feature vector $P_{proj} \in \mathbb{R}^{2 \times 1}$ (before softmax). Details for the projection branch is illustrated in Fig. 4. AsAdNet with the projection branch is further trained on all positive (mammograms with the mass, AS, or AD) and negative (mammograms with no lesion) samples. After the training finishes, the center of "root" cluster $\mu_{all} \in \mathbb{R}^{2 \times 1}$ is calculated as: $\mu_{all} = \frac{1}{M} \sum_{m=1}^{M} P_{proj}^m$, where M is the number of all positive samples.

SC^{2}F. We transfer the trained AsAdNet together with the projection branch in STP and fine-tune them with the proposed constrained contrastive loss to separate the mass, AS, and AD. A contrastive loss can divide the embedding space within one "root" cluster into three sub-clusters for the mass, AS, and

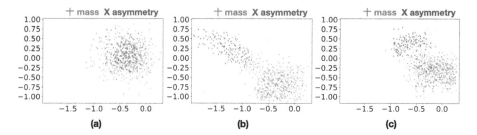

Fig. 3. Visualization of the probability vectors (predicted by the AsAdNet projection branch) on the mass and the AS samples from the test set. (a) detecting the mass and the AS as one class as in STP, (b) contrastive loss that maximizes L_2 distance, and (c) the proposed constrained contrastive loss.

AD. For clarification, we show visualizations for the mass and AS in Fig. 3 as an example. As shown in Fig. 3(a), the first step training in STP pushes the mass and AS samples into one "root" cluster in the embedding space with no clear distinction between them. However, as shown in Fig. 3(b), after applying a contrastive loss with L_2 distance, the two sub-clusters are separated too far, and that is against the radiographic fact that the AS is indeed related to the mass. Hence, we propose a novel constrained contrastive loss that separates the three sub-clusters as far as possible while still constraining them in the same "root" cluster.

For a mini-batch of N samples with two $N/2$ pairs, when the pairs are from the same class (*e.g.*, mass), we use an L_2 loss to minimize their intra-class distance in the embedding space. Otherwise, when they are from different classes (*e.g.*, mass and AS), the projection branch in AsAdNet generates a feature vector for a mass sample $P^{mass}_{proj} \in \mathbb{R}^{2\times1}$ and an AS sample $P^a_{proj} \in \mathbb{R}^{2\times1}$. Instead of directly optimizing a large distance between P^{mass}_{proj} and P^a_{proj}, we optimize a large angle between $P^{mass}_{proj} - \mu_{all}$ and $P^a_{proj} - \mu_{all}$. In this way, we set P^{mass}_{proj} and P^a_{proj} as far as possible, under the constraint that P^{mass}_{proj} and P^a_{proj} are still close to μ_{all}, so that they remain in the same "root" cluster. The inter-class constrained contrastive loss is defined as:

$$E_{con} = \left\langle P^{mass}_{proj} - \mu_{all}, P^a_{proj} - \mu_{all} \right\rangle$$
$$- \left\| P^{mass}_{proj} - \mu_{all} \right\|_2 \cdot \left\| P^a_{proj} - \mu_{all} \right\|_2 \cdot (-1) \qquad (4)$$

where $\langle,\rangle$ is the inner product of two vectors. The angle between $P^{mass}_{proj} - \mu_{all}$ and $P^a_{proj} - \mu_{all}$ is back-propagated to be π. As shown in Fig. 3(c), the proposed constrained contrastive loss separates the sub-clusters of the mass and AD as far as possible but still remains them in the "root" cluster as in Fig. 3(a).

AsAdNet. An important nature of mammograms is that they always appear in pairs, with an image of the right breast and a corresponding one of the same view from the left. This symmetry helps with abnormality detection. Hence, inspired

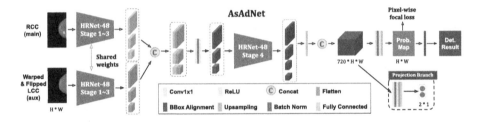

Fig. 4. Overview of the AsAdNet with the projection branch. AsAdNet is for lesion detection and the projection branch is for constrained contrastive learning.

by [26,29,30], we build a dual-view detection network - AsAdNet. The detailed network structure is shown in Fig. 4. It requires dual-view inputs from each patient - the main input (*e.g.*, right craniocaudal, RCC) which AsyDisNet outputs detection results on, and the auxiliary input (*e.g.*, left craniocaudal, LCC) which is used to provide the symmetry information to help with the detection on the main input and will be warped and flipped before being sent into the AsAdNet. The BBox Alignment binarizes the probability map under various thresholds before aligning bounding boxes on the selected-high-probability regions. We train the AsAdNet with probability map using pixel-wise focal loss instead of the final detection results, which performs better based on our experiments.

4   Experiment Design

Our data for training and validation is collected from three collaborative hospitals at distinct geographical locations using Siemens and Giotto equipment following the American College of Radiology standard and dated from 2011 to 2018[1]. A standard mammography screening case has two X-ray projection views for each breast, a craniocaudal (CC) view and a mediolateral oblique (MLO) view. The pixel-level labels are manually annotated by a junior radiologist (<5 years of experience) and fine-tuned by a senior radiologist (>10 years of experience). Public dataset DDSM [4] contains only 155 cases of combined ASs and ADs out of a total of 2,620 cases, while MIAS [24] has fewer than 30 pairs. The DDSM and MIAS are much smaller than our dataset, and their data distribution is not consistent with screening scenarios. Hence, they are not included in our study. For training, we use 2,584 mammograms fully labeled with masses, 526 with ASs, 248 with ADs, and 25,139 mammograms with no lesion. In the testing, we collect 128 mammograms fully labeled with the AS, 102 mammograms with the AD, 432 mammograms with the mass, and 3,660 mammograms with no lesion.

The ratio between the training and validation set is 8:1. Input mammograms are resized to 1008 × 800, keeping the original aspect ratio. The initial learning rate is 1×10^{-5} with 8 warming-up steps and is reduced to 1×10^{-6} after

---

[1] This study was approved by the ethics and institutional review board.

30 epochs. Adam optimizer [20] is used with a weight decay of 5×10^{-4}. We train models with 2 NVIDIA V100 GPUs with 32G memory for each. All implementation is with Python3.7 and PyTorch 1.1.0. During the STP phase, the batch size for the training is set as 12, and it is set as 6 for the SC^{2}P. In Eq. 2, α and γ are set as 0.25 and 2, respectively. It takes about 4.8 h to finish the training and validation after 80 epochs in total. The system might produce unreliable results when test mammograms are from equipment vendors different from our collaborative hospitals. When no GPU is available, the system might fail.

We evaluate the model performance with Free-Response Operating Characteristic (FROC) [7]. Different detection results are acquired by applying various thresholds. Following prior works' definition [26,30], an AS or AD is correct if it has an IoU of over 0.2 with the pixel-level label^2. We evaluate the sensitivity with various numbers of false-positive-per-image (FPPI) at 0.1, 0.5, 1, and 2.

5   Experimental Results

Table 1. Comparison of the proposed AsAdNet with other methods.

Methods	FPPI for AS				FPPI for AD			
	0.1	0.5	1.0	2.0	0.1	0.5	1.0	2.0
Mass SOTA [30]	0.138	0.462	0.601	0.689	0.142	0.437	0.575	0.697
AS baseline [31]	0.154	0.488	0.598	0.711	–	–	–	–
AD baseline [2]	–	–	–	–	0.155	0.464	0.602	0.688
Vanilla AsAdNet SEP	0.159	0.498	0.646	0.732	0.166	0.534	0.649	0.700
Vanilla AsAdNet	0.155	0.491	0.612	0.719	0.157	0.508	0.615	0.695
Ours SEP	0.165	0.503	**0.663**	0.742	0.173	0.548	0.675	0.750
Ours	**0.172**	**0.513**	0.662	**0.746**	**0.179**	**0.554**	**0.676**	**0.753**
Ours 95% CI	±0.002	±0.003	±0.002	±0.001	±0.003	±0.003	±0.002	±0.000

5.1   Comparison with Other Methods

Detailed results of various methods are shown in Table 1. The proposed method (*Ours SEP* trains two AsAdNets for detecting the AS and AD respectively while *Ours* trains one AsAdNet for detecting the AS and AD at the same time) is compared with the *Mass SOTA* [30], *AS baseline* [31] and *AD baseline* [2]. For comparison reasons, we re-implemented methods as in [2,30,31] and applied them to our datasets. The difference between *Ours* and *Vanilla AsAdNet* is that *Ours* is with STP + SC^{2}F while *Vanilla AsAdNet* directly trains the network structure in Fig. 4 with images and labels. Due to the space limitation, only the 95% confidence interval of the *Ours* is shown. Other methods' 95% confidence intervals are similar. We can see that the proposed *Vanilla AsAdNet* structure performs

---

^{2} Our cooperating medical institutes also agree with this definition.

Table 2. Ablation study for the STP and SC^{2}F.

		FPPI for AS				FPPI for AD			
		0.1	0.5	1.0	2.0	0.1	0.5	1.0	2.0
STP	ImageNet	0.151	0.466	0.595	0.708	0.149	0.457	0.588	0.676
	AsAd Pretrain	0.160	0.497	0.651	0.738	0.160	0.533	0.665	0.719
	Ours	**0.172**	**0.513**	**0.662**	**0.746**	**0.179**	**0.554**	**0.676**	**0.753**
SC^{2}F	No Fine-tuning	0.155	0.491	0.612	0.719	0.157	0.508	0.615	0.695
	FC Layer	0.156	0.498	0.609	0.731	0.162	0.509	0.626	0.713
	DenseNet [17]	0.158	0.495	0.618	0.724	0.160	0.513	0.621	0.705
	Contrastive [L2]	0.154	0.488	0.598	0.710	0.154	0.508	0.606	0.692
	Ours	**0.172**	**0.513**	**0.662**	**0.746**	**0.179**	**0.554**	**0.676**	**0.753**

better than the *Mass SOTA* [30], *AS baseline* [31], and *AD baseline* [2]. Training the *Vanilla AsAdNets SEP* on the AS and AD separately achieves higher FROC than training the AS and AD together in *Vanilla AsAdNet* because one network for each facilitates specific feature mining. However, with the proposed STP and SC^{2}F, *Ours* demonstrates better ability than *Ours SEP*. This is because that both the STP and SC^{2}F benefit from the mixing of the mass, AS, and AD. Overall, *Ours* out-performs all other method with noticeable margin, which indicates the value of our proposed STP, SC^{2}F and AsAdNet.

5.2   Ablation Study

We show ablation study results in Table 2. To demonstrate the value of the proposed STP, we replace it with *ImageNet*, which uses ImageNet pre-trained parameters in AsAdNet. Besides, we also experiment on *AsAd Pretrain*, which uses the AS and AD for pre-training without including the mass data. We can see that the *ImageNet* performs worst, as it does not include the medical images in the pre-training, while *AsAd Pretrain* under-performs *Ours* as it includes only the AS and AD in the pre-training. It can be concluded that the proposed STP that leverages the largely available mass data to transfer knowledge onto the detection of the rarely available AS and AD is helpful.

To show the value of the proposed SC^{2}F, we replace it with *No Fine-tuning*, which directly trains one AsAdNet to detect the AS and AD. *FC Layer* uses fc layers to regress the lesion type. *DenseNet* uses a DenseNet [17] to classify the detected ROI. *Contrastive [L2]* uses L2 distance loss for contrastive learning. Details are listed in Table 2. We see that *Ours* out-performs all other alternatives with a noticeable margin, which indicates that the proposed SC^{2}F effectively separates samples from different classes as far as possible in the embedding space while still constraining them in the same "root" cluster from STP.

6   Conclusions

We present a novel framework of STP + SC^{2}F with a detection model AsAd-Net to solve the AS and AD detection on mammograms. Our experiments on 29,159 mammograms prove that both leveraging mass data in pre-training and applying constrained contrastive learning for fine-tuning can effectively improve the detection performance. Superior results have been achieved in comparison with previously reported SOTA approaches. The overall approach is scalable and applicable to hospitals' Picture Archiving and Communication System (PACS).

One limitation is that the current method can not train with weakly labeled data like medical reports, and we plan to improve on this subject in the future.

References

1. Bachman, P., Hjelm, R.D., Buchwalter, W.: Learning representations by maximizing mutual information across views. In: Advances in Neural Information Processing Systems, vol. 32, pp. 15535–15545. Curran Associates, Inc. (2019)
2. Ben-Ari, R., Akselrod-Ballin, A., Karlinsky, L., Hashoul, S.: Domain specific convolutional neural nets for detection of architectural distortion in mammograms. In: 2017 IEEE 14th International Symposium on Biomedical Imaging (ISBI 2017), pp. 552–556. IEEE (2017)
3. Berg, A.W.A., Leung, J.: Diagnostic Imaging: Breast, 3rd edn. Elsevier, Amsterdam (2019)
4. Bowyer, K., et al.: The digital database for screening mammography. In: Third International Workshop on Digital Mammography, vol. 58, p. 27 (1996)
5. Cao, Z., et al.: Supervised contrastive pre-training for mammographic triage screening models. In: de Bruijne, M., et al. (eds.) MICCAI 2021. LNCS, vol. 12907, pp. 129–139. Springer, Cham (2021). https://doi.org/10.1007/978-3-030-87234-2_13
6. Cao, Z., et al.: DeepLIMa: deep learning based lesion identification in mammograms. In: 2019 IEEE/CVF International Conference on Computer Vision Workshop (ICCVW), pp. 362–370 (2019). https://doi.org/10.1109/ICCVW.2019.00047
7. Chakraborty, D.P.: Maximum likelihood analysis of free-response receiver operating characteristic (FROC) data. Med. Phys. 16(4), 561–568 (1989)
8. Chen, T., Kornblith, S., Norouzi, M., Hinton, G.: A simple framework for contrastive learning of visual representations. In: Proceedings of the 37th International Conference on Machine Learning, vol. 119, pp. 1597–1607. PRML (2020)
9. Chen, T., Kornblith, S., Swersky, K., Norouzi, M., Hinton, G.E.: Big self-supervised models are strong semi-supervised learners. In: Advances in Neural Information Processing Systems, vol. 33, pp. 22243–22255. Curran Associates, Inc. (2020)
10. Costa, A.C., Oliveira, H.C., Borges, L.R., Vieira, M.A.: Transfer learning in deep convolutional neural networks for detection of architectural distortion in digital mammography. In: 15th International Workshop on Breast Imaging (IWBI 2020), vol. 11513, p. 115130N. International Society for Optics and Photonics (2020)
11. D'Orsi, C.: 2013 ACR BI-RADS Atlas: Breast Imaging Reporting and Data System. American College of Radiology (2014)
12. Guan, Y., et al.: Detecting asymmetric patterns and localizing cancers on mammograms. Patterns 1(7), 100106 (2020)

13. Hadsell, R., Chopra, S., LeCun, Y.: Dimensionality reduction by learning an invariant mapping. In: Proceedings of the IEEE Conference on Computer Vision and Pattern Recognition, vol. 2, pp. 1735–1742 (2006)

14. Hadsell, R., Chopra, S., LeCun, Y.: Dimensionality reduction by learning an invariant mapping. In: 2006 IEEE Computer Society Conference on Computer Vision and Pattern Recognition (CVPR 2006), vol. 2, pp. 1735–1742 (2006)

15. He, K., Fan, H., Wu, Y., Xie, S., Girshick, R.: Momentum contrast for unsupervised visual representation learning. In: Proceedings of the IEEE Conference on Computer Vision and Pattern Recognition, pp. 9729–9738 (2020)

16. Hjelm, R.D., Fedorov, A., Lavoie-Marchildon, S., Grewal, K., Trischler, A., Bengio, Y.: Learning deep representations by mutual information estimation and maximization. In: International Conference on Learning Representations (2019)

17. Iandola, F., Moskewicz, M., Karayev, S., Girshick, R., Darrell, T., Keutzer, K.: DenseNet: implementing efficient convnet descriptor pyramids. arXiv preprint arXiv:1404.1869 (2014)

18. Kelder, A., Lederman, D., Zheng, B., Zigel, Y.: A new computer-aided detection approach based on analysis of local and global mammographic feature asymmetry. Med. Phys. **45**(4), 1459–1470 (2018)

19. Khosla, P., et al.: Supervised contrastive learning. In: Advances in Neural Information Processing Systems, vol. 33, pp. 18661–18673. Curran Associates, Inc. (2020)

20. Kingma, D.P., Ba, J.: Adam: a method for stochastic optimization. In: International Conference on Learning Representations (2015)

21. Narváez, F., Alvarez, J., Garcia-Arteaga, J.D., Tarquino, J., Romero, E.: Characterizing architectural distortion in mammograms by linear saliency. J. Med. Syst. **41**(2), 1–12 (2017). https://doi.org/10.1007/s10916-016-0672-5

22. van den Oord, A., Li, Y., Vinyals, O.: Representation learning with contrastive predictive coding. arXiv preprint arXiv:1807.03748 (2018)

23. Oyelade, O.N., Ezugwu, A.E.S.: A state-of-the-art survey on deep learning methods for detection of architectural distortion from digital mammography. IEEE Access **8**, 148644–148676 (2020)

24. Suckling, J.P.: The mammographic image analysis society digital mammogram database. Digital Mammo, pp. 375–386 (1994)

25. Sung, H., et al.: Global cancer statistics 2020: GLOBOCAN estimates of incidence and mortality worldwide for 36 cancers in 185 countries. CA Cancer J. Clin. **71**(3), 209–249 (2021)

26. Tang, Y., et al.: Leveraging large-scale weakly labeled data for semi-supervised mass detection in mammograms. In: Proceedings of the IEEE/CVF Conference on Computer Vision and Pattern Recognition, pp. 3855–3864 (2021)

27. Vedalankar, A.V., Gupta, S.S., Manthalkar, R.R.: Addressing architectural distortion in mammogram using AlexNet and support vector machine. Inform. Med. Unlocked **23**, 100551 (2021)

28. Wu, Z., Xiong, Y., Yu, S.X., Lin, D.: Unsupervised feature learning via nonparametric instance discrimination. In: Proceedings of the IEEE Conference on Computer Vision and Pattern Recognition, pp. 3733–3742 (2018)

29. Yang, Z., et al.: MommiNet: mammographic multi-view mass identification networks. In: Martel, A.L., et al. (eds.) MICCAI 2020. LNCS, vol. 12266, pp. 200–210. Springer, Cham (2020). https://doi.org/10.1007/978-3-030-59725-2_20

30. Yang, Z., et al.: MommiNet-v2: mammographic multi-view mass identification networks. Med. Image Anal. **73**, 102204 (2021)

31. Zeng, Y.C.: Asymmetry recognition of mammogram images based on convolutional neural network. In: 2019 IEEE 8th Global Conference on Consumer Electronics (GCCE), pp. 738–740. IEEE (2019)
32. Zhuang, C., Zhai, A.L., Yamins, D.: Local aggregation for unsupervised learning of visual embeddings. In: Proceedings of the IEEE International Conference on Computer Vision, pp. 6002–6012 (2019)
33. Zyout, I., Togneri, R.: A computer-aided detection of the architectural distortion in digital mammograms using the fractal dimension measurements of BEMD. Comput. Med. Imaging Graph. **70**, 173–184 (2018)

Imbalanced Data
and Out-of-Distribution Generalization

Class Imbalance Correction for Improved Universal Lesion Detection and Tagging in CT

Peter D. Erickson, Tejas Sudharshan Mathai$^{(\boxtimes)}$, and Ronald M. Summers

Imaging Biomarkers and Computer-Aided Diagnosis Laboratory,
Radiology and Imaging Sciences, Clinical Center, National Institutes of Health,
Bethesda, MD, USA
mathaits@nih.gov

Abstract. Radiologists routinely detect and size lesions in CT to stage cancer and assess tumor burden. To potentially aid their efforts, multiple lesion detection algorithms have been developed with a large public dataset called DeepLesion (32,735 lesions, 32,120 CT slices, 10,594 studies, 4,427 patients, 8 body part labels). However, this dataset contains missing measurements and lesion tags, and exhibits a severe imbalance in the number of lesions per label category. In this work, we utilize a limited subset of DeepLesion (6%, 1331 lesions, 1309 slices) containing lesion annotations and body part label tags to train a VFNet model to detect lesions and tag them. We address the class imbalance by conducting three experiments: 1) Balancing data by the body part labels, 2) Balancing data by the number of lesions per patient, and 3) Balancing data by the lesion size. In contrast to a randomly sampled (unbalanced) data subset, our results indicated that balancing the body part labels always increased sensitivity for lesions ≥ 1 cm for classes with low data quantities (Bone: 80% vs. 46%, Kidney: 77% vs. 61%, Soft Tissue: 70% vs. 60%, Pelvis: 83% vs. 76%). Similar trends were seen for three other models tested (FasterRCNN, RetinaNet, FoveaBox). Balancing data by lesion size also helped the VFNet model improve recalls for all classes in contrast to an unbalanced dataset. We also provide a structured reporting guideline for a "Lesions" subsection to be entered into the "Findings" section of a radiology report. To our knowledge, we are the first to report the class imbalance in DeepLesion, and have taken data-driven steps to address it in the context of joint lesion detection and tagging.

Keywords: CT · Universal lesion detection · Class imbalance · Deep learning · DeepLesion

1 Introduction

Tumor burden assessment and staging of cancer is critical for patient treatment [1,2]. The first step towards this goal is lesion localization, which enables

---

Supplementary Information The online version contains supplementary material available at https://doi.org/10.1007/978-3-031-16760-7_17.

G. Zamzmi et al. (Eds.): MILLanD 2022, LNCS 13559, pp. 177–186, 2022.
https://doi.org/10.1007/978-3-031-16760-7_17

lesion size measurement and assessment of malignancy risk. Typically, in clinical practice, computed tomography (CT) and positron emission tomography (PET) are preferred for lesion analysis [1]. Radiologists scroll through a volume to find lesions of size ≥ 10 mm and treat them as suspicious for metastasis [1,2]. They also identify lesions across multiple patient visits and track their progression (growth, shrinkage, or unchanged status) based on treatment response. Lesions can have heterogeneous shapes, sizes, and appearances in CT, and this further compounds assessment as there are a variety of imaging scanners and inconsistent exam protocols in use at different institutions. Moreover, sizing lesions during a busy clinical day is cumbersome for a radiologist due to observer measurement variabilities, especially when treatment guidelines for examining metastasis evolve, and some potentially metastatic lesions can be missed.

Recently, many automated approaches have been proposed for universal lesion detection [3–9] on the DeepLesion dataset with state-of-the-art results. The DeepLesion dataset contains 32,735 lesions annotated by radiologists in 32,120 axial CT slices from 10,594 studies of 4,427 patients. The dataset is divided into 70% train, 15% validation, and 15% test splits respectively. Eight (8) lesion-level tags (bone, abdomen, mediastinum, liver, lung, kidney, soft tissue, and pelvis) are available for only the validation and test splits. Prior works utilize the entire dataset for development and testing, while only a handful have gone beyond lesion detection and addressed clinical issues [8–11]. However, as shown in Fig. 1(a), there is a severe class imbalance in the DeepLesion dataset with over-representation of certain classes (lung, abdomen, mediastinum, and liver) in contrast to other under-represented classes (pelvis, soft tissue, kidney, bone). This imbalance has not been addressed in prior work; e.g., in [3], public datasets for lung nodules (LUNA dataset [12]), liver tumors (LITS dataset [13]), and lymph nodes (NIH Lymph Node dataset [14]) were added to improve detection. However, this solely increased the data quantities (and detection performance) of the over-represented classes without affecting the under-represented classes. Tackling class imbalances has potential clinical implications, such as improving interval change detection (lesion tracking over time) [8,9].

In this paper, we addressed the class imbalance in the DeepLesion dataset by using only the annotated subset (30%) to train a state-of-the-art VFNet model [15] for lesion detection and classification. In a limited data-driven manner, we conducted experiments that balanced the training data according to: 1) the body part that the lesion was identified in, 2) the number of lesions observed in a patient, and 3) the size of the lesions. Through balancing the data by the body part label, we have shown a consistent increase in detection sensitivity for under-represented (UR) classes along with a minimal sensitivity drop for over-represented (OR) classes. This trend was also seen with other detectors, such as Faster RCNN [16], RetinaNet [17], and FoveaBox [18]. Additionally, we saw recalls for all classes improve with the VFNet model through our experiment that balanced the lesions according to their size. Moreover, we provide a structured reporting guideline by creating a dedicated "Lesions" sub-section for entry into the "Findings" section of a radiology report. The "Lesions" sub-section contains a structured list of detected lesions along with their body part tags, detection confidence, and series and slice numbers. To the best of our knowledge, we are the first to show a class imbalance in the DeepLesion dataset and have taken data-driven steps to address it in the context of lesion detection and classification.

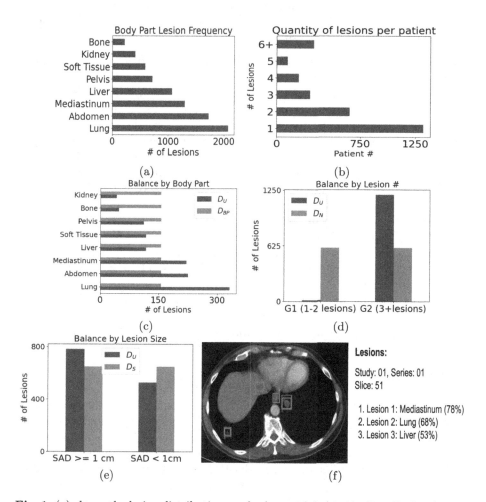

Fig. 1. (a) shows the lesion distribution per body part label in the DeepLesion dataset [22] with certain over-represented and under-represented classes. (b) shows the number of patients with a specific number of lesions annotated. (c) Compared to the unbalanced dataset D_U, our dataset D_{BP} balanced the number of lesions across the different body part classes (orange). (d) shows the lesion distribution for patients who were divided into two groups: G1 had patients with 1–2 lesions and G2 had patients with 3+ lesions. Compared to D_U, dataset D_N (orange) had an equal number of lesions in G1 and G2. The number of patients in each group was not balanced. (e) shows the lesion distribution categorized by the short axis diameter (SAD) length. Compared to D_U, in dataset D_S the number of lesions with SAD ≥ 1 cm and SAD < 1 cm were balanced (orange). (f) Four lesions were detected in the chest area. Green boxes: GT, yellow boxes: TP, red boxes: FP. The top-3 predictions, their labels, and confidence scores were compiled into a structured "Lesions" sub-section for entry into the "Findings" section of a radiology report. Only lesions that were predicted with confidences $\geq 50\%$ are shown. Figure is best viewed electronically in color. (Color figure online)

2   Methods

In this section, we briefly describe the neural networks that were employed for lesion detection and tagging. Our goal is to improve an existing model's robustness against class imbalances using data-driven approaches.

State-of-the-Art Detectors. Various state-of-the-art detectors were employed for lesion detection and tagging in CT slices. Notably, we used: 1) VFNet [15], 2) Faster RCNN [16], 3) RetinaNet [17], and 4) FoveaBox [18]. Faster RCNN is a two-stage anchor-based detector in which region proposals for regions-of-interest (ROI) were generated by the first stage, followed by a second stage that classified these proposals and regressed the bounding box coordinates. RetinaNet [17] is an anchor-free detector that utilized the focal loss to solve a common class imbalance problem in detection, wherein proposals were sampled in non-informative ROIs of the image instead of salient object locations. FoveaBox used a ResNet-50 backbone to generate feature maps from the input and a fovea head network that estimated the coordinates in an image that may be potentially covered by an object ROI. Finally, VFNet combined a Fully Convolutional One-Stage Object (FCOS) detector [19] (without the centerness branch), an Adaptive Training Sample Selection (ATSS) mechanism [20], which selected high quality ROI candidates during training, and a novel IoU-aware varifocal loss [15] to detect ROI. After model training was completed, Weighted Boxes Fusion (WBF) [21] was used to combine the numerous predictions and improve the precision/recall metric. Supplementary material contains implementation details for the models.

3   Experiments

Dataset. The NIH DeepLesion dataset [22] contains keyslices that were annotated with 1–3 lesions per slice and 30 mm of context above and below the keyslice was provided. Annotations were made using RECIST measurements [2], from which 2D bounding boxes were extracted for each lesion. Eight (8) lesion-level tags (bone - 1, abdomen - 2, mediastinum - 3, liver - 4, lung - 5, kidney - 6, soft tissue - 7, and pelvis - 8) were available for only the validation and test splits. The lesion tags were obtained through a body part regressor [23], which provided a continuous score that represented the normalized position of the body part for a slice in a CT volume (e.g., liver, lung, kidney etc.). The body part label for the slice was assigned to any lesion annotated in that slice [22,23]. As the DeepLesion dataset contained multiple visits of the same patient, only lesions from the first patient visit were kept [8] to maintain uniqueness during training. This process left 26,034 lesions from 25,568 slices in the dataset. Next, we removed lesions that did not contain a body part label (the training split) leaving us with a limited dataset D_L containing 8,104 lesions from 7,953 slices. D_L contained $\sim$24.75% of the original DeepLesion dataset, and was split into 60% training, 20% validation, 20% testing splits with unique patients in each split. This 60% training split was still unbalanced and in our experiments (see below), we utilized only $\sim$6% of DeepLesion (1331 lesions, 1309 slices).

Experimental Design. The unbalanced lesion distribution per body part label in Fig. 1(a) and distribution of lesion quantities per patient in Fig. 1(b) led us to design four experiments with a limited annotated dataset D_L. In the first experiment E_{BP}, we generated a dataset balanced by body part label D_{BP}; As seen in Figs. 1(a) and 1(c), the body part label with the lowest data quantity ("Bone") was identified and the data quantities in the remaining labels were matched to the lowest quantity. The intent was to emphasize that all lesion classes were equally likely during training through sample selection. In the second experiment E_N, we created a dataset balanced by the number of lesions D_N any given patient had. From Fig. 1(b), there are a large number of patients with 1–2 lesions and fewer patients with 3+ lesions. For E_N, we first created two groups (G1 and G2) and sampled patients for each group such that each group contained the same number of lesions as shown in Fig. 1(d). The aim was to provide a balanced number of lesions per patient such that the model witnessed patients with varying number of lesions at test time with equal likelihood. Our third experiment E_S was clinically oriented, and we produced a dataset balanced by the lesion size D_S. Lesions with SAD ≥ 10 mm were collected in one group while those with SAD < 10 mm were present in the second group. The objective was to create a dataset with equal numbers of lesions divided according to their size as both smaller and larger lesions are equally likely at test time. In our fourth and final experiment E_U, we generated an unbalanced dataset D_U with a random sample of the training split of D_L, such that it had similar distributions (random) of labels as shown in Figs. 1(c)–(e).

4   Results and Discussion

Results. Table 1 and Fig. 2 display the results of our experiments at 4 FP and 30% IoU overlap [24] on lesions with SAD ≥ 1 cm, which are generally more clinically significant lesions. Table 1 in the supplementary material reflects our experimental results on lesions with SAD < 1 cm. In contrast to the experiment with unbalanced data D_U, our experiment balancing body part labels E_{BP} improved recalls for 4/4 under-represented (UR) classes (Bone: 80% vs. 46%, Kidney: 77% vs. 61%, Soft Tissue: 70% vs. 60%, Pelvis: 83% vs. 76%) across all the models tested. These results are evident for both SAD $\geq$ and < 1 cm. Among the over-represented (OR) classes, we see consistent improvements for the "Lung" category across all models and for "Mediastinum" label for all models except FoveaBox. However, the "Abdomen" and "Liver" categories show a decrease in sensitivity across all models. The sensitivity reduction is expected as the number of training samples used for OR classes have been reduced as shown in Fig. 1(c). Although to understand this phenomenon better, we calculated the confusion matrices for each experiment (see supplementary material) using the VFNet model. From the DeepLesion dataset description [22], the "Soft Tissue" class encompassed lesions found in the muscle, skin, or fat, while the "Abdomen" class was a "catch-all" term for all abdominal lesions that were not "Kidney" or "Liver" masses. Anatomically however, "Kidney" and "Liver" are organs in close proximity to one another and axial slices often show cross-sections of both organs in the same slice. This is reflected in the confusion matrix as the "Abdomen", "Kidney" and "Liver" labels are confused with each other most often. Comparing E_U with E_N (balancing by lesion number), recalls improved for only 1/4 UR classes (Kidney) for Faster RCNN and FoveaBox, and 2/4 UR classes for RetinaNet (Kidney and Soft Tissue) and VFNet (Kidney, soft tissue) respectively. For the OR classes, only "Liver" improved for VFNet, 2/4 classes improved for Faster RCNN and FoveaBox (Abdomen, Lung) respectively, and 3/4 classes improved for RetinaNet (Mediastinum, Lung, Liver). Compared against E_{BP}, recalls were lower for all UR classes except for VFNet, which did well on 2/4 classes (Soft Tissue and Pelvis). For the OR classes, 2/4 classes improved for Faster RCNN (Abdomen, Liver), 3/4 classes improved for VFNet and RetinaNet (Abdomen, Mediastinum and Liver), and all 4 classes improved for FoveaBox.

Table 1. Detection sensitivities of different detectors based on different experiments are shown @ 4 FP and an IOU of 0.3 for lesions with a SAD $\geq$ 1 cm.

Experiment	Bone	Kidney	Soft Tissue	Pelvis	Abdomen	Mediastinum	Lung	Liver
E_U - Faster R-CNN [16]	23.3	40.5	50.4	67.5	57.7	79.6	66.8	**77.3**
E_{BP} - Faster R-CNN [16]	**63.3**	**75.1**	**58.1**	**68.5**	55.6	**83.3**	**74.9**	69.8
E_N - Faster R-CNN [16]	16.6	49.3	44.1	63.2	**65.5**	78.7	72.6	76.9
E_S - Faster R-CNN [16]	30.0	49.7	51.7	56.4	61.1	74.8	74.5	73.1
E_U - RetinaNet [17]	21.7	38.4	48.2	55.8	**70.5**	82.8	76.1	75.9
E_{BP} - RetinaNet [17]	**66.7**	**66.7**	**60.3**	**59.8**	62.3	85.3	**79.7**	71.0
E_N - RetinaNet [17]	27.5	53.1	26.1	49.6	68.7	**86.2**	77.4	**76.5**
E_S - RetinaNet [17]	26.2	22.4	25.0	21.1	51.9	61.7	58.8	58.2
E_U - FoveaBox [18]	28.3	46.4	54.2	59.2	64.8	**88.3**	69.2	**76.7**
E_{BP} - FoveaBox [18]	**65.0**	**67.9**	**66.7**	**63.4**	56.2	84.5	**76.9**	70.0
E_N - FoveaBox [18]	18.3	56.5	46.9	34.1	70.1	85.1	74.7	71.5
E_S - FoveaBox [18]	41.66	40.9	46.3	47.6	**71.1**	86.8	75.1	74.9
E_U - VFNet [15]	46.7	61.6	60.0	76.0	76.8	85.6	70.8	77.7
E_{BP} - VFNet [15]	**80.0**	**77.6**	**70.7**	83.4	69.5	87.7	78.9	76.3
E_N - VFNet [15]	28.8	63.3	63.6	73.5	69.6	78.8	68.2	**91.0**
E_S - VFNet [15]	51.6	67.0	67.3	**87.2**	**82.1**	**89.8**	**82.7**	82.1

In contrast to the E_U experiment, in the E_S experiment (balancing by lesion size), VFNet recalls were always better across all classes for both SAD $\geq$ 1 cm and $<$ 1 cm. Only one UR class showed improved recall for RetinaNet and FoveaBox (Bone) respectively, while 3/4 UR classes did better for Faster RCNN (Bone, Kidney, Soft Tissue). In the OR classes, RetinaNet did worse on all classes, and 2/4 OR classes showed improvements for Faster RCNN and FoveaBox (Abdomen, Lung). In contrast to the E_{BP} experiment, sensitivities were lower for all UR classes except for the "Pelvis" class with VFNet. For the OR classes, RetinaNet did not show improvements for any class, 2/4 classes improved for Faster RCNN (Abdomen, Liver), and 3/4 classes improved for FoveaBox (Abdomen, Mediastinum, Liver). Compared against the E_N experiment, sensitivities were worse for all UR classes

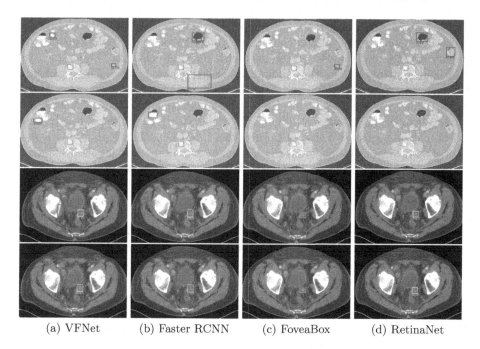

(a) VFNet   (b) Faster RCNN   (c) FoveaBox   (d) RetinaNet

Fig. 2. Columns (a)–(d) show outputs of the various models on slices from CT volumes of two different patients. The first row of each pairing represents the model output after being trained on an unbalanced D_U dataset, while the second row shows results when trained on a dataset balanced by body part labels D_{BP}. Green boxes: GT, yellow boxes: TP, red boxes: FP. The predicted classes and confidence scores are also shown. The first pair shows that models trained with D_U did not identify and classify a "Bone" lesion correctly (first row), whereas one trained on D_{BP} did (second row). Particularly, VFNet trained on D_{BP} predicted correctly with a confidence on 97%. The second pair shows fewer FP for VFNet with D_{BP}, and a missed detection for FoveaBox (last row). (Color figure online)

with RetinaNet. They were better for 2/4 UR classes for FoveaBox (Bone and Pelvis), and 3/4 UR classes for Faster RCNN (Bone, Kidney, Soft Tissue). On the OR classes, recall was worse for all classes with RetinaNet, improved for 1/4 OR classes with Faster RCNN (Lung), and 3/4 classes for VFNet (Abdomen, Mediastinum, Lung) and all classes for FoveaBox.

Discussion. In contrast to previous work, we have shown that through effective data exploration of the DeepLesion dataset, the recalls for all models across all the under-represented classes were improved. Specifically, our E_{BP} experiment (balancing data by body part labels) displayed this clear improvement. We also saw an increase in sensitivity for the OR classes "Lung" and "Mediastinum" with Faster RCNN, RetinaNet and VFNet respectively. The "Abdomen" and "Liver" classes were confused with each other most often. We contend that the "Abdomen" and "Soft Tissue" labels were generated through a body part regressor, and are ambiguous and non-specific labels that broadly encompass multiple regions in the abdomen. In fact, after we asked a radiologist to re-classify a random sample of 100 lesions with the original term "Abdomen", we identified multiple lesions that should be assigned new labels such as "Liver", "Pancreas", "Spleen", "Muscle", "Stomach" etc. There are many other anno-tated lesions in DeepLesion for whom the assigned labels may change upon manual inspection. In our experiment E_N (balancing by number of lesions), we did not see a consistent trend of improvement and hypothesize that this is due to not simultaneously balancing the lesions by the body part labels. Balancing the data by both body part labels and number of lesions proved difficult as it was difficult to categorize patients when they had multiple lesions with different labels. In our E_S experiment (balancing the lesion size), the recalls for all classes improved with the VFNet model.

We were unable to compare against prior works as limited approaches exist to jointly detect and tag lesion [10,11]. One approach [11] used a Mask-RCNN model that required segmentation labels, which we did not create in this work. Furthermore, this approach also provided more descriptive tags, which would require a sophisticated ontology derived from radiology reports (unavailable in DeepLesion dataset) to map them to the body part tags used in this work. To circumvent this issue, we implemented other detection models to prove our consistent results. We also present a clinically useful structured reporting guide-line by creating a dedicated "Lesions" sub-section for entry into the "Findings" section of a radiology report. The "Lesions" sub-section contains a structured list of detected lesions along with their body part tags, detection confidence, and series and slice numbers. Furthermore, DeepLesion contains both contrast and non-contrast enhanced CT volumes, but the exact phase information is unavail-able in the dataset. Thus, we have not been able to balance the data according to the phase of the CT volume, and this is a limitation of our work. For future work, we plan to conduct an experiment that upsamples the classes with low data points, and balance the data by both the body part label and lesion size.

5   Conclusion

In this paper, we have shown that the DeepLesion dataset exhibits a severe imbalance in the number of lesions per body part label. It also contains missing annotations and label tags. We have utilized a limited data subset (6%, 1331 lesions, 1309 slices) to train a VFNet model to detect lesions and tag them. We conducted three experiments to address the class imbalance and have shown a consistent increase in recalls for UR labels through our experiment E_{BP} (Bone: 80% vs. 46%, Kidney: 77% vs. 61%, Soft Tissue: 70% vs. 60%, Pelvis: 83% vs. 76%) in contrast to E_U. We have also shown that FasterRCNN, RetinaNet, and FoveaBox perform similarly. In addition, we have shown that balancing data by lesion size helped the VFNet model improve recalls for all classes. To our knowledge, we are the first to show a class imbalance in the DeepLesion dataset and have taken data-driven steps to address it in the context of lesion detection and classification.

Acknowledgements. This work was supported by the Intramural Research Program of the National Institutes of Health (NIH) Clinical Center.

References

1. Eisenhauer, E., et al.: New response evaluation criteria in solid tumours: revised RECIST guideline (version 1.1). Eur. J. Cancer **45**(2), 228–247 (2009)
2. Schwartz, L., et al.: RECIST 1.1-update and clarification: from the RECIST committee. Eur. J. Cancer **62**, 132–137 (2016)
3. Yan, K., et al.: Learning from multiple datasets with heterogeneous and partial labels for universal lesion detection in CT. IEEE TMI **40**(10), 2759–2770 (2021)
4. Cai, J., et al.: Lesion harvester: iteratively mining unlabeled lesions and hard-negative examples at scale. IEEE TMI **40**(1), 59–70 (2021)
5. Yang, J., et al.: *AlignShift*: bridging the gap of imaging thickness in 3D anisotropic volumes. In: Martel, A.L., et al. (eds.) MICCAI 2020. LNCS, vol. 12264, pp. 562–572. Springer, Cham (2020). https://doi.org/10.1007/978-3-030-59719-1_55
6. Yang, J., He, Y., Kuang, K., Lin, Z., Pfister, H., Ni, B.: Asymmetric 3D context fusion for universal lesion detection. In: de Bruijne, M., et al. (eds.) MICCAI 2021. LNCS, vol. 12905, pp. 571–580. Springer, Cham (2021). https://doi.org/10.1007/978-3-030-87240-3_55
7. Han, L., et al.: SATr: Slice Attention with Transformer for Universal Lesion Detection. arXiv (2022)
8. Cai, J., et al.: Deep lesion tracker: monitoring lesions in 4D longitudinal imaging studies. In: IEEE CVPR (2020)
9. Tang, W., et al.: Transformer Lesion Tracker. arXiv (2022)
10. Yan, K., et al.: Holistic and comprehensive annotation of clinically significant findings on diverse CT images: learning from radiology reports and label ontology. In: IEEE CVPR (2019)
11. Yan, K., et al.: MULAN: multitask universal lesion analysis network for joint lesion detection, tagging, and segmentation. In: Shen, D., et al. (eds.) MICCAI 2019. LNCS, vol. 11769, pp. 194–202. Springer, Cham (2019). https://doi.org/10.1007/978-3-030-32226-7_22
12. Setio, A.A.A., et al.: Validation, comparison, and combination of algorithms for automatic detection of pulmonary nodules in computed tomography images: the LUNA16 challenge. Med. Image Anal. **42**, 1–13 (2017)
13. Bilic, P., et al.: The Liver Tumor Segmentation Benchmark (LiTS). CoRR (2019)
14. Roth, H.R., et al.: A new 2.5D representation for lymph node detection using random sets of deep convolutional neural network observations. In: Golland, P., Hata, N., Barillot, C., Hornegger, J., Howe, R. (eds.) MICCAI 2014. LNCS, vol. 8673, pp. 520–527. Springer, Cham (2014). https://doi.org/10.1007/978-3-319-10404-1_65
15. Zhang, H., et al.: VarifocalNet: an IoU-aware dense object detector. In: IEEE CVPR, pp. 8514–8523 (2021)
16. Ren, S., et al.: Faster R-CNN: towards real-time object detection with region proposal networks. IEEE PAMI **39**(6), 1137–1149 (2017)
17. Lin, T.Y., et al.: Focal loss for dense object detection. In: IEEE ICCV, pp. 2999–3007 (2017)
18. Kong, T., et al.: FoveaBox: Beyond Anchor-based Object Detector. arXiv (2019)
19. Tian, Z., et al.: FCOS: fully convolutional one-stage object detection. In: IEEE ICCV, pp. 9627–9636 (2019)

20. Zhang, S., et al.: Bridging the Gap Between Anchor-based and Anchor-free Detection via Adaptive Training Sample Selection. CoRR (2019)
21. Solovyev, R., et al.: Weighted boxes fusion: ensembling boxes from different object detection models. Image Vis. Comput. **107**, 104117 (2021)
22. Yan, K., et al.: DeepLesion: automated mining of large-scale lesion annotations and universal lesion detection with deep learning. J. Med. Imaging **5**(3), 1–11 (2018)
23. Yan, K., et al.: Unsupervised body part regression via spatially self-ordering convolutional neural networks. In: IEEE ISBI, pp. 1022–1025 (2018)
24. Mattikalli, T., et al.: Universal lesion detection in CT scans using neural network ensembles. In: SPIE Medical Imaging: Computer-Aided Diagnosis, vol. 12033 (2022)

CVAD: An Anomaly Detector for Medical Images Based on Cascade VAE

Xiaoyuan Guo[1]([✉]), Judy Wawira Gichoya[2], Saptarshi Purkayastha[3],
and Imon Banerjee[4,5]

[1] Department of Computer Science, Emory University, Atlanta, GA, USA
xiaoyuan.guo@emory.edu
[2] School of Medicine, Emory University, Atlanta, GA, USA
judywawira@emory.edu
[3] School of Informatics and Computing, Indiana University-Purdue University
Indianapolis, Indianapolis, IN, USA
saptpurk@iupui.edu
[4] Department of Radiology, Mayo clinic, Phoenix, AZ, USA
[5] School of Computing and Augmented Intelligence, Arizona State University,
Phoenix, AZ, USA
banerjee.imon@mayo.edu

Abstract. Anomaly detection in medical imaging plays an important role to ensure AI generalization. However, existing out-of-distribution (OOD) detection approaches fail to account for OOD data granularity in medical images, where identifying both intra-class and inter-class OOD data is essential to the generalizability in the medical domain. We focus on the generalizability of outlier detection for medical images and propose a generic **C**ascade **V**ariational autoencoder-based **A**nomaly **D**etector (CVAD). We use variational autoencoders' cascade architecture, which combines latent representation at multiple scales, before being fed to a discriminator to distinguish the OOD data from the in-distribution data. Finally, both the reconstruction error and the OOD probability predicted by the binary discriminator are used to determine the anomalies. We compare the performance with the state-of-the-art deep learning models to demonstrate our model's efficacy on various open-access natural and medical imaging datasets for intra- and inter-class OOD. Extensive experimental results on multiple datasets show our model's effectiveness and generalizability. The code will be publicly available.

Keywords: Anomaly detection · Cascade Variational autoencoder · Medical images · OOD detection

1 Introduction

Despite recent advances in deep learning that have contributed to solving various complex real-world problems [5], the safety and reliability of AI technologies remain a big concern in medical applications [6,20]. Deep learning models for medical tasks are often trained with known classes, which are called in-distribution

G. Zamzmi et al. (Eds.): MILLanD 2022, LNCS 13559, pp. 187–196, 2022.
https://doi.org/10.1007/978-3-031-16760-7_18

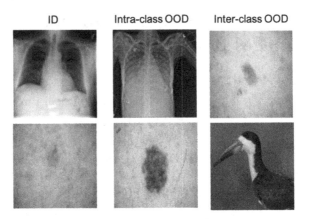

ID   Intra-class OOD   Inter-class OOD

Fig. 1. ID, Intra- and Inter-class OOD examples for medical images. Compared to natural images, medical OOD samples exhibit more subtle intra-class variations (e.g., normal vs pneumonia in the 1st row and benign vs malignant in the 2nd row).

(ID) data, but fail to identify the cases with significant quality variances, unseen classes, and unknown categories, which are out-of-distribution (OOD) inputs. To ensure the reliability of deep models' predictions, it is necessary to identify unknown types of data that are different from the training data distribution. Therefore, anomaly detectors should be able to distinguish unpredictable outliers based the learnt knowledge of ID. However, the core challenges for medical anomaly detection are – (1) the OOD data is usually unavailable during training; (2) there are infinite numbers of variations of OOD data; and (3) different types of OOD data can be identified with varying difficulties. To facilitate future performance measurement and quantification, we categorize the outliers into **inter-class** and **intra-class** OOD types based on the variation difference. As exemplified in Fig. 1, inter-class OOD data are from categories different from the ID data[1], e.g. a skin cancer image v.s. a lung X-ray image; intra-class OOD data belong to the same category as the ID data but different classes, e.g. a normal skin image v.s. a skin image with cancer. Therefore, inter-class OOD data often has larger variations from the ID data, whereas the intra-class OOD data is close to ID data. Thus, identifying intra-class OOD data is more difficult than the inter-class OOD data given subtle differences with ID data.

Models based on Variational Autoencoders (VAEs) and Generative Adversarial Networks (GANs) are promising as the deep generative models can learn latent features of training data and generate synthetic data with similar features to known classes [9]. Although VAEs are theoretically elegant and easy to train with nice manifold representations, they usually produce blurry images that lack detailed information [3,13,14,23]. GANs usually generate much sharper images and have been used for anomaly detection [22], such as AnoGAN [19] and

---

[1] By default, we mean a category can contain several distinct classes. For example, a Chest Xray category can include different types of diseases.

GANomaly [1]. However, GANs often face challenges in training stability and sampling diversity [8]. [7] proposed to use an ensembles of GANs for more stable performance, which adds the model complexity. Besides, there are hybrid models that detect anomalies by combining a VE/VAE with a GAN [3,12]. Moreover, many other approaches have contributed to OOD detection, for example, UTRAD [4], a Transformer-based OOD detection method is also developed, but aiming for 3D medical images. Nonetheless, OOD detectors that consider the outliers' granularity are still lacking. Although [10] also detects both the inter- and intra-class OOD data, but different from our definitions, the work focuses on skin lesion data specifically and defines its inter-class variation as the variations in visual appearance across separate lesion diseases, which belongs to our intra-class OOD detection.

To cope with the OOD unavailability and uncertainty challenges, we adopt an unsupervised way to design our anomaly detector. For intra-class OOD data, we expect the model can be sensitive to minor variations and thus screen the dissimilar inputs. To acquire such high identification of hard OOD cases, we propose a **C**ascade **V**ariational autoencoder based **A**nomaly **D**etector (CVAD) to learn both coarser and finer features inspired by [3,15], which have demonstrated effectiveness in enhancing the reconstruction ability by using a cascade architecture. Based on the observation, we design a similar cascased VAE architecture backbone, with which CAVD gains superior reconstructions and learns good-quality features to threshold out the OOD data. To enhance the detection ability of inter-class OOD data, we further train a binary discriminator with the reconstructed data as the fake OOD category. In this paper, our contributions are three-fold:

- We propose a specifically designed medical OOD detector – CVAD. By utilizing a cascade VAE to learn latent variables of in-distribution data, CVAD owns good reconstruction ability of in-distribution inputs and obtains discriminative ability for OOD data based on the reconstruction error.
- We adopt a binary discriminator to further separate the in-distribution data from the OOD data by taking the reconstructed image as fake OOD samples. Thus, our model has better discriminative capability for the inter-class as well as intra-class OOD cases.
- We conduct extensive experiments on multiple public medical image datasets to demonstrate the generalization ability of our proposed model. We evaluate comprehensively against state-of-the-art anomaly detectors in detecting both intra-class and inter-class OOD data, showing improved performance. The implementation technical report including original code and usage instructions has been publicly available.

2   Method

2.1   CVAD Architecture

Figure 2 shows the design of CVAD. Inspired by the GAN's architecture, we adopt a cascade VAE architecture as the "generator" for modeling ID repre-

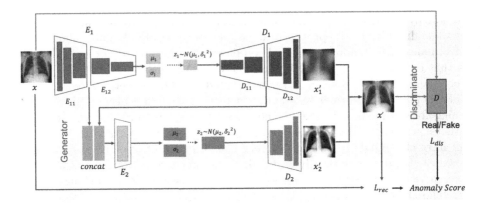

Fig. 2. Proposed CVAD architecture - a cascade VAE as the generator and a separate binary classifier (D) as the discriminator.

sentations and a separate classifier as the "discriminator" to strengthen OOD discrimination.

Generator: Different from the standard VAE, our "generator" has two encoders E_1, E_2 and two decoders D_1, D_2. To learn the high-level features, a deep and standard VAE architecture constructed by E_1 and D_1 formulates the deep latent variables z_1 by sampling parameters μ_1 and σ_1 of size K. Meanwhile, the low-level features are learnt by the branch VAE. Instead of using the original input, branch VAE utilizes the concatenation of two intermediate features from E_{11} and D_{11}. Given original input variables x, the input of branch VAE can be represented as $f(x)$. The encoder of branch VAE E_2 is simpler than E_1 whereas the decoder D_2 owns the same architecture as D_{12}. This branch VAE formulates latent Gaussian distributions with parameters μ_2, σ_2 of size $4K$. After sampling, two sets of latent variables, i.e., z_1, z_2 are acquired and decoded to image contexts x'_1 and finer details x'_2 respectively. x is the combination of x'_1 and x'_2.

Discriminator: Since the "generator" itself has no awareness of distinguishing outliers, we add a binary discriminator D to distinguish the reconstructed image x' from the original input image x. As x' shares very similar features with x after the first-stage training of the image generator, the discriminator is much more sensitive to minor differences from the in-distribution data, enhancing the accuracy of identifying both intra-class OOD data and inter-class OOD data.

2.2   Combined Loss Function

Instead of training CVAD in an adversarial way, we train the generator and the discriminator in two stages. The reason is that training with adversarial losses often leads to much sharper reconstructions but ignores the low-level information of ID data, incurring high reconstruction errors and potential dangerous decisions for medical applications. Therefore, CAVD is designed to first train the image generator and then the binary discriminator to detect OOD data. This non-adversarial training enables CVAD to inherit the merit of VAEs and avoid the instability of GANs.

To optimize the generator, we minimize two objectives for the primary VAE part in Eq. 1 and the branch VAE part in Eq. 2, KL refers to Kullback-Leibler divergence.

$$L(x; \phi_1, \theta_1) = -E_{z_1 \sim q_{\phi_1}(z_1|x)}[log \, p_{\theta_1}(x|z_1)] + D_{KL}(q_{\phi_1}(z_1|x)||p_{\theta_1}(z_1)) \quad (1)$$

$$L(x; \phi_2, \theta_2) = -E_{z_2 \sim q_{\phi_2}(z_2|f(x))}[log \, p_{\theta_2}(x|z_2)] + D_{KL}(q_{\phi_2}(z_2|f(x))||p_{\theta_2}(z_2)) \quad (2)$$

Therefore, the "generator" loss can be formulated as Eq. 3. α_1 and α_2 to balance the weights of the two individual terms.

$$L_G = \alpha_1 L(x; \phi_1, \theta_1) + \alpha_2 L(x; \phi_2, \theta_2) \quad (3)$$

The binary discriminator is trained to distinguish true/fake images using binary cross entropy.

An anomaly score S is defined in Eq. 4 based on errors during inference and includes two parts: the reconstruction error L_G output by the "generator" and the probability of being the anomaly class S_D output by the discriminator. Instead of simply adding the two parts together, we first scale the "generator" reconstruction errors into [0,1] for the whole dataset and get the average score value to avoid assigning imbalanced weights between the two parts:

$$S = 0.5 * \left(\frac{L_G - L_{Gmin}}{L_{Gmax} - L_{Gmin}} + S_D \right) \quad (4)$$

2.3   Network Details

As illustrated in Fig. 2, our generator has a standard VAE part which consists of E_{11}, E_{12}, D_{11} and D_{12} and a branch VAE composed by a shallow encoder E_2 and a decoder D_2. The primary VAE is a symmetric network with five 4×4 convolutions with stride 2 and padding 1 followed by five transposed convolutions. Respectively, E_{11} stands for the first three convolution layers; E_{12} refers the last two convolution layers; D_{11} is for the first three transposed convolution layers and D_{12} means the last two transposed convolution layers. The input of the branch VAE is the intermediate features of E_{11} and the middle decoded features of D_{11}. E_2 here is a convolution layer which has a same 4×4 kernel with stride 2 and padding 1. D_2 shares the same decoder architecture as D_{12}. All convolutions and transposed-convolutions are followed by batch normalization and leaky ReLU (with slope 0.2) operations. We used a base channel size of 16 and increased number of channels by a factor of 2 with every encoder layer and decreased the number of channels to half for each decoder layer. The latent dimension K of z_1 is set as 512 and z_2 is with $4K$, i.e., 2048 dimensions. The parameters are selected empirically as we found that smaller latent dimensions weaken the fine-grained details learning and larger latent dimensions are resource-expensive to train. The binary discriminator is composed of five convolution layers with the same settings as above and a final fully connected layer to make a binary prediction. After a sigmoid function, the final ID/OOD class probability is obtained.

Table 1. AUC scores predicted by OOD detectors for inter-class identification on RSNA, IVC-Filter and SIIM datasets. Bold indicates the best performance. The total number of samples of each dataset is reported in the bracket of *Details* column.

Dataset	Details	Methods	AUROC score		
			InterClass1	*InterClass2*	*InterClass3*
RSNA	In-class: normal (8,851)	AE [18]	$0.677^{\pm0.006}$	$0.608^{\pm0.005}$	$0.616^{\pm0.004}$
	Intra-class: pneumonia (9,555), abnormal (11,821)	VAE [2]	$0.752^{\pm0.004}$	$0.604^{\pm0.007}$	$0.613^{\pm0.006}$
	InterClass1: BIRD (37,715)	DeepSVDD [17]	$0.838^{\pm0.005}$	$\mathbf{0.834^{\pm0.004}}$	$0.604^{\pm0.006}$
	InterClass2: SIIM (33,125)	GANomaly [1]	$0.733^{\pm0.005}$	$0.816^{\pm0.004}$	$0.597^{\pm0.007}$
	InterClass3: IVC-Filter (1,258)	f-AnoGAN [19]	$0.842^{\pm0.001}$	$0.693^{\pm0.001}$	$0.682^{\pm0.002}$
		CVAD (ours)	$\mathbf{0.863^{\pm0.003}}$	$0.803^{\pm0.004}$	$\mathbf{0.703^{\pm0.005}}$
IVC-Filter	In-class: type 11 (196)	AE [18]	$0.372^{\pm0.051}$	$0.342^{\pm0.041}$	$0.237^{\pm0.051}$
	Intra-class: type 0-10, 12,13 (1,062)	VAE [2]	$0.666^{\pm0.026}$	$0.400^{\pm0.039}$	$0.706^{\pm0.027}$
	InterClass1: BIRD (37,715)	DeepSVDD [17]	$0.861^{\pm0.051}$	$0.724^{\pm0.060}$	$0.883^{\pm0.102}$
	InterClass2: SIIM (33,125)	GANomaly [1]	$0.803^{\pm0.018}$	$0.827^{\pm0.190}$	$0.922^{\pm0.072}$
	InterClass3: RSNA (30,227)	f-AnoGAN [19]	$0.911^{\pm0.020}$	$0.625^{\pm0.043}$	$0.864^{\pm0.042}$
		CVAD	$\mathbf{0.984}^{\pm0.002}$	$\mathbf{0.911}^{\pm0.017}$	$\mathbf{0.985}^{\pm0.001}$
SIIM	In-class: benign (32,541)	AE [18]	$0.572^{\pm0.004}$	$0.013^{\pm0.000}$	$0.752^{\pm0.005}$
	Intra-class: malignant (584)	VAE [2]	$0.712^{\pm0.006}$	$0.021^{\pm0.002}$	$0.759^{\pm0.003}$
	InterClass1: BIRD (37,715)	DeepSVDD [17]	$0.980^{\pm0.001}$	$\mathbf{0.992^{\pm0.000}}$	$0.804^{\pm0.002}$
	InterClass2: IVC-Filter (1,258)	GANomaly [1]	$0.688^{\pm0.005}$	$0.989^{\pm0.000}$	$0.442^{\pm0.006}$
	InterClass3: RSNA (30,227)	f-AnoGAN [19]	$0.951^{\pm0.001}$	$0.924^{\pm0.002}$	$0.606^{\pm0.003}$
		CVAD	$\mathbf{0.983^{\pm0.001}}$	$0.978^{\pm0.001}$	$\mathbf{0.869^{\pm0.003}}$

3 Experiments

3.1 Datasets and Implementation Details

We conducted extensive experiments on multiple open-access medical image datasets for intra- and inter-class OOD detection. In total, we used three medical image datasets – RSNA Pneumonia dataset [21], inferior vena cava filters (IVC-Filter in short) on radiographs [11] and SIIM-ISIC Melanoma dataset [16] (identify melanoma in lesion images) and one natural image datasets – Bird Species[2]. Column *Details* of Table 1 lists the class information and number of images for each dataset and the corresponding usage. Bird dataset was only used as inter-class OOD for detection validation, which is an extension evaluation of medical OOD detectors in identifying OOD inputs from a very different domain, e.g., natural world objects. To unify the OOD detection pipeline and facilitate evaluation, we resized both the medical images and the validation inter-class OOD images to a unified $256 \times 256 \times channel$ size. To train the anomaly detectors, we split the ID data into training and valuation parts in the ratio of 80% v.s. 20%. All the OOD data will only be used during evaluation phase. We implemented our model by setting both α_1 and α_2 as 1. We evaluated our anomaly detection model performance in terms of standard statistical metrics - (i) area under the receiver operating characteristic (AUROC, AUC in short); (ii) True Positive rate (TPR); (iii) False positive rate (FPR). To classify ID and OOD classes, a threshold should be defined for the anomaly scores. Notably, the AUC

---

[2] https://www.kaggle.com/gpiosenka/100-bird-species.

Table 2. Intra-class OOD detection results (FPR, TPR and AUC values) of various anomaly detectors trained on RSNA, IVC-Filter and SIIM datasets. Best results are highlighted. Standard deviations are calculated via 10 rounds of bootstrapping estimations.

Methods	RSNA			IVC-Filter			SIIM		
	↓FPR	↑TPR	↑AUC	↓FPR	↑TPR	↑AUC	↓FPR	↑TPR	↑AUC
AE [18]	$0.318^{\pm0.014}$	$0.461^{\pm0.009}$	$0.566^{\pm0.004}$	$0.198^{\pm0.104}$	$0.350^{\pm0.075}$	$0.436^{\pm0.040}$	$0.420^{\pm0.024}$	$0.714^{\pm0.030}$	$0.673^{\pm0.006}$
VAE [2]	$0.473^{\pm0.001}$	$0.462^{\pm0.001}$	$0.487^{\pm0.001}$	$0.489^{\pm0.097}$	$0.707^{\pm0.076}$	$0.542^{\pm0.080}$	$0.442^{\pm0.008}$	$0.740^{\pm0.006}$	$0.676^{\pm0.023}$
DeepSVDD [17]	$0.508^{\pm0.021}$	$0.413^{\pm0.023}$	$0.421^{\pm0.009}$	$0.503^{\pm0.106}$	$0.672^{\pm0.042}$	$0.500^{\pm0.075}$	$0.276^{\pm0.036}$	$0.683^{\pm0.050}$	$0.740^{\pm0.010}$
GANomaly [1]	$0.524^{\pm0.005}$	$0.678^{\pm0.015}$	$0.576^{\pm0.005}$	$0.446^{\pm0.172}$	$0.627^{\pm0.227}$	$0.518^{\pm0.103}$	$0.553^{\pm0.103}$	$0.495^{\pm0.108}$	$0.418^{\pm0.016}$
f-AnoGAN [19]	$0.365^{\pm0.033}$	$0.541^{\pm0.029}$	$0.614^{\pm0.005}$	$0.419^{\pm0.077}$	$0.611^{\pm0.054}$	$0.544^{\pm0.042}$	$0.381^{\pm0.000}$	$0.624^{\pm0.033}$	$0.721^{\pm0.015}$
CVAD (ours)	$0.327^{\pm0.016}$	$0.646^{\pm0.017}$	$\mathbf{0.696}^{\pm0.005}$	$0.541^{\pm0.094}$	$0.706^{\pm0.091}$	$\mathbf{0.582}^{\pm0.031}$	$0.376^{\pm0.020}$	$0.766^{\pm0.021}$	$\mathbf{0.749}^{\pm0.010}$

value is threshold-invariant, while the TPR and FPR are determined by the selection of the anomaly threshold. We adopted the Geometric Mean (G-Mean) method to determine an optimal threshold for the ROC curve by tuning the decision thresholds and reported the resulting FPR and TPR values. To be fair and thorough, we ran all the experiments on both intra-class OOD and inter-class OOD to further analyze the performance of anomaly detectors on the specific type of OOD detection.

3.2 Results

We set the vanilla AE and VAE architectures as baselines and compared our CVAD model with several representative models with varying architectures – a classifier-based approach DeepSVDD [17], and two GAN-based methods, i.e., GANomaly [1] and f-AnoGAN [19]. Table 1 primarily presents the inter-class OOD performance and Table 2 shows the models' performance for the intra-class OOD detection.

Results for Inter-class OOD Detection. To fairly evaluate all the models, we test them on multiple inter-class OOD data types and present the corresponding AUC scores in Table 1. CVAD obtains the highest AUC values on RSNA and SIIM datasets (except for inter-class2), and performs the best for IVC-Filter dataset across three inter-class OOD detection evaluations. Especially, CVAD remains highest ability to detect Bird OOD data, which indicates its potentials in excluding the OOD samples that are from very different domains. Generally, the inter-class OOD detection of CVAD is satisfied with stable performance.

Results for Intra-class OOD Detection. On the RSNA dataset, CVAD achieves the best AUC score 0.696 (+0.275 from DeepSVDD's AUC score 0.421, +0.120 from GANomaly's AUC score 0.576, +0.082 from f-AnoGAN's AUC score 0.614); for IVC-Filter, CVAD obtains the highest AUC values 0.582; for SIIM dataset, although DeepSVDD and f-AnoGAN show competitive performance, CVAD acquires the optimal AUC score 0.749. Overall, CVAD performs stably and effectively for intra-class OOD detection, while the other methods fail to maintain their advantages over all the tasks (both inter- and intra-class OOD detection) .

Table 3. AUC scores predicted by the "generator" CVAD_G, the discriminator CVAD_D and CVAD for inter-class identification on RSNA, IVC-Filter and SIIM datasets respectively.

Dataset	Methods	AUROC score			
		IntraClass	*InterClass1*	*InterClass2*	*InterClass3*
RSNA	*CVAD_ G (ours)*	$0.602^{\pm0.006}$	$0.854^{\pm0.003}$	$0.517^{\pm0.004}$	$0.601^{\pm0.005}$
	CVAD_D (ours)	$0.672^{\pm0.005}$	$0.793^{\pm0.003}$	$0.809^{\pm0.003}$	$0.679^{\pm0.005}$
	CVAD (ours)	$0.696^{\pm0.005}$	$0.863^{\pm0.003}$	$0.803^{\pm0.004}$	$0.703^{\pm0.005}$
IVC-Filter	*CVAD_ G (ours)*	$0.568^{\pm0.031}$	$0.981^{\pm0.003}$	$0.787^{\pm0.023}$	$0.983^{\pm0.002}$
	CVAD_D (ours)	$0.543^{\pm0.041}$	$0.661^{\pm0.018}$	$0.925^{\pm0.011}$	$0.834^{\pm0.013}$
	CVAD (ours)	$0.582^{\pm0.031}$	$0.984^{\pm0.002}$	$0.911^{\pm0.017}$	$0.985^{\pm0.001}$
SIIM	*CVAD_ G (ours)*	$0.746^{\pm0.010}$	$0.995^{\pm0.000}$	$0.995^{\pm0.000}$	$0.827^{\pm0.004}$
	CVAD_D (ours)	$0.724^{\pm0.008}$	$0.874^{\pm0.002}$	$0.055^{\pm0.001}$	$0.862^{\pm0.005}$
	CVAD (ours)	$0.749^{\pm0.010}$	$0.983^{\pm0.001}$	$0.978^{\pm0.001}$	$0.869^{\pm0.003}$

Effectiveness of CVAD's Components. We here demonstrate the importance of each component of CVAD. Table 3 shows the performance difference under the intra-class and three inter-class OOD data situations. CVAD_G represents the "generator", CVAD_D stands for only using the predictions of the discriminator. CVAD balances the two components' prediction. As can be observed, CVAD_G and CVAD_D show certain variations for different cases. For example, CVAD_D generally works better than CVAD_G for RSNA dataset but behaves worse than CVAD_G in SIIM scenario. Nevertheless, each component owns its unique OOD discriminative ability, and combining their advantages entitles CVAD the capability of capturing both intra-class and inter-class dissimilarities. For which sake, CVAD has better generalization and can perform well and stably under different situations.

Anomaly Detection. Figure 3 shows two experimental results for RSNA dataset. Each row stands for one case and each column represents a specific type of input data. From left to right, they are in-distribution data, intra-class OOD data, inter-class OOD1 data, inter-class OOD2 data and inter-class OOD3 data, respectively. The corresponding anomaly score predicted by CVAD is on top of each example. Higher anomaly scores mean more likely the inputs are OOD. As can be seen in Fig. 3, the two intra-class OOD samples (2nd column) are alike as the in-distribution data but the inter-class OOD examples show very different appearance from in-distribution data. Correspondingly, the anomaly scores of intra-class OOD are close to the scores of ID samples and difficult to separate whereas the intra-class OOD cases with clear variations are assigned higher anomaly scores and are easy to identify. This phenomenon further demonstrates the challenges of identifying intra-class OOD data.

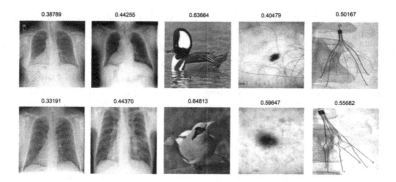

Fig. 3. Anomaly scores output by CVAD for different types of input data (experiments for RNSA dataset). Columns from left to right, ID, intra-class OOD, inter-class OOD1, inter-class OOD2, inter-class OOD3.

4 Conclusion

We propose an effective medical anomaly detector CVAD that can reconstruct coarse and fine image components by learning multi-scale latent representations. The high quality of generated images enhances the discriminative ability of the binary discriminator in identifying unknown OOD data. We demonstrate the OOD detection efficacy for both intra-class and inter-class OOD data on various medical and natural image datasets. Our model has no prior constraints on the input images and application scenarios for OOD, thus can be applied to detect OOD samples in a generic way for multiple scenarios. A detailed technical report about the code implementation and parameter usages of CVAD has been publicly available for easy reproduction.

Acknowledgements. The work is supported by the National Institute of Biomedical Imaging and Bioengineering (NIBIB) MIDRC grant of the National Institutes of Health under contracts 75N92020C00008 and 75N92020C00021 and the US National Science Foundation #1928481 from the Division of Electrical, Communication & Cyber Systems.

References

1. Akcay, S., Atapour-Abarghouei, A., Breckon, T.P.: GANomaly: semi-supervised anomaly detection via adversarial training. In: Jawahar, C.V., Li, H., Mori, G., Schindler, K. (eds.) ACCV 2018. LNCS, vol. 11363, pp. 622–637. Springer, Cham (2019). https://doi.org/10.1007/978-3-030-20893-6_39
2. An, J., Cho, S.: Variational autoencoder based anomaly detection using reconstruction probability. Spec. Lect. IE **2**(1), 1–18 (2015)
3. Bao, J., Chen, D., Wen, F., Li, H., Hua, G.: CVAE-GAN: fine-grained image generation through asymmetric training. In: Proceedings of the IEEE International Conference on Computer Vision, pp. 2745–2754 (2017)

4. Chen, L., You, Z., Zhang, N., Xi, J., Le, X.: UTRAD: anomaly detection and localization with u-transformer. Neural Netw. **147**, 53–62 (2022)

5. Duan, J., et al.: Bridging gap between image pixels and semantics via supervision: a survey. APSIPA Trans. Signal Inf. Process. **11**(1), 1–9 (2022)

6. Guo, X., Gichoya, J.W., Purkayastha, S., Banerjee, I.: Margin-aware intraclass novelty identification for medical images. J. Med. Imaging **9**(1), 014004 (2022)

7. Han, X., Chen, X., Liu, L.P.: Gan ensemble for anomaly detection. In: Proceedings of the AAAI Conference on Artificial Intelligence. vol. 35, pp. 4090–4097 (2021)

8. Huang, H., et al.: Introvae: Introspective variational autoencoders for photographic image synthesis. Adv. Neural Inf. Process. Syst. **31**, 1–11 (2018)

9. Li, D., Chen, D., Goh, J., Ng, S.k.: Anomaly detection with generative adversarial networks for multivariate time series. arXiv preprint arXiv:1809.04758 (2018)

10. Li, X., Desrosiers, C., Liu, X.: Symmetric contrastive loss for out-of-distribution skin lesion detection. In: 2022 IEEE 19th International Symposium on Biomedical Imaging (ISBI), pp. 1–5. IEEE (2022)

11. Ni, J.C., et al.: Deep learning for automated classification of inferior vena cava filter types on radiographs. J. Vasc. Interv. Radiol. **31**(1), 66–73 (2020)

12. Perera, P., Nallapati, R., Xiang, B.: OCGAN: one-class novelty detection using GANs with constrained latent representations. In: Proceedings of the IEEE/CVF Conference on Computer Vision and Pattern Recognition, pp. 2898–2906 (2019)

13. Pol, A.A., Berger, V., Germain, C., Cerminara, G., Pierini, M.: Anomaly detection with conditional variational autoencoders. In: 2019 18th IEEE International Conference on Machine Learning and Applications (ICMLA), pp. 1651–1657. IEEE (2019)

14. Ran, X., Xu, M., Mei, L., Xu, Q., Liu, Q.: Detecting out-of-distribution samples via variational auto-encoder with reliable uncertainty estimation. Neural Netw. **145**, 199–208 (2022)

15. Razavi, A., Van den Oord, A., Vinyals, O.: Generating diverse high-fidelity images with VQ-VAE-2. Adv. Neural Inf. Process. Syst. **32**, 1–9 (2019)

16. Rotemberg, V., et al.: A patient-centric dataset of images and metadata for identifying melanomas using clinical context. Sci. Data **8**(1), 1–8 (2021)

17. Ruff, L., et al.: Deep one-class classification. In: International Conference on Machine Learning, pp. 4393–4402. PMLR (2018)

18. Sakurada, M., Yairi, T.: Anomaly detection using autoencoders with nonlinear dimensionality reduction. In: Proceedings of the MLSDA 2014 2nd workshop on machine learning for sensory data analysis, pp. 4–11 (2014)

19. Schlegl, T., Seeböck, P., Waldstein, S.M., Langs, G., Schmidt-Erfurth, U.: f-AnoGAN: fast unsupervised anomaly detection with generative adversarial networks. Med. Image Anal. **54**, 30–44 (2019)

20. Tschuchnig, M.E., Gadermayr, M.: Anomaly detection in medical imaging-a mini review. Data Sci. Anal. Appl. 33–38 (2022)

21. Wang, X., Peng, Y., Lu, L., Lu, Z., Bagheri, M., Summers, R.M.: Chest X-ray8: Hospital-scale chest X-ray database and benchmarks on weakly-supervised classification and localization of common thorax diseases. In: Proceedings of the IEEE Conference on Computer Vision and Pattern Recognition, pp. 2097–2106 (2017)

22. Xia, X., et al.: GAN-based anomaly detection: a review. Neurocomputing **493**, 497–535 (2022)

23. Zimmerer, D., Petersen, J., Maier-Hein, K.: High-and low-level image component decomposition using VAES for improved reconstruction and anomaly detection. arXiv preprint arXiv:1911.12161 (2019)

Approaches for Noisy, Missing, and Low Quality Data

Visual Field Prediction with Missing and Noisy Data Based on Distance-Based Loss

Quang T. M. Pham[1], Jong Chul Han[2,3], and Jitae Shin[1(✉)]

[1] Department of Electrical and Computer Engineering, Sungkyunkwan University,
Suwon 16419, Korea
jtshin@skku.edu
[2] Department of Ophthalmology, Samsung Medical Center, Sungkyunkwan
University School of Medicine, Seoul 03181, Korea
[3] Department of Medical Device, Management and Research, SAIHST,
Sungkyunkwan University, Seoul 03181, Korea

Abstract. Glaucoma is a threatening eye disease that can cause blindness. It is common to use visual field (VF) tests and optical coherence tomography (OCT) images for monitoring glaucoma. However, it is hard to utilize both VF tests and OCT images because of the limitation of data. The missing data can be a challenge for deep learning models. Moreover, the instability of VF tests also leads to a degradation of the dataset. It can make models learn wrong patterns. Therefore, we propose a deep learning model to predict future VF based on both previous VF tests and OCT images regardless of the missing data. To deal with unstable VF data, a distance-based loss function is introduced. As the result, our proposed model shows a significant improvement in the future VF prediction task.

Keywords: Visual field · Future prediction · Deep learning

1 Introduction

Glaucoma is an eye disease that damages the optic nerve [11]. It is one of the main causes of blindness worldwide, especially in the elderly group [5]. To monitor the development of glaucoma, doctors commonly conduct visual field (VF) tests. However, the VF test is a time-consuming process. The test can give poor reliability since it depends on patient comprehension or cooperation. Thus, the damaged point on VF tests can be shuffled between test times (Fig. 1). The unreliable data can degrade the performance of the deep learning model since the mean square loss function requires the accurate ground truth at the point-wise level.

Besides the VF test, the OCT test also can be used to keep track of glaucoma [10]. The advantages of the OCT test are fast and reliable. However, the OCT test is expensive. For that reason, there is less OCT data available compared to VF data. In order to exploit both VF and OCT data, we have to deal with the missing data issue.

© The Author(s), under exclusive license to Springer Nature Switzerland AG 2022
G. Zamzmi et al. (Eds.): MILLanD 2022, LNCS 13559, pp. 199–205, 2022.
https://doi.org/10.1007/978-3-031-16760-7_19

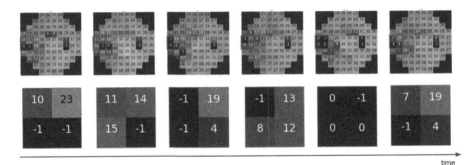

Fig. 1. The instability of VF tests.

The previous studies mainly used a series of VFs to predict glaucoma progression. Yousefi et al. [13] introduced a Gaussian model for glaucoma progression detection while a 3D convolution model is applied in [9]. For the future VFs prediction task, several deep learning models are exploited [2,12]. An RNN model is used in [6] while Berchuck et al. [2] proposed a VAE model. However, those works only utilize VFs data. To exploit both VFs and OCT images, a deeply-regularized latent-space linear regression model is introduced in [1,14]. However, the limitation of medical data still remains.

In this research, we propose a deep learning model to predict future VF. We use both the VF test and OCT test as input. Our model can deal with the missing data problem by providing mask data. On the other hand, a new loss function is introduced to handle the instability of VF tests.

2   Method

The model is based on the baseline model [7] which combines Convolution Neural Network (CNN) and Long Short-Term Memory (LSTM) [4]. The input includes previous VF tests, OCT images, and mask information. The OCT images are the set of RNFL thickness maps, horizontal tomograms, and vertical tomograms. The baseline model includes two main parts. The CNN part is a ResNet-50 extractor [3], which is used for extracting features from OCT images. Then, the series of image features and VF data are fed into an LSTM module. Instead of using Mean Square Error (MSE), a weighted MSE is applied to handle noisy data. Firstly, each VF test is evaluated to detect noisy data. Based on that, we assign the weight of VF tests for training. The good samples have weights of 1 while the noisy samples have lower weights. It helps the model pay less attention to noisy data so the effect of noise is reduced.

While the baseline model only accepts paired data (both VF and OCT data are available), our model can deal with missing data by using mask information. The missing OCT images are filled as black images. The mask information is a vector that indicates whether that OCT image is missing or available.

Commonly, we define 1 as available and 0 as missing data in masks. In our case, we use the weights obtained from the weighted MSE as values for masks (Fig. 2). It is more helpful since those values reflect the impact of each VF test during training. Consequently, it helps our model to pay less attention to noisy VF tests. The mask information is fed into the LSTM module along with OCT features and VF data.

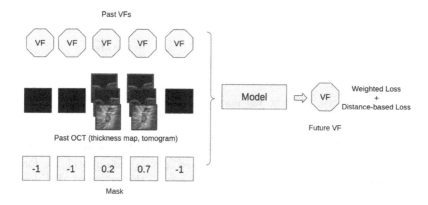

Fig. 2. The overview of the proposed model.

2.1   Distance-Based Loss

The weighted MSE is good for detecting noisy data. However, it can only handle noisy data at the sample level. In the VF test, the result strongly depends on patient cooperation. It gives small deviations to the results. Therefore, it is possible that the damaged points are not in the same position between different test times. But we can assume that the deviations are narrow. Thus, we propose a new loss function, called distance-based loss, to deal with this issue. This loss function can relax the point-wise criterion while comparing the ground truth and VF prediction. As the result, the distance-based loss can perform better than the MSE in such cases.

The distance-based loss can be described in Fig. 3. Firstly, we should detect the damaged point in the VF test. In our case, we apply a fixed threshold. The normal sensitivity is 32.8 dB [8]. Therefore, we consider that all the points below 30 are considered damaged points. Next step, we define a set of neighbors of damaged points. These neighbors are regions where deviations can occur. Since the deviations are small, only the next-to points of damaged points are set as neighbors (distance is 1). After that, we calculate the difference between the ground truth and VF prediction of each point in neighbor regions. We set a lower weight, β, for the points that have negative differences (the predicted value is lower than the ground-truth value, $\beta < 1$). For the other points, we set weights as 1. Finally, we apply the weighted MSE with those weights. Note that, the distance-based loss is more efficient than the weighted MSE loss used

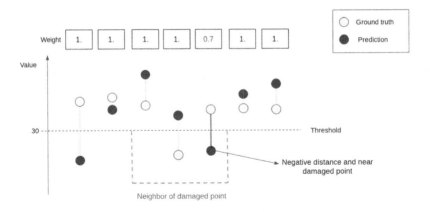

Fig. 3. The distance-based loss.

in the baseline model. While the same weight is applied to all points in the case of weighted MSE loss, the distance-based loss gives different weights for each point. For training the proposed model, we use both the weighted MSE loss and the distance-based loss:

$$L_{main} = \alpha_1 L_{weightedMSE} + \alpha_2 L_{distance-based} \tag{1}$$

where α_1 and α_2 are weights for each loss.

3   Experiments

3.1   Dataset and Implementation

Our dataset includes 1527 paired 30-2 visual field maps and OCT tests from 266 patients. The average age of patients is 57 years old. The number of visits of each patient is 5.7 on average. The visual field test and OCT test can be taken on different dates. Therefore, we consider a paired visual field - thickness map as the time interval between two tests is less than 6 months. All left eyes are flipped horizontally (for RNFL thickness maps, horizontal tomograms, and visual field maps). The visual field data is normalized with zero centering. All the image data are resized to 224 × 224.

For training, we apply common data augmentation techniques (shift, scale, and rotate). With limited data, our model is trained with only 15 epochs to avoid overfitting, the Adam optimizer is used. The initial learning rate is 0.001 and is divided by 10 after 7 epochs. We use cross-validation with 5 folds to get the final results. The weights for each loss are 1 and 1.7 for α_1 and α_2, respectively. In distance-based loss, β is set to 0.7. For more detail, the source code can be found at the Github repository https://github.com/QuangBK/future_VF_prediction.

3.2 Results

The metrics we use for experiments are Root Mean Square Error (RMSE) mean absolute error (MAE) as below:

$$RMSE = \sqrt{\frac{\sum_{i=0}^{75}\left(x_{GT}^i - x_{pred}^i\right)^2)}{76}} \tag{2}$$

$$MAE = \frac{\sum_{i=0}^{75}\left|x_{GT}^i - x_{pred}^i\right|)}{76} \tag{3}$$

We first do an ablation study in Table 1. The results show that both mask information and distance-based loss are helpful. The MAE and RMSE scores are improved with them. Moreover, it is true that the OCT images can increase the performance compared with using only VFs data.

Table 1. The ablation study.

Input	Missing data	Distance-based loss	MAE	RMSE
VFs	✗	✗	3.33 ± 1.38	4.60 ± 1.77
VFs	✓	✗	3.29 ± 1.38	4.54 ± 1.77
VFs + images	✗	✗	3.31 ± 1.50	4.58 ± 1.84
VFs + images	✓	✗	3.16 ± 1.30	4.48 ± 1.73
VFs + images	✓	✓	3.14 ± 1.37	4.43 ± 1.77

In comparison, we refer to Berchuck's [2] and Park's [6] works. Note that, we use the same input (224×224 OCT images) for all compared methods. In Table 2, the baseline model with only weighted MSE loss can outperform the two compared methods. Our proposed method with mask information and distance-based loss gives the best performance with an MSE of 3.14 and an RMSE of 4.43. To verify the statistical significance of the results, we apply one-sided Wilcoxon tests with $p < 0.05$.

Table 2. The comparison of MAE and RMSE results (dB).

Model	MAE	RMSE
Berchuck et al. [2]	4.76 ± 2.09	6.34 ± 2.44
Park et al. [6]	3.51 ± 1.46	4.81 ± 1.83
Baseline	3.31 ± 1.37	4.58 ± 1.77
Our model	3.14 ± 1.35	4.43 ± 1.77

4   Conclusion

In this study, we propose a deep learning model for predicting future VF maps from previous VFs and OCT images (RNFL thickness maps, horizontal tomograms, and vertical tomograms). Several techniques are applied to deal with the limited data in the medical domain. Firstly, we use mask information to handle the missing data problem. Next, since VF data is not reliable, a distance-based loss is introduced. It helps to reduce the noise at the point-wise level during training with noisy VF data. The quantitative results show that our model achieves the best performance compared to other methods.

Acknowledgements. This study was partly supported by SMC-SKKU Future Convergence Research Program Grant and was partly supported by the MSIT (Ministry of Science and ICT), Korea, under the ITRC (Information Technology Research Center) support program (IITP-2022-0-01798) supervised by the IITP (Institute for Information & Communications Technology Planning Evaluation).

References

1. Asaoka, R., et al.: A joint multitask learning model for cross-sectional and longitudinal predictions of visual field using oct. Ophthalmol. Sci. **1**(4), 100055 (2021). https://doi.org/10.1016/j.xops.2021.100055. https://www.sciencedirect.com/science/article/pii/S2666914521000531

2. Berchuck, S.I., Mukherjee, S., Medeiros, F.A.: Estimating rates of progression and predicting future visual fields in glaucoma using a deep variational autoencoder. Sci. Rep. **9**(1), 18113 (2019). https://doi.org/10.1038/s41598-019-54653-6

3. He, K., Zhang, X., Ren, S., Sun, J.: Deep residual learning for image recognition. In: 2016 IEEE Conference on Computer Vision and Pattern Recognition (CVPR), pp. 770–778 (2016). https://doi.org/10.1109/CVPR.2016.90

4. Hochreiter, S., Schmidhuber, J.: Long short-term memory. Neural Comput. **9**(8), 1735–1780 (1997). https://doi.org/10.1162/neco.1997.9.8.1735

5. Kapetanakis, V.V., Chan, M.P.Y., Foster, P.J., Cook, D.G., Owen, C.G., Rudnicka, A.R.: Global variations and time trends in the prevalence of primary open angle glaucoma (POAG): a systematic review and meta-analysis. Br. J. Ophthalmol. **100**(1), 86–93 (2016). https://doi.org/10.1136/bjophthalmol-2015-307223. https://bjo.bmj.com/content/100/1/86

6. Park, K., Kim, J., Lee, J.: Visual field prediction using recurrent neural network. Sci. Rep. **9**(1), 8385 (2019). https://doi.org/10.1038/s41598-019-44852-6

7. Pham, Q.T., Han, J.C., Shin, J.: A multimodal deep learning model for predicting future visual field in glaucoma patients. https://doi.org/10.21203/rs.3.rs-1236761/v1

8. Racette, L., Fischer, M., Bebie, H., Holló, G., Johnson, C., Matsumoto, C.: Visual Field Digest. Haag-Streit AG, January 2016

9. Shon, K., Sung, K.R., Shin, J.W.: Can artificial intelligence predict glaucomatous visual field progression? A spatial-ordinal convolutional neural network model. Am. J. Ophthalmol. **233**, 124–134 (2022). https://doi.org/10.1016/j.ajo.2021.06.025. https://www.sciencedirect.com/science/article/pii/S0002939421003548

10. Tan, O., et al.: Detection of macular ganglion cell loss in glaucoma by Fourier-domain optical coherence tomography. Ophthalmology **116**(12), 2305-2314.e2 (2009). https://doi.org/10.1016/j.ophtha.2009.05.025. https://www.sciencedirect.com/science/article/pii/S0161642009005442
11. Weinreb, R.N., Aung, T., Medeiros, F.A.: The pathophysiology and treatment of glaucoma: a review. JAMA **311**(18), 1901–1911 (2014)
12. Wen, J.C., et al.: Forecasting future Humphrey visual fields using deep learning. PLoS ONE **14**(4), 1–14 (2019). https://doi.org/10.1371/journal.pone.0214875
13. Yousefi, S., et al.: Detection of longitudinal visual field progression in glaucoma using machine learning. Am. J. Ophthalmol. **193**, 71–79 (2018). https://doi.org/10.1016/j.ajo.2018.06.007.   https://www.sciencedirect.com/science/article/pii/S000293941830271X
14. Zheng, Y., et al.: Glaucoma progression prediction using retinal thickness via latent space linear regression. In: Proceedings of the 25th ACM SIGKDD International Conference on Knowledge Discovery and Data Mining, KDD 2019, pp. 2278–2286. Association for Computing Machinery, New York (2019). https://doi.org/10.1145/3292500.3330757

Image Quality Classification for Automated Visual Evaluation of Cervical Precancer

Zhiyun Xue[1]([⊠]), Sandeep Angara[1], Peng Guo[1], Sivaramakrishnan Rajaraman[1],
Jose Jeronimo[2], Ana Cecilia Rodriguez[2], Karla Alfaro[3], Kittipat Charoenkwan[4],
Chemtai Mungo[5], Joel Fokom Domgue[6,7,8], Nicolas Wentzensen[2], Kanan T. Desai[2],
Kayode Olusegun Ajenifuja[9], Elisabeth Wikström[10], Brian Befano[11],
Silvia de Sanjosé[2], Mark Schiffman[2], and Sameer Antani[1]

[1] National Library of Medicine, National Institutes of Health, Bethesda, MD 20894, USA
zhiyun.xue@nih.gov
[2] National Cancer Institute, National Institutes of Health, Rockville, MD 20850, USA
[3] Basic Health International, San Salvador, El Salvador
[4] Department of Obstetrics and Gynecology, Chiang Mai University, Chiang Mai 50200,
Thailand
[5] Department of Obstetrics and Gynecology, University of North Carolina-Chapel Hill School
of Medicine, Chapel Hill, NC, USA
[6] Cameroon Baptist Convention Health Services, Bamenda, North West Region, Cameroon
[7] Department of Obstetrics and Gynecology, Faculty of Medicine and Biomedical Sciences,
University of Yaoundé, Yaoundé, Cameroon
[8] Department of Epidemiology, The University of Texas MD Anderson Cancer Center,
Houston, TX, USA
[9] Obafemi Awolowo University Teaching Hospital Complex, Ile Ife, Nigeria
[10] Department of Women's and Children's Health, Karolinska Institutet, Stockholm, Sweden
[11] Information Management Services, Calverton, MD, USA

Abstract. Image quality control is a critical element in the process of data collection and cleaning. Both manual and automated analyses alike are adversely impacted by bad quality data. There are several factors that can degrade image quality and, correspondingly, there are many approaches to mitigate their negative impact. In this paper, we address image quality control toward our goal of improving the performance of automated visual evaluation (AVE) for cervical precancer screening. Specifically, we report efforts made toward classifying images into four quality categories ("unusable", "unsatisfactory", "limited", and "evaluable") and improving the quality classification performance by automatically identifying mislabeled and overly ambiguous images. The proposed new deep learning ensemble framework is an integration of several networks that consists of three main components: cervix detection, mislabel identification, and quality classification. We evaluated our method using a large dataset that comprises 87,420 images obtained from 14,183 patients through several cervical cancer studies conducted by different providers using different imaging devices in different geographic regions worldwide. The proposed ensemble approach achieved higher performance than the baseline approaches.

Keywords: Image quality · Uterine cervix image · Automated visual
evaluation · Mislabel identification · Ensemble learning

G. Zamzmi et al. (Eds.): MILLanD 2022, LNCS 13559, pp. 206–217, 2022.
https://doi.org/10.1007/978-3-031-16760-7_20

1 Introduction

Cervical cancer is mainly caused by persistent infection of carcinogenic human papillomavirus (HPV). It is one of the most common cancers among women. Its morbidity and mortality rates are especially high in low- and middle-income countries (LMIC). Besides HPV vaccination, effective approaches to screening and treatment of precancerous lesions play an important role in the prevention of cervical cancer. Precancer is a term that refers to the direct precursors to invasive cancer, which are the main target of cervical screening. In LMIC, due to the limited resources of medical personnel, equipment, and infrastructure, visual inspection of cervix with acetic acid (VIA) is a commonly adopted method for screening for cervical precancer (and treatable cancer). While it is simple, inexpensive, quick to get a result, and does not require expert personnel training, VIA has fairly mediocre intra- and inter- observer agreement and may result in over-treatment and under-treatment [1].

One way to improve VIA screening performance may be to combine it with a low-cost imaging device incorporated with computerized technology that uses predictive machine learning and image processing techniques, called automated visual evaluation (AVE) for the purpose of this discussion [2]. Our proof-of concept work [2, 3] that was demonstrated on two cervical image datasets showed the promise of AVE in LMIC as an adjunctive tool for VIA for screening, or triage of HPV-positive women if such testing is available. Subsequent work has revealed possible problems in implementation [4]. For instance, image quality control, among others, is a key issue.

There are many factors that can adversely affect or degrade image quality. Some are related to clinical or anatomical aspects of cervix, such as the visibility of the transformation zone where cervical cancers tend to arise, and the presence of occlusion due to vaginal tissue, blood, mucus, and medical instruments (e.g., speculum, cotton swab, intrauterine device). Some of these are related to the technical aspect of imaging device and the illumination condition, such as blur, noise, glare, shadow, discoloration, and low contrast, among others. While it is important to train care providers to take high-quality pictures, it is also of importance to develop automated techniques to limit, control, and remedy the image quality problem in existing data sets as well as during acquisition. To this end, we have been working on several aspects, such as filtering out non-cervix images [5], identifying green-filtered images and iodine-applied images [6], separating sharp images from non-sharp images [7], and deblurring blurry images [8]. We also have been working on analyzing the effects of several image quality degradation factors on the performance of AVE. These include carrying out experiments to quantitively examine and evaluate the AVE results on different levels of image noise and the effectiveness of denoising on AVE [9].

In real-world images, there are often multiple types of degradation existing simultaneously which may vary within as well as across datasets. It may be very difficult to synthesize (mimic) certain types of degradation let alone a combination of multiple degradation types which is significantly harder. Therefore, we have been interested in developing a general image quality classifier using the data labeled by expert clinician annotators based on their judgment. For the quality grading, the annotators were guided by predetermined criteria comprising several factors. They were developed by researchers at National Cancer Institute (NCI) who contributed the first-round quality filtering. Using this guide, NCI researchers assigned image quality labels ("unusable", "unsatisfactory", "limited", and "evaluable") for images in six datasets that were obtained from different studies, geographical areas, and sources. The guide was specifically designed to reduce the workload and labor time of collaborating gynecologists for annotating images with respect to diagnostic review (for AVE disease grading and treatability analysis), i.e., cutting down the number of low(bad)-quality images among the images to be reviewed by the gynecologists. We noted that the images had a large variance in appearance within each dataset and across datasets. The combined dataset contains 14,183 patients and 87,420 images. We aimed to develop a 4-class quality classifier using this multi-source data.

It is common for a large real-world dataset to be noisy and have mis-annotations due to fatigue, misunderstanding, and highly ambiguous samples. Therefore, using all the available training data sometimes may not be the best choice for achieving good generalization. In our dataset, there might be high degrees of ambiguity between some samples in the adjacent classes such as "unsatisfactory" and "limited", and "limited" and "evaluable" (as implied in the descriptions of labeling criteria in Sect. 2). We also happened to notice the existence of mislabeled images in the training dataset during random visual browsing. Like labeling itself, manual label cleaning for a large dataset is tedious and labor-intensive. To deal with noisy labels and reduce their negative effects on model performance, one can: 1) design a network that takes weak supervision into consideration; and 2) identify mislabeled or highly ambiguous data automatically. In this paper, we focus on the latter. That is, in addition, to develop an image quality classifier, we are interested in removing/cleaning data used in training to produce better generalization performance.

There are prior works in the literature aiming for mislabel identification. The majority of them monitor the training process and extract certain measures that can be used to represent the difference between clean and mislabeled samples from the training process [10–13]. For example, based on the observation that the curve of the training accuracy with the increase of training epochs is different between clean and bad samples, the authors in [10] developed an iterative approach in which a model was retrained by using only the samples having the lowest loss at the current iteration. Another such example is [11], which proposed a method to use the area under the margin (AUM) value to measure the difference in the training dynamics (as a function of training epochs) between the correctly and incorrectly labeled samples. [11] also developed an effective way (using so-called indicator samples) to find a suitable threshold value to separate the AUM values of correctly labeled samples from those of in-correctly labeled samples. For our application, we selected and applied a method [14] that is based on an alternative idea. It identifies label errors by directly estimating the joint distribution between noisy observed labels and unknown uncorrupted labels based on the model prediction probability scores [14]. We integrated this algorithm into our image quality classification ensemble framework.

The main contribution of our work is: we developed a new approach that utilizes ensemble methods for both mislabel identification and quality classification for uterine cervix images. We also carried out comparison and ablation experiments to demonstrate the effectiveness of the proposed approach. In the following sections, we first introduce the large dataset collected from multiple sources and the criteria used for manual quality annotation, next present the whole quality classification framework that contains three main components, then describe experimental tests, comparison, and discussion, and at last conclude the paper.

2 Image Quality Labeling Criteria and Data

In this section, we describe the criteria used for AVE image quality annotation and the image datasets that were labeled.

2.1 The Labeling Criteria

These labeling criteria aim to be used for guiding an image taker or health worker for their first round of image quality examination, i.e., to be used for annotating an image based on the technical quality and the ability to see acetowhite areas, not based on anatomical considerations (e.g., squamous-columnar junction (SCJ) observability). There are four image quality categories: *unusable*, *unsatisfactory*, *limited*, and *evaluable*. Images labeled as "limited" or "evaluable" will be used for diagnostic review. The brief guidelines for each category are as follows.

- **Unusable:** The image is one of the following types: non-cervix, iodine, green-filtered, post-surgery, or having an upload artifact.
- **Unsatisfactory**: The image is not "unusable", but image quality does not allow for evaluation, e.g., has too much blur, is zoomed out/in too much.
- **Limited**: The quality is high enough to allow evaluation of the image, but the image has flaws, e.g., off-center, low light, some blur, obstruction.
- **Evaluable**: The quality is high and there are no major technical flaws. If in doubt, then classify the image as "limited"

2.2 Datasets

The images that were annotated were obtained from 6 cervical cancer studies conducted by different providers with different imaging devices at different regions/countries: NET, Dutch Biopsy (Bx), ITOJU [15], Sweden, Peru, and SUCCEED [16]. The name of the device and the principal investigator (PI) of each study is listed in the Appendix Table 4. For images from the NET study, they were collected from four countries (El Salvador, Kenya, Thailand, and Cameroon) with different image id prefixes. ITOJU study was carried out in Nigeria and SUCCEED (the Study to Understand Cervical Cancer Early Endpoints and Determinants) was conducted in US. The images within each dataset or across datasets have a large appearance variance with respect to not only cervix or disease related factors (such as woman's age, parity, and cervix anatomy and condition) but also non-cervix or non-disease related factors (such as illumination, imaging device, clinical instrument, zoom, and angle). In these datasets, one patient may have a varied number of images in one visit or multiple visits. Appendix Table 5 lists the number of annotated images from each study and the number of images in each quality category.

In each study, the number of images may vary significantly among quality categories. However, the total numbers of images in the combined dataset across the categories are not highly imbalanced. The reason that Dutch Bx, Sweden and Peru datasets contain a significant percentage of unusable or unsatisfactory images is because many of them are green-filtered or Lugol's iodine applied images or close-up images. Although green filter and iodine solution are not usually used in VIA, it is a common practice to use them in colposcopy examinations for visual evaluation of cervix. In addition, practitioners in colposcopy tend to take close-up images to check, show or record regions-of-interest, but significantly zoomed-in images are not considered adequate for AVE use as each image is evaluated individually by AVE. A few examples of images in each category are shown in the Appendix Fig. 3.

3   Methods

Figure 1 shows the overall diagram of the proposed method. It consists of three main components: 1) cervix detector; 2) quality classifier; and 3) mislabel identifier. The mislabel identifier is based on the result of the quality classifier trained with cross validation. We used three quality classifiers and three corresponding mislabel identifiers. We applied ensemble learning on both the results of mislabel identification and the results of quality classifications. In this study, we aim to remove/clean bad samples from the training and validation sets only, not the test set. The cleaned training and validation sets (the candidates that are identified by all three mislabel identifiers are removed) are then used to train three quality classifiers respectively. The final label of classification is generated by combining the output probability scores of the three classifiers. In the following, we provide more details for each main component.

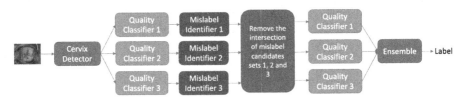

Fig. 1. Diagram of the proposed approach.

3.1   Cervix Detection

Since the cervix is the region of interest and the image may contain a significantly large area outside of the cervix, we developed a cervix locator using RetinaNet [17], a one-stage object detection network. We trained the model with a set of images in a different study (Costa Rica Vaccine Trial, conducted by the National Cancer Institute, USA [18]) whose cervices were manually marked and were not used for image quality evaluation/labeling. The detected cervix region was then cropped out and resized before being passed to a classifier. Since not all the images will have a cervix detected (for example, there are images that are not cervix images), all those images in the test set that have no cervix detected by the detector are predicted as "unusable".

3.2 Quality Classification

Image classification has been actively and extensively studied in the literature. Since the debut of AlexNet, many new algorithms or architectures have been developed in this decade of the fast-growing era of deep learning. There are two broad types of neural networks: 1) convolutional neural network (CNN) based, and 2) Transformer based. Using an ensemble of different architectures can utilize the complementary characteristics of the networks and achieve better performance. For our application, we selected three network architectures. Two of those were recent algorithms that have achieved state-of-the-art performance on large general-domain datasets: ResNeSt (ResNet50) [19] and Swin Transformer (Swin-B) [20]. We also added a simpler and smaller ResNet network (ResNet18) for comparison. For all three networks, we initialized their weights using ImageNet pre-trained models and fine-tuned them using our cervix images and labels. To combine the outputs of the three networks, we used the following ensemble method: the class whose average output probability value from all three networks is the largest value among the 4 classes is selected as the final label.

3.3 Mislabel Identification

We applied the algorithm of confident learning (CL) [14] for identifying bad samples in the training data. CL aims to identify mislabels by estimating label uncertainty, i.e., the joint distribution between the noisy and true labels. It uses predicted probability outputs from a classification model for the estimation and is data-centric instead of model-centric. Due to its model-agnostic characteristics, CL can be easily incorporated into our ensemble classification framework. To compute predicted probabilities, K-fold cross-validation is used. In CL, the class imbalance and heterogeneity in predicted probability distributions across classes are addressed by using a per-class threshold when calculating the confident joint [14]. In [21] which uses CL to identify mislabeled images in the ImageNet dataset and all the candidates were reexamined and relabeled by annotators, it showed that many of the candidates were not considered mislabeled by the annotators. Hence, to improve the precision, we used CL for all three classification networks and selected the candidates that were recommended for elimination by all three identifiers.

4 Experimental Results and Discussion

We randomly split the images at the patient level within each dataset into training/validation/test set at the ratio of 70/10/20. Table 1 lists the number of original images in the training/validation/test set in each category in each dataset, respectively. After cervix detection, there were 503, 71, and 141 images that had no cervix detected in training, validation, and test set respectively. Most of these no-cervix-detected images have ground-truth label of "unusable" and a few are of label "unsatisfactory". For the 141 test images that the cervix detector did not have output, they were all assigned with the prediction label of "unusable" (since the criteria for labeling an image as "unusable" include a "non-cervix" image).

For all the classification models (ResNeSt50, ResNet18, and Swin-B), the input images were resized to 224 × 224, and the weights were initialized with corresponding

Table 1. The number of original images in training/validation/test set.

	Unusable	Unsatisfactory	Limited	Evaluable	Total	No-cervix detected
Train	17734	18083	14376	10836	61029	503
Validation	2726	2609	2078	1548	8961	71
Test	5069	5230	4041	3090	17430	141

ImageNet pre-trained model weights. Both ResNeSt50 and ResNet18 models used the same following hyperparameters: 1) cross-entropy loss with label smoothing; 2) 64 batch size; and 3) Adam optimizer ($\beta 1 = 0.9$, $\beta 2 = 0.999$) with a learning rate of 5x10–5. For Swin-B, we used: 1) cross-entropy loss function; 2) batch size of 8; 3) Adam optimizer with a learning rate cosine scheduler (initial learning rate was 5×10^{-5} and the number of warm-up epochs was 5). All three networks used augmentation methods that include random rotation, scaling, center cropping, and horizontal and vertical flip. Each model was trained for 100 epochs and the model at the epoch with the lowest loss value on the validation set was selected.

For identifying bad samples using CL, we created 4-fold cross-validation set using the original training and validation sets and trained 4 models for each classifier. The label uncertainty of both training and validation sets was estimated from their predictions from the 4 models. For pruning, the "prune by noise rate" option was used. The number of mislabeled candidates generated by using each network from the training and validation set is given in Table 2. The number of images in the intersection is much smaller than that generated by any of the networks (6,455 vs. i.e. 13,038).

Table 2. The number of identified mislabel candidates.

	Set	Unusable	Unsatisfactory	Limited	Evaluable	Total	
ResNet18	Train	981	3037	4380	3464	11862	13602
	Val.	145	417	664	514	1740	
ResNeSt50	Train	1441	3534	5371	3518	13864	15930
	Val.	197	565	758	546	2066	
Swin-B	Train	1126	3226	4095	2947	11394	13038
	Val.	141	486	625	392	1644	
Intersection	Train	614	1346	1953	1722	5635	6455
	Val.	114	186	257	263	820	

Table 3. The classification performance on the test set (with/without bad sample removal from the training and validation set).

	Acc	Recall	Spec.	Prec.	F1	MCC	Kappa
Using original train and validation sets							
ResNeSt50	0.742	0.724	0.914	0.734	0.728	0.642	0.650
ResNet18	0.733	0.710	0.910	0.726	0.715	0.628	0.637
Swin-B	0.756	0.744	0.919	0.749	0.746	0.665	0.671
Ensemble	0.766	0.750	0.921	0.760	0.754	0.676	0.682
Using cleaned train and validation sets							
ResNeSt50	0.752	0.734	0.917	0.751	0.740	0.659	0.664
ResNet18	0.746	0.722	0.914	0.747	0.730	0.648	0.654
Swin-B	0.759	0.746	0.920	0.759	0.751	0.671	0.674
Ensemble	0.769	0.752	0.923	0.771	0.759	0.683	0.687

We used the following metrics to evaluate multi-class classification performance: accuracy and average values of recall, specificity, precision, F1 score, Matthew's correlation coefficient (MCC), and Kappa score, respectively (using the one-vs-rest approach). Table 3 lists the test set values of the above metrics for each network before and after the removal of identified mislabeled candidates from the training/validation sets. From Table 3, we observed that: 1) when the same set is used to train, the ensemble classifier achieves higher performance than any of the individual classifier; and 2) all the classifiers that are trained with the training data that excludes the mislabeled candidates obtain slightly better performance than those trained using the original data. These observations demonstrate the advantages and effectiveness of ensemble learning, as well as using more data to train may not be helpful and data quality is important. The overall improvement (ensemble plus mislabeled candidate removal) over the best baseline individual model (SwinB) is around 2.7% w.r.t. MCC ((0.683–0.665)/0.665). As shown by [21], some identified candidates may not be indeed mislabeled after the manual re-evaluation. However, to us, it is acceptable to exclude data that are in fact correctly labeled from the training process if it improves the generalization performance.

Figure 2 shows the t-SNE plot of the features extracted from ResNet18 model trained using the original training set as well as the features of the mislabeled candidates and the cleaned training set from the same t-SNE plot. It shows that the cleaned one has a better separation between classes than the original one, indicating the identified candidates may be ambiguous samples. The classification confusion matrix calculated from the test set for the ensemble classifier trained by using the cleaned training/validation set is given in the appendix. From the labeling guidelines in Sect. 2, we expect the main ambiguity to exist between the classes of "evaluable" and "limited" or the classes of "limited" and "unsatisfactory". It is confirmed by the confusion matrix (Fig. 4). As the images predicted with "limited" and "evaluable" will pass the quality check and be used for diagnostic evaluation, we also examined the binary class ("limited + evaluable" vs. "unusable + unsatisfactory") classification performance by generating the 2-class confusion matrix from the 4-class one. Its accuracy, F1 score and MCC are: 0.885, 0.859, and 0.762, respectively.

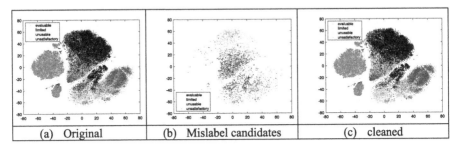

| (a)   Original | (b)   Mislabel candidates | (c)   cleaned |

Fig. 2. T-SNE plots of training set

5   Conclusions

The quality of cervix images is important to the succeeding image analysis and visual evaluation for cervix cancer screening. In this paper, we report one of our efforts toward controlling the image quality, i.e., automatically filtering out images of unacceptable quality. To this end, we developed a multi-class classifier using a large, combined dataset that was labeled with four quality categories. Due to factors including ambiguities among classes and the variance in user understanding and interpretation, it is common for a large dataset to have noisy labels. Therefore, we also aimed to improve the generalization performance by identifying and removing bad samples from the training/validation set. By integrating confident learning and ensemble learning, our proposed method achieved better prediction performance than the baseline networks.

Acknowledgement. This research was supported by the Intramural Research Program of the National Library of Medicine (NLM) and the Intramural Research Program of the National Cancer Institute (NCI). Both NLM and NCI are part of the National Institutes of Health (NIH). The NET study was supported partly by Global Good. The authors also want to thank Farideh Almani at NCI for her help.

Appendix

Table 4. The device and PI of each dataset

	Prefix		Device	PI
NET	El Salvador	Screening population	Samsung J8	Karla Alfaro kalfaro@basichealth.org
	Kenya	Screening population	Samsung J8	Chemtai Mungo chemutai.mungo@gmail.com
	Thailand	Colposcopy clinic	Samsung J8	Kittipat Charoenkwan kittipat.c@cmu.ac.th
	Cameroon	Screening population	Samsung J8	Joel Fokom Domgue fokom.domgue@gmail.com
Dutch Bx	GYFZ	Colposcopy clinic	Digital SLR Camera	Nicolas Wentzensen
ITOJU	HFLD	Screening population	Mobile ODT Eva	Kanan T. Desai and Kayode Olusegun Ajenifuja ajenifujako@yahoo.com kanan_desai2004@yahoo.com
Sweden	PUBG	Colposcopy clinic	Colposcopes	Elisabeth Wikström elisabeth.wikstrom05@gmail.com
Peru	PUBL	Colposcopy clinic	Colposcope	Jose Jeronimo
SUCCEED	SBX	Colposcopy clinic	Digital SLR Camera	Nicolas Wentzensen

Table 5. Number of images in each dataset in each quality category

	Prefix	Patients	Images	Unusable	Unsatisfactory	Limited	Evaluable
NET	BSPR	82	249	0	24	111	114
	FARH	73	356	0	91	173	92
	JBKV	159	449	3	26	201	219
	ZRQB	157	439	1	6	41	391
Dutch Bx	GYFZ	1036	7886	3839	288	1376	2383
ITOJU	HFLD	1388	19060	177	3991	7633	7259
Sweden	PUBG	878	2221	1072	362	566	221
Peru	PUBL	9736	55082	20423	20820	9568	4271
SUCCEED	SBX	674	1678	14	314	826	524
Total		14183	87420	25529	25922	20495	15474

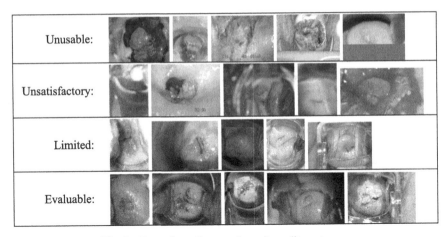

Fig. 3. Examples of images in each quality category.

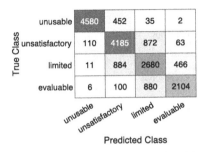

Fig. 4. The classification confusion matrix of the test set

References

1. Jeronimo, J., Massad, L.S., Castle, P.E., Wacholder, S., Schiffman, M.: Interobserver agreement in the evaluation of digitized cervical images. Obstet. Gynecol. **110**, 833–840 (2007)
2. Hu, L., Bell, D., Antani, S., Xue, Z., Yu, K., Horning, M.P., et al.: An observational study of deep learning and automated evaluation of cervical images for cancer screening. J. Natl. Cancer Inst. (JNCI) **111**(9), 923–932 (2019)
3. Xue, Z., Novetsky, A.P., Einstein, M.H., et al.: A demonstration of automated visual evaluation of cervical images taken with a smartphone camera. Int. J. Cancer (2020). https://doi.org/10.1002/ijc.33029
4. Desai, K.T., et al.: The development of "automated visual evaluation" for cervical cancer screening: the promise and challenges in adapting deep-learning for clinical testing: interdisciplinary principles of automated visual evaluation in cervical screening. Int. J. Cancer. **150**(5), 741–752 (2022). https://doi.org/10.1002/ijc.33879
5. Guo, P., et al.: Ensemble deep learning for cervix image selection toward improving reliability in automated cervical precancer screening. Diagnostics **10**(7), 451 (2020)

6. Xue, Z., et al.: Cleaning highly unbalanced multisource image dataset for quality control in cervical precancer screening. In: Santosh, K., Hegadi, R., Pal, U. (eds.) Recent Trends in Image Processing and Pattern Recognition, pp. 3–13. Springer, Cham (2021). https://doi.org/10.1007/978-3-031-07005-1_1

7. Guo, P., Singh, S., Xue, Z., Long, L.R., Antani, S.: Deep learning for assessing image focus for automated cervical cancer screening. In: IEEE EMBS International Conference on Biomedical & Health Informatics (BHI) (2019). https://doi.org/10.1109/BHI.2019.8834495

8. Ganesan, P., Xue, Z., Singh, S., Long, L.R., Ghoraani, B., Antani, S.: Performance evaluation of a generative adversarial network for deblurring mobile-phone cervical images. In: Proceedings of IEEE Engineering in Medicine and Biology Conference (EMBC), Berlin, Germany, pp. 4487–4490 (2019)

9. Xue, Z., Angara, S., Levitz, D., Antani, S.: Analysis of digital noise and reduction methods on classifiers used in automated visual evaluation in cervical cancer screening. Proc. SPIE Int. Soc. Opt. Eng. **11950**, 1195008 (2022). https://doi.org/10.1117/12.2610235

10. Shen, Y., Sanghavi, S.: Learning with bad training data via iterative trimmed loss minimization. In: ICML (2019)

11. Pleiss, G., Zhang, T., Elenberg, E., Weinberger, K.Q.: Identifying mislabeled data using the area under the margin ranking. In: Proceedings of the 34th International Conference on Neural Information Processing Systems (NeurIPS), pp. 17044–17056. Curran Associates Inc., Red Hook, Article 1430 (2020)

12. Zhang, Z., Sabuncu, M.R.: Generalized cross entropy loss for training deep neural networks with noisy labels. In: Proceedings of the 32th International Conference on Neural Information Processing Systems (NeurIPS) (2018)

13. Patrini, G., Rozza, A., Krishna Menon, A., Nock, R., Qu, L.: Making deep neural networks robust to label noise: a loss correction approach. In: Conference on Computer Vision and Pattern Recognition (CVPR) (2017)

14. Northcutt, C., Jiang, L., Chuang, I.: Confident Learning: Estimating Uncertainty in Dataset Labels. J. Artif. Intell. **70**, 1373–1411 (2021). https://doi.org/10.1613/jair.1.12125

15. Desai, K.T., et al.: Design and feasibility of a novel program of cervical screening in Nigeria: self-sampled HPV testing paired with visual triage. Infect. Agent Cancer **15**(60) (2020). https://doi.org/10.1186/s13027-020-00324-5

16. Wang, S.S., et al.: Human papillomavirus cofactors by disease progression and human papillomavirus types in the study to understand cervical cancer early endpoints and determinants. Cancer Epidemiol Biomarkers Prev. **18**(1), 113–120 (2009). https://doi.org/10.1158/1055-9965.EPI-08-0591

17. Lin, T., Goyal, P., Girshick, R., He, K., Dollar, P.: Focal loss for dense object detection. IEEE Trans. Pattern Anal. Mach. Intell. **42**(02), 318–327 (2020)

18. Herrero, R., Wacholder, S., Rodriguez, A.C., et al.: Prevention of persistent human papillomavirus infection by an HPV16/18 vaccine: a community-based randomized clinical trial in Guanacaste, Costa Rica. Cancer Discov. **1**(5), 408–419 (2011)

19. Zhang, H., et al.: ResNeSt: split-attention networks. https://arxiv.org/abs/2004.08955

20. Liu, Z., et al.: Swin transformer: hierarchical vision transformer using shifted windows. In: 2021 IEEE/CVF International Conference on Computer Vision (ICCV), Montreal, QC, Canada, pp. 9992–10002 (2021)

21. Northcutt, C., Athalye, A., Mueller, J.: Pervasive label errors in test sets destabilize machine learning benchmarks. In: The 35th Conference on Neural Information Processing Systems (NeuIPS) (2021)

A Monotonicity Constrained Attention Module for Emotion Classification with Limited EEG Data

Dongyang Kuang[1]([✉])[ID], Craig Michoski[2][ID], Wenting Li[1], and Rui Guo[1]

[1] School of Mathematics (Zhuhai), Sun Yat-sen University,
Zhuhai, Guangdong, China
dykuang@outlook.com
[2] Oden Institute for Computational Engineering and Sciences,
University of Texas at Austin, Austin, USA
michoski@oden.utexas.edu
https://dykuang.github.io/

Abstract. In this work, a parameter-efficient attention module is presented for emotion classification using a limited, or relatively small, number of electroencephalogram (EEG) signals. This module is called the Monotonicity Constrained Attention Module (MCAM) due to its capability of incorporating priors on the monotonicity when converting features' Gram matrices into attention matrices for better feature refinement. Our experiments have shown that MCAM's effectiveness is comparable to state-of-the-art attention modules in boosting the backbone network's performance in prediction while requiring less parameters. Several accompanying sensitivity analyses on trained models' prediction concerning different attacks are also performed. These attacks include various frequency domain filtering levels and gradually morphing between samples associated with multiple labels. Our results can help better understand different modules' behaviour in prediction and can provide guidance in applications where data is limited and are with noises.

Keywords: Monotonicity Constrained Attention · EEG · Emotion classification · Deep learning · Parameter efficient model

1 Introduction

Due to improved computational methodologies alongside affordable access to efficient and powerful computational and neuroimaging hardware, there has been significant enthusiasm for the development of techniques for analyzing, predicting, and understanding human behavior through brain signals recorded from neuroimaging devices. One of the most popular and widespread neuroimaging techniques is electroencephalography (EEG), which is appealing for a variety of reasons, including that electroencephalograms can capture excellent time resolution as far as neuroimaging techniques go while being recorded on pragmatic devices that are portable, available, and affordable.

© The Author(s), under exclusive license to Springer Nature Switzerland AG 2022
G. Zamzmi et al. (Eds.): MILLanD 2022, LNCS 13559, pp. 218–228, 2022.
https://doi.org/10.1007/978-3-031-16760-7_21

As stated in [21], EEG classification algorithms can be roughly divided into the following five categories: i) conventional classifiers [18–20,28], ii) matrix and tensor based classifiers [6], iii) transfer learning based methods [3,8], iv) deep learning algorithms and advanced statistical approaches [5,23], and v) multi-label classifiers [3,22,31]. Although many effective classification methods exist, particularly those utilizing deep learning techniques, many potential concerns remain for developing practical algorithms which can be deployed for general contextual use. Three such problems include: 1) large open-sourced EEG data sets are limited, making deep neural networks with a lot of parameters challenging to train and generalize effectively; 2) brain signals such as scalp EEG are known to have a high signal-to-noise ratio, effectively polluting the training and generalizability of the models [2,17,25]; and 3) the result from large and deep networks – while accurately predictive—can be challenging to interpret [1,4].

One solution to the above three concerns (1)–(3) is to construct parameter-efficient models that can be trained on relatively small and potentially noisy data sets while being lightweight enough to allow for physically/medically/clinically interpretable solutions. We note that good candidates for such approaches are attention modules in neural networks such as in [7,10,32,33]. Thus this work, inspired by the self-attention mechanism and Gram feature matrix in the context of neural style transfer [9], presents the Monotonicity Constrained Attention Module (MCAM) that can dynamically construct the attention matrix from the feature Gram matrix. With MCAM, one can set constraints on different prior monotonic patterns to guide neural networks for selectively emphasizing informative features and suppressing unfavorable ones, leading to an efficient, accurate, and ultimately more easily interpretable framework.

2   Related Work

Attention Mechanism: Many attention mechanisms exist for refining deep features in the framework of neural network models. Among them, the Squeeze-and Excitation (SE) attention module [10] and Convolutional Block Attention Module (CBAM) [33] are two representatives. The former helped win the last ImageNet contest in 2017. The latter performed attention operations both spatially and channel-wise. Both the two attention modules can be applied to any existing network. More recently, starting from the research done in [7] with attention matrix computed from query-key-value (QKV) feature branches, various types of self-attention mechanism are growing fast in different fields such as computer vision (CV), e.g. [16,27] and speech processing, e.g. [13,24].

Our Work: With the setting of limited and noisy data, our primary contributions can be summarized as follows: 1) We have developed a Monotonicity Constrained Attention Module (MCAM) suitable for EEG-based emotion classification when data is limited. Our experiments show that MCAM can help achieve performance comparable to other SOTA modules requiring fewer trainable parameters. 2) MCAM opens a portal in the backbone network so that one can conveniently incorporate priors on the monotonicity of the learned function that can effectively convert feature-based Gram matrices into attention matrices for better feature refinement. 3) For better interpretation, extra sensitivity analysis on MCAM's prediction concerning different attacks is also performed to investigate the various influences caused by inserting attention modules.

3   Proposed Method

The mechanism of our proposed attention module is summarized in Fig. 1. First, the Gram matrix C [29] is computed using the deep channel features X. Next, a function $f : [-1, 1] \rightarrow [0, 1]$ is constructed in the module, which is meant to 'learn' the mapping that effectively translates C element-wise to an attention matrix A for better classification. As the key component of MCAM, we use a 3-layer MLP for approximating f during training.

To understand the effect the trained function f has for incorporating prior information between feature correlation and attention, we test different constraints for regularizing the monotonicity of f. In this manuscript, three configurations of MCAM are considered: 1) *M1*, no constraint on f's monotonicity at all; 2) *M2*, f should be non-decreasing on $[-1, 0]$ and non-increasing on $[0, 1]$, meaning the prior that less (positively or negatively) correlated features should contribute more to the corresponding value in A; and 3) *M3*,

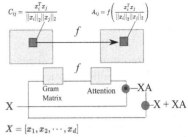

Fig. 1. The Monotonicity Constrained Attention Module (MCAM). Here $\|\cdot\|_2$ denotes the standard L^2-norm.

f should be non-increasing on $[-1, 0]$ and non-decreasing on $[0, 1]$ meaning the prior that the more correlation (positively or negatively) should result in more attention strength through A.

The monotonicity constraint is defined using a uniform grid $\{t_i\}, i = 0, \cdots, N$, on $[-1, 1]$, where for case *M2* the loss becomes:

$$\sum_{i=0}^{N/2} \frac{1}{2} \left(|f'(t_i)| - f'(t_i) \right) + \sum_{i=N/2}^{N} \frac{1}{2} \left(|f'(t_i)| + f'(t_i) \right), \tag{1}$$

and for case *M3* becomes:

$$\sum_{i=0}^{N/2} \frac{1}{2} \left(|f'(t_i)| + f'(t_i) \right) + \sum_{i=N/2}^{N} \frac{1}{2} \left(|f'(t_i)| - f'(t_i) \right). \tag{2}$$

Here f' is estimated using a simple first order finite difference scheme. Finally, the resulting attention matrix A incorporates into the deep feature refinement via the expression $X + XA$ as shown in Fig. 1.

4   Experiments

Backbone–EEGNet: EEGNet is a compact convolutional neural network for EEG-based brain-computer interfaces which was proposed by [15]. We choose EEGNet as the backbone for benchmarking different attention modules for two main reasons: 1) It is one representative model that is parameter efficient, thus very suitable for small datasets; 2) Its simple design allows for accessible examinations and interpretations on the effects of attention modules considered in this paper.

Data Collection: DEAP dataset [12] is a well known database for benchmarking various emotion classification and analysis methods [11, 14, 26, 30]. The dataset contains 32-channels EEG signals and 8-channels peripheral physiological signals from 32 volunteers who were asked to watch 40 1-min videos and report their emotion scores (varying from 1 to 9) in the four categories: valence, arousal, dominance, and liking. We will only be using the 32-channels EEG for experiments.

Data Preprocessing: We are interested in the within-subject classification task in this study. Setting the threshold at 5, we convert emotion scores from valence/arousal categories to form a 4-class classification family, comprised of {HVHA, HVLA, LVHA, LVLA} for each subject. The first three seconds of each trial are baseline data and are used to normalize the rest via $x(t) \leftarrow x(t)/max(|x(t \leq 3)|)$. Note that Subject 23 is excluded in the following experiments because this subject has only three emotion labels.

Experiment Setting: For each subject, the data is split into three parts. The first 5000 time points (from ~ 0 s to ~ 39 s) will be used in training, the following 5000–6000 (from ~ 40 s to ~ 47 s) will be used for validation, and the remaining segments (from ~ 47 s to ~ 63 s) are used for testing.

Note that in order to mitigate the problems associated to limited data and imbalanced labeling, a data generator is used to randomly crop segments of 1 s to provide batches for feeding the network during training and validation. Within each batch, the generator guarantees that each label is associated with about 25% of the total samples generated. For a valid and consistent comparison among different models, the test set will be cropped into non-overlapping segments of 1 s. For each subject and each attention module compared, training is repeated 10 times. During each training repetition, the best model in terms of validation accuracy is reloaded to make predictions on the testing set, and one instance of the performance under that configuration is stored. For all experiments, the following hyperparameters are used: the backbone EEGNet's dropout rate is set to 0.5, the batchsize is set to 256, and the optimization is performed with an Adam optimizer using a learning rate of 10^{-3}. For training with the proposed MCAM, the weight for the extra loss constraining monotonicity is set at 0.1. These hyperparameters were selected from our pre-experiments with a small amount of data. Same hyperparamters were used for all experiments. The code used for our experiments will be made available at https://github.com/dykuang/BCI-Attention.

Table 1. Mean (±std) performance with different attention modules inserted.

Method	EEGNet	+QKV	+CBAM	+SE	+M1	+M2	+M3
Params	3020	4109	3200	3102	**3061**	**3061**	**3061**
Acc.(%)	93.9±5.4	93.5±5.0	94.3±4.7	95.4±3.8	95.0±4.7	93.9±6.1	95.0±4.2
Spec.(%)	97.7±1.9	97.4±2.3	97.9±1.7	98.2±1.5	98.0±1.9	97.5±2.6	97.9±2.0
F1(%)	94.0±5.4	93.5±5.0	94.3±4.6	95.4±3.8	94.9±4.7	93.8±6.2	95.0±4.2

Benchmark: We summarize commonly used classification metrics in Table 1, using EEGNet as the backbone, and inserting all attention modules at the same location in our benchmark.

Table 2. One sided paired T-tests on the F1-score, using the following abbreviations:. A: EEGNet, B: +CBAM, C: +SE, D: +M1, E: +M2, F: +M3, μ: mean F1 score.

H_0	H_1	p-value
$\mu_A = \mu_F$	$\mu_A < \mu_F$	0.018
$\mu_B = \mu_F$	$\mu_B < \mu_F$	0.038
$\mu_F = \mu_C$	$\mu_F < \mu_C$	0.115
$\mu_D = \mu_F$	$\mu_D < \mu_F$	0.437

Notice that the QKV type self-attention performs the worst, demonstrating no improvement. We hypothesize this is due to limited training data, as pointed out in [7]. For the remainder of this section, we focus only on the attention modules where performance is equivalent to, or higher than the backbone model. For a more quantitative comparison, we also perform paired T-tests and collect the resulting p-values in Table 2. At a significance level of $\alpha = 0.02$ the alternative hypothesis H_1 is accepted, i.e. EEGNet+$M3$ has a higher F1-score than EEGNet alone. At significance level of $\alpha = 0.05$, EEGNet+$M3$ has a higher F1-score than EEGNet+CBAM. Note that there is not enough evidence (at the significance level of 0.05) to reject the null hypothesis for the rest tests. That is, EEGNet+$M3$ performs similarly to EEGNet+SE and EEGNet+$M1$.

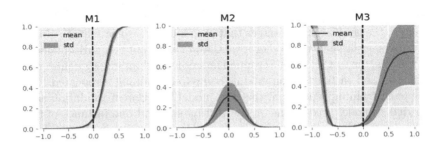

Fig. 2. Mapping from the Gram matrix's entries C_{ij} to the attention matrix's entries A_{ij} by MCAM. This plot was made from the 10 models trained from Subject 24's data.

Finally we can check the different monotonic patterns learned for different subjects during training. Figure 2 shows one example of the monotonic pattern mapping from C_{ij} to A_{ij} learned with different prior constraints.

4.1   Models' Scalp Attention Pattern

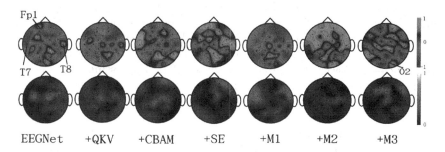

Fig. 3. Scalp map with backbone EEGNet's kernel weights for spatial attention pattern in the first depthwise convolution layer. First row: mean values calculated from 10 trained models. Second row: the standard deviation associated with the result from the first row.

The insertion of different attention modules can potentially change the spatial attention pattern of the backbone EEGNet. For comparison, we can visualize the scalp map with EEGNet's kernel weights (normalized to $[-1, 1]$) for its spatial attention pattern, i.e., kernel weights in the first depthwise convolution layer. As one can observe from Fig. 3, global patterns vary from model to model, though they share the same backbone network. Locally speaking, except for the case $+M2$, the value pair learned for channels T8 and T7 have different signs, while the case $+CBAM$ learned the opposite pattern compared to the rest. With the exception of $+M1$, all other configurations show a locally isolated island in the Fp1 area. All three variations of MCAM considered here also show a similar attention pattern around the O2 area. The standard deviation shown can be interpreted loosely as corresponding to each model's confidence in the value of its coincident kernel weights. Models compared here show high confidence in most areas, where areas of low confidence offer an interesting opportunity for deeper analysis and potentially clinical interpretation. It is also worth noting that, similar to the mean value patterns, the global patterns for standard deviation appear quite different across different models. Whether or not these patterns can be tied to clinical findings remains a question. On the other hand, robust algorithms that can help encode one's prior knowledge about clinical patterns into the models' weights is also an import research direction.

4.2   Models' Sensitivity of Prediction on Inputs' Frequency

Low pass filters are frequently used in applications to suppress noise as a pre-processing step. This section examines how frequency information in the input affects the trained model predictions with different modules inserted. With the same test data, first, a lowpass filter is used at different frequencies, and then the accuracy of different model predictions is tracked on this filtered input. Figure 4 demonstrates the result for subject 12 and subject 24. Of note is that different models show the same trend given the same data, but the trends vary across different subjects. For subject 12, a noticeable drop in performance is observed when inputs are lowpass filtered below 50 Hz, while stable performance is recovered when the frequencies are set below 30 Hz. For subject 24, a noticeable drop in performance is seen at 60 Hz, while the performance trace decreases slowly as frequencies go lower. In the case of subject 24, suppressing high-frequency noise using lowpass filters seems to compromise model performance. While each model decreases in performance as higher frequencies are filtered out, the configuration of EEGNet+$M2$ has an opposite trend in the range of 20–40 Hz. This observation raises what seems to serve as a cautionary tale that it is crucial to take care when smoothing data in the frequency domain, as the response may be complicated and hard to predict a priori.

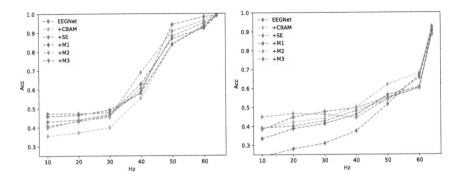

Fig. 4. The track of performance when inputs are lowpass filtered to different frequencies. Left: Subject 12, Right: Subject 24. The frequency used for the plot are 10 Hz, 20 Hz, 30 Hz, 40 Hz, 50 Hz, 60 Hz and 64 Hz.

4.3   Model Sensitivity on Morphisms Between Samples

Considering two samples x_i and x_j each associated with a different label i and j in the N classification problem, we define a morphism g_i^j parameterized by $u \in [0, 1]$ such that $x_i = g_i^j(0) * x_i$ and $x_j = g_i^j(1) * x_i$. The abstract operation $*$ will be made explicit below, as an example. We further note that in the above setting, a value u_i^j always exists such that the model's confidence score (usually represented by the softmax value from the last dense layer's output) for label i first drops below its score for label j. The lower the value of u_i^j is, the more likely the model under examination will change its prediction on sample x_i from label i to label j.

For visualization, we set u_i^j as a point in polar coordinates $(\rho, \theta) = (u_i^j, \frac{2\pi v_j}{N-1})$ where $v_j = 0, \cdots, N - 2$ is some indexing for different j. These points will serve as the vertices of an $N - 1$ polygon. The resulting summation $S_i = \sum_{j \neq i} u_i^j$ then represent how likely a model is to choose label i against all other labels under the

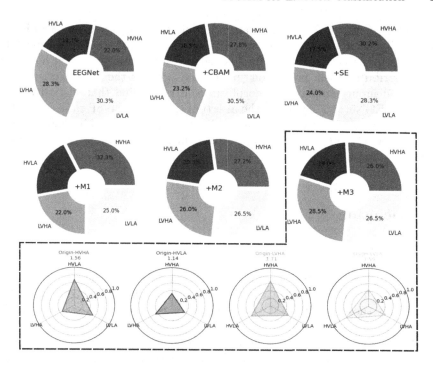

Fig. 5. Visualization of how different models tend to change prediction labels under the linearly interpolating morphism. The samples for making the plot were taken from subject 24. The colored number shown are the actual number of S_i. For example, $1.56/6 = 0.26$ recovers the percentages shown in the donut plot. (Color figure online)

considered morphism g. Furthermore, if $u_i^j + u_j^i = 1$ then $\sum_{i=0}^{N-1} S_i = \frac{N(N-1)}{2}$, in which case we can check the values of $S_i, i = 0, \cdots, N-1$ among different models on the same selected "representative" samples per label for comparing their "preferences" among candidate labels under the chosen morphism g.

As a demonstration of the above concept, we choose the simple discrete linear interpolation for g, defined by $g_i^j(u) * x_i = (1-u)x_i + ux_j$ as the morphism operation, where samples $\{x_i\}$ are selected so that all considered models have correct predictions on them. The resulting summaries are shown in Fig. 5. Each donut plot of the above two rows is the visualization of S_i for a specific model. The last row gives an example of expanding more detailed information per slice by visualizing a triangle (3-polygon) for each label. All models being compared here assign the lowest values to the HVLA category, meaning models are more likely to assign other labels for the input HVLA sample when g morphs it away to other samples of different labels. Also, note that both the backbone model and the case when CBAM is inserted have the largest value for LVLA. The insertion of the SE module, MCAM (*M1*) and MCAM (*M2*) assign the highest value to the HVHA category. Of further note is that the two configurations of MCAM (*M2* and *M3*) are surprisingly similar considering that their monotonicity mapping in the Gram matrix C's element to attention matrix A are opposite (see Fig. 2). Additionally, we examine how the scores S_i for $i = 0, 1, 2, 3$ are spread across the four labels by checking the standard deviation (std), thus indicating how each model distributes their prediction "preference" among the 4 categories given the selected input samples and morphism g. Here we find that the std for the backbone EEGNet is 0.269, while the insertion of CBAM and SE raises the std to 0.274 and 0.292, respectively, where the distributions are notably more skewed. However, MCAM (*M1*) has an std of 0.271, which is the close to the case where no attention module is inserted at all, while MCAM (*M2*) has by far the lowest value std of 0.164 followed by a std of 0.215 for the MCAM (*M3*).

5   Conclusion

We have constructed a parameter-efficient attention module called MCAM for emotion classification tasks with limited EEG data. MCAM allows one to put constraints on the embedded function's monotonicity for mapping a deep feature Gram matrix to form an effective attention matrix during feature refinements. Experiments show that MCAM's effectiveness is comparable to state-of-the-art attention modules with additional benefits. Additionally, a sensitivity analysis with different levels of lowpass filtering has been conducted, along with a novel morphing analysis designed to improve insight into the model's behavior through visualization. Future work will focus on designing more generalizable and interpretable models on limited and corrupted data sets.

Acknowledgement. This work was partially supported by the Fundamental Research Funds for the Central Universities, Sun Yat-sen University (22qntd2901).

References

1. Acharya, D., Ahmed Sayyad, R., Dwivedi, P., Shaji, A., Sriram, P., Bhardwaj, A.: EEG signal classification using deep learning. In: Tiwari, A., Ahuja, K., Yadav, A., Bansal, J.C., Deep, K., Nagar, A.K. (eds.) Soft Computing for Problem Solving. AISC, vol. 1392, pp. 393–403. Springer, Singapore (2021). https://doi.org/10.1007/978-981-16-2709-5_30
2. Bang, J.W., Choi, J.S., Park, K.R.: Noise reduction in brainwaves by using both EEG signals and frontal viewing camera images. Sensors (Basel, Switzerland) **13**, 6272–6294 (2013)
3. Blankertz, B., Kawanabe, M., Tomioka, R., Hohlefeld, F., Müller, K.r., Nikulin, V.V.: Invariant common spatial patterns: alleviating nonstationarities in brain-computer interfacing. In: Advances in Neural Information Processing Systems, pp. 113–120 (2008)
4. Cao, J., Li, J., Hu, X., Wu, X., Tan, M.: Towards interpreting deep neural networks via layer behavior understanding. Mach. Learn. **111**, 1159–1179 (2022)
5. Cecotti, H., Graser, A.: Convolutional neural networks for p300 detection with application to brain-computer interfaces. IEEE Trans. Pattern Anal. Mach. Intell. **33**(3), 433–445 (2010)

6. Congedo, M., Barachant, A., Bhatia, R.: Riemannian geometry for EEG-based brain-computer interfaces; a primer and a review. Brain-Comput. Interf. **4**(3), 155–174 (2017)
7. Dosovitskiy, A., et al.: An image is worth 16x16 words: transformers for image recognition at scale. arXiv preprint arXiv:2010.11929 (2020)
8. Fazli, S., Popescu, F., Danóczy, M., Blankertz, B., Müller, K.R., Grozea, C.: Subject-independent mental state classification in single trials. Neural Netw. **22**(9), 1305–1312 (2009)
9. Gatys, L.A., Ecker, A.S., Bethge, M.: Image style transfer using convolutional neural networks. In: Proceedings of the IEEE Conference On Computer Vision and Pattern Recognition, pp. 2414–2423 (2016)
10. Hu, J., Shen, L., Sun, G.: Squeeze-and-excitation networks. In: Proceedings of the IEEE Conference on Computer Vision and Pattern Recognition, pp. 7132–7141 (2018)
11. Khateeb, M., Anwar, S.M., Alnowami, M.R.: Multi-domain feature fusion for emotion classification using DEAP dataset. IEEE Access **9**, 12134–12142 (2021)
12. Koelstra, S., Muhl, C., Soleymani, M., Lee, J.S., Yazdani, A., Ebrahimi, T., Pun, T., Nijholt, A., Patras, I.: DEAP: A database for emotion analysis; using physiological signals. IEEE Trans. Affect. Comput. **3**(1), 18–31 (2012). https://doi.org/10.1109/T-AFFC.2011.15
13. Koizumi, Y., Yatabe, K., Delcroix, M., Masuyama, Y., Takeuchi, D.: Speech enhancement using self-adaptation and multi-head self-attention. ICASSP 2020–2020 IEEE International Conference on Acoustics, Speech and Signal Processing (ICASSP), pp. 181–185 (2020)
14. Kulkarni, S., Patil, P.R.: Analysis of DEAP dataset for emotion recognition. In: Bhattacharyya, S., Nayak, J., Prakash, K.B., Naik, B., Abraham, A. (eds.) International Conference on Intelligent and Smart Computing in Data Analytics. AISC, vol. 1312, pp. 67–76. Springer, Singapore (2021). https://doi.org/10.1007/978-981-33-6176-8_8
15. Lawhern, V.J., Solon, A.J., Waytowich, N.R., Gordon, S.M., Hung, C.P., Lance, B.J.: EEGNet: a compact convolutional network for EEG-based brain-computer interfaces. CoRR abs/1611.08024 (2016), http://arxiv.org/abs/1611.08024
16. Lee, J., Lee, I., Kang, J.: Self-attention graph pooling. ArXiv abs/1904.08082 (2019)
17. Leite, N.M.N., Pereira, E.T., Gurjao, E.C., Veloso, L.R.: Deep convolutional autoencoder for EEG noise filtering. In: 2018 IEEE International Conference on Bioinformatics and Biomedicine (BIBM), pp. 2605–2612. IEEE (2018)
18. Li, J., Zhang, L.: Bilateral adaptation and neurofeedback for brain computer interface system. J. Neurosci. Methods **193**(2), 373–379 (2010)
19. Liu, G., Huang, G., Meng, J., Zhang, D., Zhu, X.: Improved GMM with parameter initialization for unsupervised adaptation of brain-computer interface. Int. J. Num. Methods Biomed. Eng. **26**(6), 681–691 (2010)
20. Liu, G., Zhang, D., Meng, J., Huang, G., Zhu, X.: Unsupervised adaptation of electroencephalogram signal processing based on fuzzy c-means algorithm. Int. J. Adapt. Control Sig. Process. **26**(6), 482–495 (2012)
21. Lotte, F., Bougrain, L., Cichocki, A., Clerc, M., Congedo, M., Rakotomamonjy, A., Yger, F.: A review of classification algorithms for EEG-based brain-computer interfaces: a 10 year update. J. Neural Eng. **15**(3) (2018)
22. Lotte, F., Congedo, M., Lécuyer, A., Lamarche, F., Arnaldi, B.: A review of classification algorithms for EEG-based brain-computer interfaces. J. Neural Eng. **4**(2), R (2007)

23. Lu, N., Li, T., Ren, X., Miao, H.: A deep learning scheme for motor imagery classification based on restricted boltzmann machines. IEEE Trans. Neural Syst. Rehab. Eng. **25**(6), 566–576 (2016)
24. Mittag, G., Naderi, B., Chehadi, A., Möller, S.: Nisqa: A deep CNN-self-attention model for multidimensional speech quality prediction with crowdsourced datasets. In: Interspeech (2021)
25. Repov, G.: Dealing with noise in EEG recording and data analysis. Inform. Medica Slovenica **15** (2010)
26. Thejaswini, Ravi Kumar, K.M., Aditya Nataraj, J.L.: Analysis of EEG based emotion detection of DEAP and SEED-IV databases using SVM. SSRN Electr. J. **8** (2019)
27. Sankar, A., Wu, Y., Gou, L., Zhang, W., Yang, H.: DySAT: deep neural representation learning on dynamic graphs via self-attention networks. Proceedings of the 13th International Conference on Web Search and Data Mining (2020)
28. Schlögl, A., Vidaurre, C., Müller, K.R.: Adaptive methods in BCI research - an introductory tutorial. In: Graimann, B., Pfurtscheller, G., Allison, B. (eds.) Brain-Computer Interfaces. The Frontiers Collection, pp. 331–355. Springer, Heidelberg (2009). https://doi.org/10.1007/978-3-642-02091-9_18
29. Sreeram, V., Agathoklis, P.: On the properties of gram matrix. IEEE Trans. Circ. Syst. I Fundam. Theory Appl. **41**(3), 234–237 (1994)
30. Stajić, T., Jovanović, J., Jovanović, N., Jankovic, M.M.: Emotion recognition based on DEAP database physiological signals. In: 2021 29th Telecommunications Forum (TELFOR), pp. 1–4 (2021)
31. Steyrl, D., Scherer, R., Faller, J., Müller-Putz, G.R.: Random forests in non-invasive sensorimotor rhythm brain-computer interfaces: a practical and convenient non-linear classifier. Biomed. Eng./Biomedizinische Technik **61**(1), 77–86 (2016)
32. Vaswani, A., et al.: Attention is all you need. CoRR abs/1706.03762 (2017). http://arxiv.org/abs/1706.03762
33. Woo, S., Park, J., Lee, J.Y., Kweon, I.S.: CBAM: convolutional block attention module. In: Proceedings of the European conference on computer vision (ECCV), pp. 3–19 (2018)

Automated Skin Biopsy Analysis with Limited Data

Yung-Chieh Chan, Jerry Zhang$^{(\boxtimes)}$, Katie Frizzi, Nigel Calcutt, and Garrison Cottrell

University of California, San Diego, USA
{ychan,jcz001}@ucsd.edu, gary@eng.ucsd.edu

Abstract. In patients with diabetic and other peripheral neuropathies, the number of nerve fibers that originate in the dermis and cross the dermal-epidermal boundary is an important metric for diagnosis of early small fiber neuropathy and determination of the efficacy of interventions that promote nerve regeneration. To aid in the time-consuming and often variable process of manually counting these measurements, we propose an end-to-end fully automated method to count dermal-epidermal boundary nerve crossings. Working with images of skin biopsies immunostained to identify peripheral nerves using current standard operating procedures, we used image segmentation neural networks to distinguish between the dermis and epidermis and an edge detection neural network to identify nerves. We then applied an unsupervised clustering algorithm to identify nerve crossings, producing an automated count. Since our dataset is very small—containing less than one hundred images—we use pre-trained models in combination with several image augmentation methods to improve performance on training and inference. The model learns from a human expert's training data better than a human trained by the same expert.

1 Introduction

Automated systems for aiding clinical diagnoses and treatment research have been long sought after both to increase the speed of procedures as well as offer consistent quantification. In particular, semantic segmentation finds applications in many parts of the clinical process.

For the specific challenge of detecting neuropathy, there are already several methods that can automatically identify nerve-like structures. Al-Fahdawi et al. [7] showed that this task can be automated using image preprocessing and edge detection on corneal images. More recent work using deep learning shows improvements over these traditional methods [13]. In particular, several groups have applied U-Nets, an architecture designed for semantic segmentation, to skin biopsies, exactly the problem we approach here [2,10]. In [2], the authors additionally use U-Nets for tracing nerves in skin biopsies. However, in order for the U-Net to work, they enhanced the manually-traced nerves in the training set images with a 6-pixel-wide boundary in order to make the problem simpler for the U-Net. In our work, we found that U-Nets perform less well than using a state-of-the-art edge detector for nerve tracing, and no enhancement of the nerve traces was necessary.

We build off of these previous approaches using a similar deep learning semantic segmentation method. However, to overcome the problem of very limited data, we employ further methods to ensure that the model will have good performance on unseen data.

In addition, to achieve a fully automated system for detecting neuropathy and measuring nerve growth in images of skin biopsies, we factor the task into two sub-tasks: identifying nerve fibers in the skin, and identifying the dermal-epidermal boundary. For each sub-task, we employ a specialized model, and we combine their results using an unsupervised method to obtain the final nerve crossing annotations.

2   Methods

2.1   Dataset

The dataset consists of 94 images of skin biopsies collected from 13 HIV-infected patients and 11 control participants as part of a study on HIV infection and neuropathy in the United States. Each 1600×1200 image contains a portion of the biopsy at $20\times$ magnification. Many focal layers are flattened into a single image to capture depth. A human expert traced the nerves and the boundary between the dermis and epidermis.

Given the limited number of training examples, we perform the following random data augmentations during training: horizontal and vertical translation from –100 to 100 pixels, rotation from –10 to 10°, shearing from –5 to 5°, orientation (the image can be rotated to 0, 90, 180, or 270°), cropping, and horizontal and vertical flipping. For cropping, 800×800 patches are taken from each 1600×1200 image; this size generates different images with each application of the augmentation algorithm while still retaining enough of the dermis and epidermis to be useful for the model. Similarly, the other applied image augmentations ensure that each training example has an essentially unique configuration of pixels, while retaining vital information about skin structure and not distorting the image beyond what an expert technician would normally be able to work with.

The augmentation algorithm is applied as the model is training such that a random set of parameters is generated and applied for each transformation. As a result, the model is trained on a unique version of every image with each iteration. In combination with this online approach, the wide array of random image augmentation methods is one of the primary ways that we improve the model's generalization and prevent over-fitting.

2.2   Nerve Labeling

In our dataset, nerve labels are about three pixels wide and constitute only a very small portion of the image. Conventional semantic segmentation models

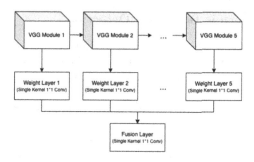

Fig. 1. Architecture of holistically-nested edge detection (HED)

suffer when there is an extreme class imbalance, failing to capture pixel-level details. After experimenting with various models, we decided to approach the task with an edge detection model.

Architecture. We use the Holistically-Nested Edge Detection (HED) [12] system. A simple illustration of the HED architecture is shown in Fig. 1. HED is a feed-forward deep convolutional neural network based on VGGNet [11]. The model consists of a series of VGG modules with an increasing number of kernels. The input image is processed by these modules sequentially and the multi-channel output of each VGG module is compressed to a single-channel side-output by a convolutional layer with a 1×1 kernel. These 1×1 convolution layers also serve as weights of the side-outputs. Each side-output focuses on a different scale of edges as deeper VGG modules, with larger receptive fields, capture larger edges. The final edge map is generated by fusing the side-outputs by one 1×1 convolution layer.

Loss Function. The loss function we used to train our model is Dice Loss, a commonly used loss for segmentation. Let P be the two-dimensional model output and T be the ground truth. The equation for Dice Loss is

$$L_{Dice}(P,T) = 1 - \frac{2 * \sum_{i,j} P_{ij} T_{ij} + 1}{\sum_{i,j} P_{ij} + \sum_{i,j} T_{ij} + 1}$$

Training Procedure. Due to the scarcity of labeled data and the sparsity of learning signals in each image, we perform transfer learning to improve the model's performance and reduce training time. We adopted the HED model pretrained on BSDS500 dataset [1] from pytorch-hed [9] and fine-tune it on our dataset. The pretrained model was already able to identify the majority of the nerves but also labeled other non-nerve edges. Hence fine-tuning on our data corrected this. We set the learning rate to 10^{-4} and a weight decay penalty of $L_2 = 10^{-3}$, determined by grid search cross-validation. The weight decay parameter is especially important in our case in order to minimize over-fitting on our small dataset. We trained the model for 200 epochs with a learning rate scheduler, which decreases the learning rate when the loss flattens.

2.3   Dermis-Epidermis Boundary Detection

As is the case with the segmentation of nerve fibers, labeling the boundary line between the dermis and epidermis can be very difficult due to class imbalance. However, this boundary is not as easily detected as nerve fibers, since the boundary is not as clearly defined.

To circumvent this problem, we reformulate the labeling scheme: instead of labeling the boundary between the dermis and epidermis, we only task the model with labeling the dermis. From this label, a boundary line between the dermis and epidermis can be generated using standard image processing techniques. In order to transform the labeling scheme, we manually extend the line in the given label to surround the whole dermis, then flood-fill the dermis region. An example is shown in Fig. 2.

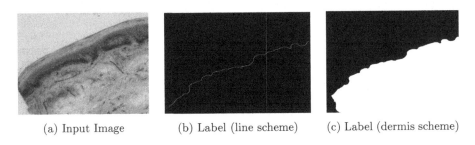

(a) Input Image   (b) Label (line scheme)   (c) Label (dermis scheme)

Fig. 2. An example label for the dermis

Therefore, using the transformed data, the task can be formulated as binary classification between dermis and non-dermis regions, a straightforward task for semantic segmentation, and the categories are relatively balanced. We use a DeepLabV3 model, a recent state-of-the-art approach for semantic segmentation [4]. In particular, we use a pre-trained instance of the model with a ResNet-101 [8] backbone, which we then fine-tune on our dataset.

Architecture. The model is a deep residual convolutional neural network with atrous (also referred to as dilated) convolutions, a key feature that allows the model to have a wider receptive field in the later layers without sacrificing feature map resolution, which is essential for semantic segmentation [4]. Atrous spatial pyramid pooling, a method similar to spatial pyramid pooling but using filters with various atrous rates, further improves the model's capacity to process both global contexts as well as small-scale detail.

Loss Function. We use the standard binary cross-entropy loss function evaluated on a per-pixel basis at the output for training the model on the dermis. To evaluate performance, we use the Dice coefficient, which is discussed in more detail in subsequent sections.

Training Procedure. Since the number of training examples is small, we leverage a version of the model that is pre-trained on PASCAL Visual Object Classes dataset [6], a set of natural images with 20 categories.

From grid search using cross-validation over learning rate and L_2 penalty, we use an initial learning rate of 3×10^{-4} and an L_2 weight decay penalty of 10^{-3}, which again helps to minimize over-fitting. The model is trained on the labeled dermis data using binary cross-entropy loss for 300 iterations, using the same learning rate schedule as above. For fine-tuning, we wrap the model with an initial and final convolutional layer and train the whole model end-to-end on the dataset. In this case, the initial convolutional layer has 3 input channels and 3 output channels, with a kernel size of 3 and padding width of 1 to maintain the resolution of the input. The output convolutional layer uses a kernel size of 1 with 21 input channels and 1 output channel, in order to reduce the dimensionality of the pretrained model's output.

2.4   Nerve Crossing Identification

Our approach for counting nerve crossings consists of three steps: transforming dermis label to dermis-epidermis boundary, clustering intersections, and filtering out invalid crossings. All parameters in this section were optimized by running the same process on the ground truth data and the model output on the same images, and maximizing their consistency.

Transform Dermis Label to Boundary. To obtain a boundary line for the segmented dermis label, we first smooth the boundary by applying a Gaussian filter with $\sigma = 10$ pixels onto the dermis map and binarizing it with a threshold of 0.6. Then, we scan the map for enclosed areas smaller than 0.2 of the image in the dermis map and flip the label for all pixels in that area. This step removes noisy patches from the model's prediction within the dermis. Finally, we extract the dermis-epidermis boundary by selecting the pixels close to the edge of the dermis area with a controllable boundary width. An example is shown in Fig. 3.

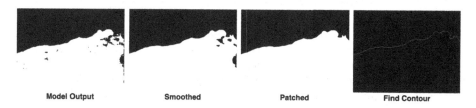

| Model Output | Smoothed | Patched | Find Contour |

Fig. 3. An example of transforming dermis label to boundary line

Cluster Intersections. In this step, we extract the overlapping pixels of the filtered nerve labels and the dermis-epidermis boundary. The coordinates of the overlapping pixels is then clustered by Density-Based Spatial Clustering of Applications with Noise (DBSCAN) [5] with $\epsilon = 3$ and the minimum number of points in a cluster set to 4. Each cluster is considered a crossing, and the coordinate of each crossing is calculated by averaging all pixels coordinated in the corresponding cluster.

Filter Crossings. For each crossing, we count the number of nerve pixels in a 17×17 pixel area centered at the crossing. We filtered out crossings that have less than 5 nerve pixels on both sides of the boundary. This step filters out nerve fibers that do not cross into the dermis but border it.

3 Experimental Setup

3.1 Evaluating the Nerve Tracing Model

The first evaluation metric we used is Dice score. For each image with P as the set of nerve pixels predicted by our model and T as the set of nerve pixels labeled by a human expert, the Dice score is calculated as:

$$Dice(P, T) = \frac{|P \cap T|}{(|P| + |T|)/2}$$

However, this metric is not very effective in measuring the quality of the model's output. The target label was manually labeled and was not precise on a pixel level. For example, the hand-drawn label does not adapt to nerve fibers with different widths, so pixels on the edge of a thick nerve fiber might not be labeled. The effect of a mislabeled pixel prominently affects the Dice score because of the scarcity of nerve labels. This results in the model's predictions getting poor Dice scores on visually identical nerve labels. The width of nerve fibers is irrelevant for identifying the crossings. Thus, we designed a more forgiving scoring metric based on a Dice score that tolerates predicted pixels to be k pixels off the ground truth. We counted predicted pixels that are k pixels away from any ground truth pixel as TP_k (True Positive within k)and defined a modified Dice score as:

$$Modified\_Dice(k, P, T) = \frac{|TP_k|}{(|P| + |T \cup TP_k|)/2}$$

When k is 0, the normal Dice score is a special case of this measure.

For nerve labeling, we compared the accuracy of three models: A U-Net pretrained for abnormality segmentation on a dataset of brain MRI volumes [3] fine-tuned on our dataset, a randomly initialized Holistic Edge Detector (HED) (i.e., trained from scratch on our data), and HED pre-trained on BSDS500 and fine-tuned on our data. The hyperparameters for training the networks were determined by grid search as above (learning rate and weight decay). We trained the models for 200 epochs using data augmentation, and evaluated the models' predictions on the test set using the Dice score and the modified Dice score with k set to 1 and 3. All models were trained on two NVIDIA GeForce GTX 1080 Ti's in about an hour.

3.2 Evaluating Dermis Model

For the dermis models, we compared the performance of three versions: the same U-Net model as above, a randomly initialized DeepLabV3 model, and a pre-trained DeepLabV3 fine-tuned on our dataset. Each is similarly tuned and trained using grid search over the hyperparameters. The U-Net model was trained on four NVIDIA GeForce GTX 1080 Ti cards in about half an hour. The DeepLabV3 model trained on a single NVIDIA GeForce GTX 3090 for 1.5 h.

4   Results

We evaluate our model at two levels. For the end-to-end counting pipeline, we use 5-fold cross validation and compare the results of the model with that of a human expert using Pearson correlation. To evaluate the individual components, for the sake of time, we train on a subset of the data for each model and compare their performance on a held-out portion. For this comparison, we use 84 training images and 10 held-out images.

4.1 Nerve Labeling Results

The results of the nerve models on the 10 held-out images are shown in Table 1. Under all evaluation metrics, the HED model pre-trained on BSDS500 dataset outperforms the pre-trained U-Net model and randomly initialized HED model.

Table 1. Nerve labeling scores shown in format mean (standard deviation)

Model	Dice score	Modified dice score k = 1	Modified dice score k = 3
U-Net	0.585 (0.083)	0.814 (0.085)	0.918 (0.079)
HED not pretrained	0.549 (0.083)	0.778 (0.089)	0.885 (0.085)
HED transfer learning	**0.611** (0.067)	**0.845** (0.054)	**0.950** (0.036)

4.2 Dermis Labeling Results

The resulting performance of each dermis model on the 10 held-out images is shown Table 2. The DeepLabV3 model shows a clear performance increase over U-Net, with a slight improvement (numerically) by using transfer learning.

Table 2. Dermis labeling scores shown in format mean (standard deviation)

Model	Dice score
U-Net	0.958 (0.027)
DeepLabV3 not pretrained	0.979 (0.012)
DeepLabV3 transfer learning	**0.986** (0.007)

4.3   Crossing Count Results

The results of the correlation comparison on the whole pipeline on each of the 5 folds are shown in Table 3. Each line indicates a model trained on a subset of the data and its correlation with the training expert on held-out data, so each score represents the model's generalization performance.

Table 3. Correlation between model prediction and ground truth over each fold. p-values below 0.001 are shown as 0.

Fold	Correlation	p
1	0.835	0.00
2	0.465	0.04
3	0.772	0.00
4	0.931	0.00
5	0.760	0.00

The model's counts were correlated with the training expert at an average of 0.753 with standard deviation 0.156 over the 5 folds. To compare the model's performance with a second expert, we obtained another set of counts on the 10 validation images used for the evaluation of the components, and trained the pipeline on the 84 training images. The two experts' counts were correlated with each other at 0.467 ($p = 0.173$), while our model is correlated with the training expert at 0.834 ($p = 0.002$). This demonstrates that the model correlates strongly with the training expert—even more than the second expert, who was trained by the first!

Examples of the model results are shown in Fig. 4. Overall, the model produces quality output that resembles the expert's label and gives a more consistent count than a human expert. Most variations are caused by the model making a different but reasonable judgment of the dermal-epidermal boundary, for example in the second image pair.

Model   Target

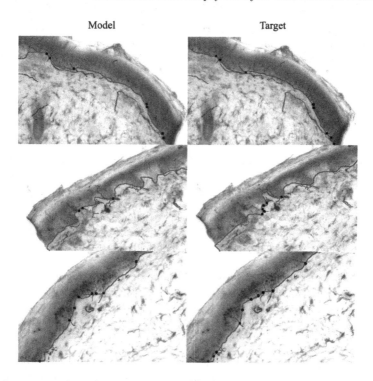

Fig. 4. Comparison between model output (left) and training target labeled by expert (right) on the test set. Blue: nerves; Green: dermal-epidermal boundary; Red: nerve crossings. (Color figure online)

5   Discussion

We proposed a fully automated, end-to-end system for detecting and counting nerve fibers in the skin which cross the dermal-epidermal boundary. We found that the model was highly correlated with the expert's labeling of the data, while a second evaluator was not statistically significantly correlated with the expert. Finally, using augmentation and cross-validation we show that even with very limited training data, the model still has good performance and generalization. A possible direction for future work is to generalize the model to different magnifications and microscope resolutions—this is not automatically handled by the model since varying these factors does not preserve the proportion of physical distance to pixel distance. One approach which does not require any changes to the model is to take a picture of a ruler with the microscope at the desired magnification and resolution to obtain this physical to pixel distance measure, and scale the input image accordingly. Another opportunity for improvement is to generalize to different colors of stains used in the samples, since this could vary between labs. These limitations could be simply solved by obtaining and training on more data, but perhaps other methods such as scale and color augmentations could be investigated.

Acknowledgements. Liam Tan contributed to the nerve crossing detection algorithm, and Maria Rodriguez and Yasmine Oliva-Illera completed manual annotations of the data. Computational support from NSF grants 2120019, 1730158, 1541349 and 2100237.

References

1. Arbeláez, P., Maire, M., Fowlkes, C., Malik, J.: Contour detection and hierarchical image segmentation. IEEE Trans. Pattern Anal. Mach. Intell. **33**, 898–916 (2011)
2. Bergwerf, H., Bechakra, M., Smal, I., Jongen, J.L.M., Meijering, E.: Nerve fiber segmentation in bright-field microscopy images of skin biopsies using deep learning. In: 2019 IEEE 16th International Symposium on Biomedical Imaging (ISBI 2019), pp. 232–215. https://doi.org/10.1109/ISBI.2019.8759504
3. Buda, M., Saha, A., Mazurowski, M.A.: Association of genomic subtypes of low-ergrade gliomas with shape features automatically extracted by a deep learning algorithm. Comput. Biol. Med. **109**, 218–225 (2019)
4. Chen, L., Papandreou, G., Schroff, F., Adam, H.: Rethinking atrous convolution for semantic image segmentation. CoRR, arXiv:abs/1706.05587 (2017)
5. Ester, M., Kriegel, H.P., Sander, J., Xu, X.: A density-based algorithm for discovering clusters in large spatial databases with noise. In: Proceedings of the 2nd International Conference on Knowledge Discovery and Data Mining, pp. 226–231 (1996)
6. Everingham, M., Eslami, S.M.A., Van Gool, L., Williams, C.K.I., Winn, J., Zisserman, A.: the pascal visual object classes challenge: a retrospective. Int. J. Comput. Vis. **111**, 98–136 (2015)
7. Al-Fahdawi, S., Qahwaji, R., Al-Waisy, A.S., et al.: A fully automatic nerve segmentation and morphometric parameter quantification system for early diagnosis of diabetic neuropathy in corneal images. Comput. Methods Prog. Biomed. **135**, 151–166 (2016)
8. He, K., Zhang, X., Ren, S., Sun, J.: Deep residual learning for image recognition. CoRR; abs/1512.03385 (2015)
9. Niklaus S.: A Reimplementation of HED using PyTorch (2018). https://github.com/sniklaus/pytorch-hed
10. Pal, A., Garain, U., Chandra, A., Chatterjee, R., Senapati, S.: Psoriasis skin biopsy image segmentation using Deep Convolutional Neural Network. Comput. Methods Prog. Biomed. **159**, 59–69 (2018)
11. Simonyan, K., Zisserman, A.: Very deep convolutional networks for large-scale image recognition. arXiv preprint arXiv:1409.1556 (2014)
12. Xie, S., Tu, Z.: Holistically-nested edge detection. CoRR ;abs/1504.06375 (2015)
13. Zhang, D., Huang, F., Khansari, M., et al.: Automatic corneal nerve fiber segmentation and geometric biomarker quantification. Euro. Phys. J. Plus **135**, 266 (2020)

Author Index

Printed in the United States
by Baker & Taylor Publisher Services